365

SKINNY
SMOOTHIES

365 SKINNY SMOOTHIES

**Healthy, Never-Boring Recipes
and 52 Weekly Shopping Lists
for Stress-Free Weight Loss**

DANIELLA CHACE, MSc, CN

The Countryman Press
A Division of W. W. Norton & Company
Independent Publishers Since 1923

This book is intended as a general information resource for healthy adults. It is not a substitute for individualized professional advice and no recommendation in this book to eat or drink anything is intended to substitute for any prescribed medication or dietary or other healthcare regimen.

Whether consuming any or all of the smoothies in this book will help you lose weight will depend on several variables, including, without limitation, your age, your individual physical condition, your individual propensity to gain weight, whether you are eating a healthy diet and exercising regularly, and how you integrate the smoothies into your diet.

Consult your healthcare provider before changing your diet in any significant way and before eating any new foods or ingredients in significant quantities, especially if you are diabetic or suffer from any other health condition, are taking any prescription medication, are pregnant or nursing, or have food or other allergies.

URLs displayed in this book link or refer to websites that existed as of press time. The publisher is not responsible for, and should not be deemed to endorse or recommend, any website other than its own or any content not created by it. The author, also, is not responsible for any third-party material. Any products recommended reflect the personal preferences of the author, who does not have a financial interest in any of the manufacturers or distributors of those products. Do your own research when it comes to choosing products for your own use.

For information about permission to reproduce selections from this book, write to Permissions, The Countryman Press, 500 Fifth Avenue, New York, NY 10110

For information about special discounts for bulk purchases, please contact W. W. Norton Special Sales at specialsales@wwnorton.com or 800-233-4830

Manufacturing by Versa Press
Book design by Allison Chi
Production manager: Devon Zahn

The Countryman Press
www.countrymanpress.com

A division of W. W. Norton & Company, Inc.
500 Fifth Avenue, New York, NY 10110
www.wwnorton.com

978-1-68268-606-5 (pbk.)

10 9 8 7 6 5 4 3 2 1

In gratitude to Helen Gray for her
enthusiasm, research, nutrition analyses,
and most of all her friendship.

CONTENTS

ACKNOWLEDGMENTS

I am grateful for the inspiration and support from colleagues and friends throughout the development of this seemingly simple, yet complex, book. First, and foremost, I thank Ann Treistman and Isabel McCarthy, my editors at The Countryman Press, for their vision and Ashley Patrick for her attention to detail throughout the copy-editing process. I also thank Jessica R. Friedman, Esq., with W. W. Norton & Company, for her thoughtful review of the manuscript, and my seasoned literary agent, Linda Konner, for her belief in the longevity of this book. And I thank my lead test team, Linda Landkammer and Robin Nye, who tasted hundreds of smoothies until the combinations were just right.

introduction

RECIPES FOR A SKINNY LIFE

The recipes in *365 Skinny Smoothies* are nutritious elixirs designed to promote weight loss and increase energy. As a nutritionist, I know that smoothies are great tools in a weight-loss program because they are easy to make, they taste good, and they can be a vehicle for macronutrients, such as protein, essential fatty acids (EFAs), and complex carbohydrates, as well micronutrients, including vitamins, minerals, and phytonutrients.

While creating the smoothies in *365 Skinny Smoothies*, I culled through hundreds of food-nutrient studies to find the foods that have the potential to increase muscle, reduce water weight, and decrease body fat. Of course, the findings of any food-nutrient study depend on the specific variables of that study, such as the physical characteristics of the study subjects (who may actually be mice or rats or even cells, although generally I try not to rely on studies with animal subjects). Study results also depend on the specific dietary regimen that the study imposed, and, if we're talking about human subjects, what else they were doing to lose weight during the study; and sometimes different studies of a single food or substance produce conflicting results. So when I say that a particular food or nutrient "boosts" or "promotes" weight loss or causes a particular physical effect related to weight loss, if you want to know exactly what evidence there is for that conclusion and what variables were involved in the study or studies at issue, seek further research. (There is a list of references at the back of the book.) But I think it is fair to say that the smoothie recipes in this book can help you lose weight in various ways, such as reducing body fat storage by decreasing insulin stimulation, reducing inflammation by triggering the release of stored water, and increasing enzymes that may help shed body fat. When you incorporate these smoothies into your daily routine, along with regular exercise and a healthy diet, these recipes are likely to have a positive effect on your weight and your overall health.

YOUR KITCHEN AS A LEARNING LAB

By trying out the recipes in this book, you are essentially creating a lab in your kitchen where you will be experimenting with various nutrients that boost weight loss. Each recipe is based on one or more weight-loss concepts, such as adding probiotic supplements and cultured foods; increasing phytochemicals found in greens and berries; boosting spices that reduce inflammation; hydrating with electrolytes; and adding protein such as hemp, chia, or protein supplement powders to support muscle development.

You'll quickly master the basics of your blender, and you'll soon be ready to start customizing your own smoothies based on your taste preferences and nutrient needs. For example, you may be attempting to increase your vitamin C intake to reduce oxidative stress, because this oxidation makes it harder to lose body fat. You can choose between many vitamin C–rich ingredients, including citrus, greens, or cherries, as antioxidant boosters in your daily smoothie, altering recipes to fit your tastes.

HOW TO USE THIS BOOK

The recipes are numbered and grouped by week and are organized by perishable ingredients—this means that recipes are grouped together according to their staple ingredient in order to keep grocery shopping to a minimum. If you follow the book from beginning to end, you will be buying the minimal amount of new foods each week. You will use up the fresh foods that you've purchased so there is less waste, and you won't have to fill your refrigerator with too many new products all at once.

You could follow the recipes through the calendar year: start with recipe #1 on January first and make the smoothies in order, with one smoothie recipe per day that introduces seasonal flavors and ingredients. Alternatively, you could jump around in the book based on the ingredients you crave or have on hand. You can always alter a recipe if you can't find a particular ingredient, so it's not necessary for you to hunt down anything unusual or hard to find in your area. I've provided ideas for alternates to use when you're out of a particular item that can be found in the Smoothie Ingredient Reference List.

Under each recipe you'll find the nutrition facts, with the calories, fat, carbohydrate, fiber, and protein content for each smoothie. The goal in creating a balanced smoothie is to keep the calorie and fat content low, while also incorporating fiber and protein. This balance of protein and fiber helps slow the digestion of the carbohydrates, which gives your body time to burn the calories as energy rather than storing them as body fat.

The amount of calories in these recipes varies, so that some make excellent additions to your diet and can be thought of as snacks or desserts. Smoothies with fewer than 250 calories are perfect little energizers between meals. You can enjoy these drinks throughout the day to keep you nutrient-balanced and nourished, but they should not be used as meals. The higher calorie smoothies provide enough energy to replace a meal. These energy-dense smoothies with more than 250 calories can be used as meal replacements. Keep in mind that 250 to 350 is still fairly low in calories, and you may need to eat an additional snack if you are active or have a higher calorie need. By replacing one to two meals a day with these nourishing drinks, you can boost your metabolism and reduce your overall caloric intake.

All you really need to get started is a blender, a liquid (which can be as simple as water), fresh or frozen produce (such as a banana) and some protein (nuts, seeds, protein powder). Toss them in your blender or food processor and blend until smooth, then drink right away.

Grocery lists are also provided for each week so you can glance at the ingredients you'll need and then check to see what you have on hand before shopping. The produce items are rounded up to whole items—so even though you may only need a half of banana for one recipe in that week, a whole banana is listed in the grocery list. This is because you'll be buying whole produce, so it will leave you with a little extra on hand. The same is true for liquids on the grocery list. The amounts have been rounded up to whole or half cups so you will have extra to use when needed to change the texture. If you like to garnish your smoothies, for example by topping them with a pinch of chia seed, pomegranate arils, or a lemon wedge, you'll want to keep a little extra on hand. The spices have also been rounded up, as the amount used in the recipes is conservative when it comes to intensity. If you like a little more spice, add as much as you can handle, as spices are nutrient-dense and provide high levels of weight-loss antioxidants. Shopping for extra ingredients will become second nature as you get into the habit of making your daily smoothies. For ease of use, the grocery lists can be photocopied, items you already have can be checked, and the list can be taken to the store to help you stay organized when shopping each week.

A YEAR OF WEIGHT LOSS

Everyone's taste buds are different. Some prefer hot and spicy, some prefer green and earthy, and others prefer sweet and creamy. This book has something for everyone. My intention is to introduce you to several new flavors and combinations each week so that you can try them until you find your favorites.

In the following chapter I have illuminated some little-known nutrition secrets. I reveal tips that I share with clients to help them lose weight. As you work your way through the recipes in this book, you will be incorporating these strategies and learning from your own experience which weight loss foods are most effective for you.

This one small lifestyle choice can even help improve overall health, disease risk, and mood. I hope you enjoy every sip, get more out of life with your renewed energy, and feel inspired by having the control to achieve your ideal body weight and maintain a healthier, fitter you for many years to come.

Chapter 1

NUTRITION SECRETS FOR LOSING WEIGHT WITH SMOOTHIES

THIS CHAPTER COVERS the myriad ways that smoothies can increase weight loss. We each have varying and specific nutritional needs. For example, at any given point in time we may have nutrient deficiencies, our metabolism may be affected by toxins, and inflammation may be triggered by food allergens. You can test your metabolism by experimenting with the following strategies to see what works for you. For example, reducing exposure to toxins will help some people shed pounds immediately, while others see their weight drop when they avoid allergenic foods. You will know you're making the right dietary changes when you start to shed pounds. When you find the formulas that are most effective for your body type, stay with them and make them a part of your weekly smoothies. This is the most straightforward way to identify what your body needs to lose stubborn pounds without expensive lab tests.

Each smoothie recipe has been formulated with bioactive nutrients for weight loss and using specific weight-loss strategies. The research used to inform the formulations can be technical, so the terms are defined for clarification in the glossary (page 304).

BOOST NUTRIENTS

We use nutrients in our bodies 24/7. If we develop nutrient deficiencies, this can slow our metabolism down and even halt some systems. For example, protein, glutathione, zinc, chromium, and B vitamins are all critical nutrients in metabolism. Berries and other superfoods, like pomegranate, cinnamon, and basil, are so rich in nutrients that they're like an antioxidant supplement in themselves, especially when eaten daily.

Smoothies do not travel well. Freshly made smoothies can't be kept for long, as after blending, the ingredients start to separate and oxidize almost immediately and break down quickly once the enzymes from the produce are released when pureed by the blender blade. Try to drink your smoothies within a few minutes after blending, while the nutrients are still fresh and vital. If you can't drink it all, you can pour your leftover smoothie into an ice cube tray and freeze. Your smoothie cubes can be tossed back into a blender later with liquid to make a quick, thick, frosty drink with those leftovers. You can also drop the frozen smoothie cubes into a glass of juice or water to add flavor and nutrients.

MINIMIZE SUGAR

Simple sugars are unhealthy because they deliver empty calories (calories without nutrients) and raise cholesterol and triglyceride levels, causing insulin resistance, inflammation, and insulin fluctuations that can lead to weight gain. To monitor your intake of sugar, check the sugar content on food labels. Keep in mind that sugars are simple carbohydrates and are included in the total number of carbohydrates listed on a label. For example, some yogurts have as much sugar as a candy bar. And don't assume that less sugar equals low calorie. Often, sugar-free or reduced-sugar foods have even more calories than their original counterparts and may contain harmful artificial sweeteners. These can be avoided by reading labels.

Our daily recommended carbohydrate intake, which includes fruits and vegetables, is calculated based on our size and activity level. The American Diabetes Association recommends about 45–60 grams of carbohydrate at a meal. All of the smoothies in this book provide the number of grams of carbs per serving in the nutrition facts. This carb number includes both complex carbohydrates, such as those from whole fruits, as well as sugars from fruit juices. My recipes generally contain less than 30 carbs per smoothie, which is clearly well under the ADA's recommended intake. I have carefully designed the smoothies in this book to be low carb and low calorie.

INCREASE PROTEIN

The ideal weight-loss smoothie is low calorie and protein-enhanced to supply just enough fuel for consistent energy, without the fat storage. Protein is a key macronutrient for weight loss, as it supplies amino acids, which are the building blocks for many of the biological functions in our bodies. Protein and fat help to slow the breakdown of an entire meal, thus reducing the amount of sugar from the carbohydrate being released into the bloodstream at one time. Therefore, the protein helps give our metabolic processes time to use the calories from our food as energy rather than storing the calories as body fat. Protein foods, such as chia seed, hulled hemp seed, and protein powders, can be added to smoothies to help balance the carbohydrates.

Studies show that protein reduces appetite as well as food cravings, and it also provides the amino acids that drive metabolism. Muscle cells are very active and burn calories at a high rate, even when we're sleeping. When we develop even 5 pounds of new muscle, it can help burn an extra 500–750 calories in a 24-hour period, even when we are resting.

PROTEIN FOR SMOOTHIES

The following chart provides some examples of my favorite sources of protein for smoothies.

Protein Sources	Grams of Protein Per Serving
Protein powders	14–32 grams in 3 tablespoons
Greek yogurt	16–20 grams in ½ cup
Yogurt	10 grams in ½ cup
Chia seed	6 grams in 2 tablespoons
Hulled hemp seed	5–7 grams in 2 tablespoons
Hemp protein powder	5 grams in 2 tablespoons
Nuts	5 grams in ¼ cup

The amount of protein we need varies depending on our activity level, age, and hormone levels. To give you a general idea, most adults need about 50 grams of dietary protein daily.

INCREASE SPICES

Unfortunately, we don't use many culinary herbs in the United States. In fact, the standard American diet relies heavily on sugar, fat, and salt rather than nutritionally dense spices for flavor. By adding spices, we create flavor and increase the phytonutrients that help us lose weight and keep us healthy.

Herbs and spices like basil, turmeric, and black pepper provide powerful nutrients for weight loss. The world's oldest medical system, the Ayurvedic medicine practices of India, uses culinary herbs daily for the prevention and treatment of disease and imbalance. In India, they use turmeric and black pepper to reduce inflammation, and holy basil to help manage hypoglycemia and diabetes. Basil and holy basil are medicinally potent herbs with a heady fragrance and flavor that happen to be perfect for smoothies. Studies have found that basil antioxidants have a positive effect on blood sugar levels. Basil also contains active compounds, such as ursolic acid, rosmarinic acid, carvacrol, and linalool, which, studies indicate, can help alleviate anxiety and inflammation.

SWEETEN WITH FIBER

Sometimes we want to add a little sweetness to a smoothie. But how can you add sweetness without compromising your goal to minimize sugar? This can be done with fiber-rich foods such as dates, prunes, and figs. They add sweet flavor, but they break down slowly in our bodies because of their fiber. This is a huge benefit because slowing the digestion of the carbohydrates gives our bodies longer-lasting energy and less storage of body fat.

When we make smoothies, we're blending rather than juicing, so we retain the fiber from the fruits and vegetables we're including. This is beneficial because essential minerals attach themselves to this fiber. Also, fiber holds on to water as it moves through the digestive tract, helping us hydrate. This allows the body to absorb water as needed, which vastly improves hydration.

Hydration is important for weight loss for many reasons. Dehydration may give us the false signal that we are hungry when actually we are simply thirsty and in need of water and possibly electrolytes. By adding coconut water, green tea, decaffeinated herbal teas, fruits, and vegetables to your smoothies, you can add flavor and boost the water content and electrolytes to keep yourself hydrated. You can also stay hydrated by drinking filtered water throughout the day and adding ice to your smoothies. As a bonus, ice helps emulsify (blend together) the smoothie, in addition to providing easy hydration.

Additionally, when fiber is added to a smoothie, it helps reduce the glycemic load of the entire drink. The glycemic load is a system that assigns a number to specific foods based on how much they will increase a person's blood sugar level when eaten. For example, oranges are low at a glycemic load of 40, while refined table sugar is high at 100. When we add fiber to our meals, we can reduce the overall glycemic load of that meal, as fiber slows the breakdown of foods in the digestive tract. This slows the release of nutrients into the bloodstream, thus reducing the risk for a spike in blood sugar, which triggers the pancreas to respond with insulin. Once insulin has been released into the bloodstream, its job is to shunt the sugar into cells for energy, and the excess is stored away as fat. Therefore, increasing fiber in our meals and smoothies helps reduce the insulin response, which helps reduce the potential for calories to be stored away as body fat. There are many high-quality fiber products on the market these days—such as glucomannan, pectin, chicory fiber, and acacia fiber—that are gentle and dissolve well in smoothies.

SUPPORT FAT-BURNING ENZYMES

We need essential fatty acids (EFAs)—which are healthful fats from foods such as avocado, nuts, and seeds—for our skin and cells, nerves, and fat-burning enzymes. EFAs are the essential oils/fats that we need to take in through our diet, as we can't produce these internally. Just 1 gram of EFAs per day appears to increase the production of fat-burning enzymes. One gram of EFAs is the amount in

1 teaspoon of chia seed or 2 teaspoons of hulled hemp seed. In the recipes that follow, I generally recommend adding 1 to 2 tablespoons of chia seed or hulled hemp seed to each smoothie to boost the fat-burning potential of each smoothie.

READ NUTRITION LABELS

Now that you've taken in the information above, you can approach food with a keener eye for nutrition. When you buy food products for your smoothies, such as yogurt, be sure to read the nutrition fact labels to see how much sugar, protein, fiber, and fat is in each serving.

Nutrition facts and food labels are on most food products and make it possible to calculate the macronutrient (carbohydrates, protein, and fat) levels in each serving. It's important to be aware that the numbers listed reflect one serving. Always take a quick glance at the number of servings per container, even when it seems like it should be obvious. For example, small bottles of juice that most of us would intend to drink as one serving are often designated as two or even three servings. This is common with food labeling. You can avoid this trap by simply being aware and looking at the number of servings, and then multiplying the number of carbs by the servings number to get the total number of carbs for that product.

AVOID TOXINS

Some toxins have a direct link to obesity because they affect the liver, so avoiding toxins may help you lose weight faster. When the liver is busy cleaning up toxins, it can't properly break down insulin, which continues to circulate longer in the bloodstream, grabbing up sugar and storing it away as fat. The more toxins, the more body fat storage! Eating clean, organic, whole, and unprocessed plant foods is a fast track to weight loss.

Agricultural chemicals are toxins that can be found in nonorganic produce. The Environmental Working Group (ewg.org) has a handy list of the "Dirty Dozen," which signifies the most heavily sprayed types of produce. For example, apples, celery, cherries, tomatoes, cucumbers, grapes, hot peppers, nectarines, peaches, spinach, and strawberries are all heavily sprayed, so it's best to buy organic. The USDA's organic seal also lets you know a product is free of genetically modified organisms (GMOs), which is important because GMOs are by definition grown with the use of more agricultural chemicals than other types of crops. The EWG also provides a "Clean Fifteen" list, which designates the least sprayed types of produce, such as avocado, cantaloupe, grapefruit, kiwi, mango, papaya, and pineapple. It's not as important to buy organic when it comes to these foods.

Avoid phthalates, such as bisphenol A (BPA), which are toxins found in most plastics. Studies have found that exposure to these compounds through our food and water may be a causative factor in the development of obesity. Phthalates are endocrine disruptors that we now understand play a significant role in our obesity epidemic. You can minimize your exposure to these compounds by purchasing and storing foods and juices in glass rather than plastic. Small particles of plastic pollution are making their way into our food supply and are now found in dairy products. This is just one more reason to move toward a plant-based diet. Opt for homemade nut milks, rather than dairy, to avoid these microplastics and nanoplastics.

REDUCE INFLAMMATION

Inflammation is becoming a common health issue, as so many people suffer from food allergies, autoimmune conditions, heart disease, diabetes, and cancer. Inflammation can cause bloating, joint pain, headaches, stiff back, edema, and inflammation of fat tissue that causes the appearance of cellulite. By reducing the body's inflammation, puffy tissue seems to magically tighten as we excrete extra water weight. Therefore, avoid inflammation triggers, such as toxins, food allergens, and unhealthy food. Some of the most common allergenic foods are wheat and gluten, corn, eggs, refined sugar, milk, and soy. Many people who react to dairy foods can still digest yogurt, however. Yogurt is a cultured product, which means it contains probiotic organisms that help break down the natural sugars—the lactose—making it easier to digest and assimilate. In my nutrition practice, my clients have reported losing up to fifteen pounds of water weight within days of removing an allergenic food from the diet. Keep this in mind, as inflammation can look like body fat.

SUPPORT DIGESTION

There are thousands of different healthy bacteria that live in our gut, orchestrating our metabolic functions. Without proper gut flora we can't absorb nutrients such as polyphenols. We need healthy gut flora for proper digestion and nutrient metabolism. We get these important organisms via cultured products such as cultured coconut milk, yogurt, kefir, and supplements.

A HEALTHY DAILY HABIT

A morning smoothie is a quick way to jump-start metabolism for the day to come. Once you leave the house, it's natural that the day can get pretty busy. Maybe you eat out, forget to take supplements, or just get caught up in everyday responsibilities. Having a daily morning smoothie is an effective weight-loss strategy. It ensures that you get that morning boost of nutrients and protein, which gets your metabolic motor revving by taking your body out of a fasting state and adding nutrients to your metabolic system, where they work to create energy from calories and from stored body fat. Eating breakfast, especially a protein-rich meal, can also help keep the weight off once you reach your weight goal.

Studies on the weight-loss effects of different food nutrients are continuously being reported. The research is very exciting, but keep in mind that the results are based on daily exposure to those nutrients. For example, we can't expect fiber or turmeric to help us lose weight if we ingest them only once a week. However, when we incorporate these nutrients into our daily routine, they can have a huge impact on our health. Our bodies are in a constant process of cell turnover, hormone production, and fat gain and release. By incorporating certain nutrients into our daily smoothies, we support our bodies in the continual process of fat loss and muscle gain. The food nutrients we take in through our diets are absorbed into the bloodstream, where they are delivered to the cells and tissues throughout the body that need them for myriad functions, including to help convert fat into energy.

Drinking a daily smoothie made with nutrient-dense ingredients is one of the most powerful strategies for quick weight loss. The next step is setting up your life in a way that makes it easy for you to stay with your new daily smoothie habit. Enjoy every sip and know that you are taking a giant leap in your self-care.

Chapter 2

THE SMOOTHIE-MAKER'S KITCHEN

THIS CHAPTER IS A GUIDE for setting up your kitchen, so you'll have what you need to easily whip up nutritious smoothies every day.

This chapter provides categories of weight-loss smoothie ingredients, quick tips for prepping them, and a review of the basic kitchen tools needed for smoothie making. When shopping for smoothie ingredients, choose a few items from each category to stock your pantry. That way you'll be able to make smoothies in minutes, right when you're craving them, without having to make a trip to the store.

Many of these smoothie ingredients have a long shelf life, or they will last for months in the freezer, which makes it easy to stock up. Frozen fruit can seem ideal because the berries are pre-pitted; fruits such as mangoes, peaches, and pineapples are chopped into small pieces that are easy on our blenders, and they're generally frozen at the peak of ripeness, so the fruit is sweet and juicy. The downside to buying frozen fruit is that they are often packaged in plastic bags. Look for frozen fruit in your co-op's bulk freezer section and use fresh produce when available to avoid the plastic.

A few ingredients will need to be purchased fresh as they have a shorter shelf life. You may want to start with the grocery lists provided in the recipe chapter to minimize the number of trips to the grocery store.

WEIGHT-LOSS SMOOTHIE INGREDIENTS

Flavor Extracts

Concentrated flavorings made from pure ingredients are not only flavorful but contain concentrated nutrients. Here are a few favorites for smoothies.

Almond extract	Hazelnut extract	Pure vanilla
Cherry extract	Orange oil	extract

Fruit

You are limited only by the availability of fruit in your area. Most fresh and dried fruits make excellent smoothie ingredients.

Apples	Cranberries	Papayas
Avocado	Figs	Pears
Bananas	Grapes	Pineapples
Berries	Honeydew	Plums
Cantaloupe	Huckleberries	Pomegranate
Cherries	Kiwis	Star fruit
Citrus	Lingonberries	Stone fruit
Coconut	Mangoes	Watermelon

Juices, Nectars, and Concentrates

Juices, juice nectars, and juice concentrates all contain fruit nutrients and flavor. Many fruits have been made into these liquid products; the list is seemingly endless. Check your local co-op to see which types are available to you.

JUICES

Apple juice (unfiltered)	Orange juice	Tangerine juice
	Pineapple juice	Tomato juice
Grapefruit juice	Pomegranate juice	Vegetable juice
Lemon juice		
Lime juice	Prune juice	

NECTARS

Apricot nectar	Blueberry nectar	Passion fruit nectar
Black currant nectar	Mango nectar	
	Papaya nectar	Peach nectar

CONCENTRATES

Black cherry concentrate
Blueberry concentrate
Cranberry concentrate

Vegetables

Many vegetables blend well and taste great when raw, but others are best cooked first, such as squash. Test the flavor of potent plant foods such as garlic, turmeric, or hot peppers by adding a small amount, blending, and tasting. Then add more if desired.

Beets	Cucumbers	Pumpkin
Carrots	Garlic	Squash
Celery	Ginger root	Tomatoes
Chili peppers	Greens	Turmeric root

Milks

Avoid flavored milk, such as chocolate and vanilla, as they generally have a higher sugar content.

ANIMAL MILKS

Milk from animals, such as cows and goats, contains protein, but also saturated fats, cholesterol, synthetic hormones, and the animal's natural hormones, as well as antibiotics and microplastics. You can find organic RBST-free and antiobiotic-free animal milks, which are better for you; check labels carefully to make sure they meet these standards. However, nut milks and other plant milks are much healthier choices.

Cow milk
Goat milk
Sheep milk

PLANT MILKS

Milks made from plant foods are rich in minerals and free of cholesterol.

Oat milk
Rice milk
Soy milk

NUT MILKS

Nut milks are ideal plant milks because nuts are oily and make creamy textured milk.

Almond milk	Flaxseed milk	Macadamia milk
Cashew milk	Hazelnut milk	Pistachio milk
Coconut milk	Hemp milk	Walnut milk

HOMEMADE NUT MILK

Soak 1 cup nuts, such as almonds, cashews, or hazelnuts, overnight in water, then pour off the soaking water and place the nuts in a blender. Add 3 cups purified water and blend well. Strain mixture through cheesecloth or nut milk bag to remove the pulpy fiber, then pour the liquid into a glass container to store in the refrigerator. Freshly made nut milk only stays fresh for about two days, so use it quickly by adding it to smoothies or tea, pouring over oatmeal, or drinking as a delicious cold beverage.

Nuts and Seeds

Whole nuts, seeds, and nut butters can be used in smoothies to add fiber, protein, and flavor. Nuts are nutritious but can add a lot of calories. Therefore, when adding nuts, aim for 2 tablespoons per serving for maximum nutrition.

Almonds	Hazelnuts	Pistachios
Cashews	Hulled hemp seed	Pumpkin seeds
Chia seed	Peanuts	Sesame seeds
Flaxseed	Pecans	Walnuts

Protein Boosters

Just 1 to 2 tablespoons of protein per smoothie is ideal.

Chia seed	Plant protein
Hulled hemp seed	powder
Nuts	Seeds

Herbs and Spices

Just a handful of herbs or a pinch of spice adds flavor, fragrance, and powerful weight-loss nutrients.

Basil	Cocoa	Peppercorns
Cilantro	Five-spice powder	Star anise
Cinnamon	Ginger (ground)	Turmeric
Cloves	Mint	(ground)

Sweeteners

Minimize sweeteners. A small amount goes a long way; for example, using just a few drops of liquid stevia will sweeten a smoothie.

Agave	Honey	Stevia
Coconut palm	Prunes	Xylitol
nectar		

Tea and Coffee

Brewed tea leaves and coffee beans make tasty and nutrient-dense bases for smoothies.

Coffee (fresh-brewed)	Coffee (instant, granules)	Green tea Herbal tea

Water and Ice

Add as much water and ice to each recipe as needed to blend your smoothie to desired consistency.

FILTERED WATER

Purified tap water is the ideal, eco-conscious choice for a liquid base for smoothies.

FILTERED-WATER ICE CUBES

Ice cubes add water to smoothies to boost hydration and give drinks a cold and frosty texture. Use filtered water to remove toxins before freezing. For added flavor, you can also freeze tea to use as ice cubes.

COCONUT WATER

Coconut water can be used as a liquid base and provides electrolytes and a nutty flavor.

SPARKLING WATER

Sparkling bottled water can be added to fruit (non-cream-based) smoothies after they've been blended.

PREPPING YOUR PRODUCE

Fresh produce is perishable and will need to be purchased within days of use. Pick up the fresh items you'll need at your local farmers' market or in the produce section of the grocery store. After shopping, spend a little time prepping the produce. This will reduce the amount of time it takes to whip up your favorite smoothie in the morning, when you're likely to be tired and pressed for time.

Wash These

Wash all produce by rinsing under running water for a few seconds.

Peel These

Tough peels need to be removed from some produce before blending or freezing. These items need some degree of peeling.

Avocado (pitted)	Grapefruit	Meyer lemons
Bananas	Kiwis	Oranges
Clementines	Lemons	Pineapple
Cucumbers	Limes	Tangerines
Garlic	Mandarin oranges	Turmeric
Ginger root	Mangoes (pitted)	

Pit These

Remove the pits but leave the skin intact unless otherwise noted, as most blenders can handle the delicate skin on this type of produce.

Avocado (peeled)	Donut peaches	Plums
Apricot	Mangoes (peeled)	Prunes
Cherries	Nectarines	
Dates	Peaches	

Core These

Remove the core but leave the skin intact, as most blenders can handle the skin on this type of produce.

Apples
Pears

Freeze These

Freeze fresh berries, bananas, and small seeds so they'll last longer and provide a frosty texture to smoothies.

Bananas (peeled)	Hulled hemp seed	Tea (brewed) ice
Berries	Stone fruit	cubes
Cherries	(pitted)	
Chia seed		

Grate These

Depending on the power and style of your blender, you may need to grate peels and roots before blending. A microplane rasp works well, or a cheese grater works in a pinch. Whole nutmeg is very hard and will always requires grating. Nutmeg mills, microplanes, and nutmeg graters are made for this purpose and make the task easy.

Citrus peel	Nutmeg (whole)
Ginger root	Turmeric root

Grind These

Use a spice grinder or coffee grinder to pre-grind fresh spices and seeds if you don't have a high-power blender.

Cardamom pods	Cloves (whole)	Star anise
Chia seed	Flaxseed	Vanilla beans
Cinnamon sticks	Holy basil (dried)	

KITCHEN TOOLS FOR SMOOTHIES

Just a few simple tools are needed to make smoothies. You'll need a blender with a strong motor and sharp blades; otherwise, your ice and tough ingredients will just bounce around in the blender's pitcher. A high-power motor easily grinds through ice, frozen fruit, nuts, and vegetables.

Opt for glass rather than plastic whenever possible to avoid obesogenic chemicals, such as BPA, that can be leached from plastics into our food. Choose blenders with glass pitchers, glass food-storage containers, glass measuring cups, etc.

You'll also want a cutting board for prepping fruits and vegetables. I'm thrilled with the Epicurean boards. You may need to buy a couple of these, as it's important to have one cutting board to use for produce only. I run them through the dishwasher almost every day, and they show very little wear, even after many years of daily use. Epicurean also makes gorgeous and easily washable silicone spatulas.

A sharp knife for chopping, coring, and peeling will make produce prep a breeze.

Happy blending!

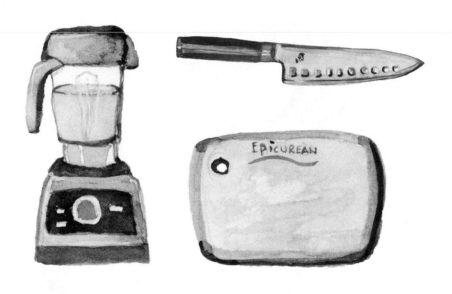

Chapter 3

SMOOTHIE RECIPES

Week 1

Grocery List

- ☐ 6 apples
- ☐ 1 banana
- ☐ 1 garlic clove
- ☐ 3 teaspoons lemon juice
- ☐ 1 mango
- ☐ 5 inches fresh ginger root
- ☐ 1 inch fresh turmeric root
- ☐ ½ cup wild blueberries
- ☐ 3 cups coconut water
- ☐ 4 tablespoons chia seed
- ☐ 3 tablespoons hulled hemp seed
- ☐ 2 tablespoons protein powder
- ☐ 1 tablespoon loose leaf green tea
- ☐ 1 teaspoon ground cinnamon
- ☐ 1 teaspoon ground cardamom

1. APPLE GINGER WARM-UP

The delicate apple and coconut flavors in this smoothie get a zesty kick from ginger, with a hot bite from the fresh garlic. Apples provide quercetin, which is a flavonoid that helps clear the body of environmental chemicals that can cause obesity, such as phthalates like BPA.

½ apple
½ small garlic clove
½ cup coconut water
¼ cup ice
1 tablespoon chia seed
1 inch fresh ginger root

Combine all ingredients in a high-power blender or food processor and blend until smooth. Drink immediately.

CALORIES: 111 FAT: 5 CARBS: 11 FIBER: 9 PROTEIN: 3

2. THE GOLDEN BANANA

In this recipe, banana and turmeric are deliciously sweet accompaniments that pair with the tartness of the apple. And of course, flavor is not the only benefit we get here. Turmeric is a root grown in South Asia that is ground into a bright yellow powder and used extensively as a medicinal spice. It is an ideal addition to all weight-loss smoothies, as it contains bioactive curcumin, which is a COX-2 inhibitor and has been shown to act as an anti-inflammatory.

½ apple
½ frozen banana
½ cup coconut water
¼ cup ice
1 tablespoon hulled hemp seed
½ inch fresh turmeric root
½ teaspoon lemon juice

Combine all ingredients in a high-power blender or food processor and blend until smooth. Drink immediately.

CALORIES: 136 FAT: 3 CARBS: 21 FIBER: 6 PROTEIN: 3

3. GINGERED APPLE

This smoothie features a golden turmeric color, sweet apple flavor, and warm ginger undertones. Bioactive nutrients in turmeric are more powerful in the fresh root than dried powder.

1 apple
1 cup coconut water
¼ cup ice
1 tablespoon chia seed
1 inch fresh ginger root
½ inch fresh turmeric root
1 pinch of ground cinnamon

Combine all ingredients in a high-power blender or food processor and blend until smooth. Drink immediately.

CALORIES: 190 **FAT:** 4 **CARBS:** 30 **FIBER:** 7 **PROTEIN:** 3

4. GINGERED APPLE MANGO

This smoothie is tropical and light with a little ginger heat! Adding protein to smoothies helps preserve lean body mass, which is the best fat burner of all.

1 apple
½ cup frozen mango
½ cup ice
2 tablespoons protein powder
1 inch fresh ginger root

Combine all ingredients in a high-power blender or food processor and blend until smooth. Drink immediately.

CALORIES: 148 **FAT:** 0 **CARBS:** 23 **FIBER:** 7 **PROTEIN:** 10

5. APPLE GINGER LEMON

This smoothie provides a light blend, with fresh ginger flavor and heat. Apples provide malic acid, tartaric acid, and soluble fiber, such as pectin, which detoxify the gastrointestinal tract. Reducing toxins in the digestive tract supports the liver's ability to deactivate insulin, which reduces body fat buildup.

1 apple

1 cup coconut water

½ cup ice

1 tablespoon hulled hemp seed

1 inch fresh ginger root

2 teaspoons lemon juice

Combine all ingredients in a high-power blender or food processor and blend until smooth. Drink immediately.

CALORIES: 124 **FAT:** 3 **CARBS:** 25 **FIBER:** 8 **PROTEIN:** 3

If you're using a high-power blender, you should be able to simply remove the skin from the ginger root and let your blender do the rest of the work. Otherwise, you may need to chop your ginger root first before adding it to the blender.

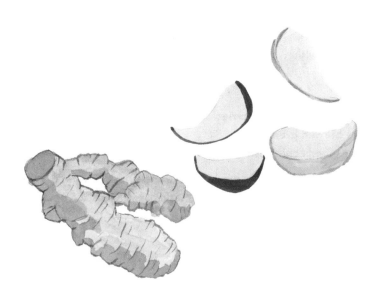

6. SPICED APPLE

This cold refresher is aromatic, spicy, and frosty. Cardamom seeds contain a range of essential oils that provide active compounds that stimulate digestion, boost metabolism, and support the body to burn body fat more effectively.

1 apple
½ cup ice
1 tablespoon hulled hemp seed
1 inch fresh ginger root
1 pinch of ground cardamom
1 pinch of ground cinnamon

Combine all ingredients in a high-power blender or food processor and blend until smooth. Drink immediately.

CALORIES: 103 **FAT:** 3 **CARBS:** 29 **FIBER:** 6 **PROTEIN:** 3

Add more ginger if you prefer more heat. You can also add up to 3 tablespoons of hulled hemp seed if you like the nutty flavor of hemp and want to boost protein.

7. GREEN TEA AND CHIA

This refreshing smoothie is like a slightly sweetened iced tea. The apples and wild blueberries provide the polyphenol antioxidant quercetin, which is an anti-inflammatory. Just 1½ cups of green tea consumed per day triggers weight loss.

1 apple
½ cup frozen wild blueberries
2 cups brewed green tea
2 tablespoons chia seed

Combine all ingredients in a high-power blender or food processor and blend until smooth. Drink immediately.

CALORIES: 240 **FAT:** 7 **CARBS:** 44 **FIBER:** 15 **PROTEIN:** 5

Week 2

Grocery List

- ☐ 2 dates
- ☐ 2 apples
- ☐ ¼ cup minced fresh basil leaves
- ☐ ½ inch turmeric root
- ☐ 1 cup frozen cherries
- ☐ 1½ cups applesauce
- ☐ 3½ cups hazelnut milk
- ☐ 1 cup nonfat Greek yogurt
- ☐ ½ cup coconut water
- ☐ ½ cup grapefruit juice
- ☐ 8 tablespoons chia seed
- ☐ 4 tablespoons protein powder
- ☐ 1 whole vanilla bean
- ☐ 4 teaspoons pure vanilla extract
- ☐ 2 teaspoons hazelnut extract
- ☐ 1 teaspoon ground cinnamon

8. APPLE BASIL BOOSTER

This smoothie provides a fresh apple flavor with the herbal scent of basil. Basil supports blood-sugar regulation, as it contains concentrations of nutrients that help boost the metabolism.

1 cup water
1 cup applesauce
½ cup ice
¼ cup minced fresh basil leaves
2 tablespoons chia seed
1 teaspoon vanilla extract

Combine all ingredients in a high-power blender or food processor and blend until smooth. Drink immediately.

CALORIES: 242 **FAT:** 10 **CARBS:** 30 **FIBER:** 14 **PROTEIN:** 6

9. CHERRY GRAPEFRUIT VANILLA

This recipe is a play on the popular grapefruit-vanilla jelly doughnuts that are often available around the holidays. Fresh turmeric root helps your body release stored water from body fat tissue.

½ apple
½ cup frozen cherries
¼ cup grapefruit juice
2 tablespoons chia seed
1 teaspoon vanilla extract
½ inch fresh turmeric root

Combine all ingredients in a high-power blender or food processor and blend until smooth. Drink immediately.

CALORIES: 220 **FAT:** 7 **CARBS:** 36 **FIBER:** 11 **PROTEIN:** 5

10. CHILLY CHERRY SLUSH

This smoothie has luscious, sweet apple and cherry flavors. It's perfect as a dessert after dinner to help improve your beauty sleep, as the sweet cherries are a rich source of sleep-supporting melatonin, which is beneficial as deep sleep is needed for effective weight loss.

½ cup frozen cherries
½ cup applesauce
½ cup coconut water
½ cup ice
2 tablespoons chia seed

Combine all ingredients in a high-power blender or food processor and blend until smooth. Drink immediately.

CALORIES: 210 **FAT:** 7 **CARBS:** 36 **FIBER:** 10 **PROTEIN:** 5

11. SPICED HAZELNUT APPLE

This delicious smoothie is dessert-like, fragrant, and satisfying. Those who eat apples daily have increased levels of healthy antioxidant enzymes, such as glutathione peroxidase, in their blood. These enzymes protect the body from environmental toxins that are linked to obesity.

1 apple
1 whole vanilla bean
1 cup hazelnut milk
½ cup ice
2 tablespoons chia seed
1 pinch of ground cinnamon

Combine all ingredients in a high-power blender or food processor and blend until smooth. Drink immediately.

CALORIES: 310 **FAT:** 10 **CARBS:** 42 **FIBER:** 12 **PROTEIN:** 6

12. SWEET VANILLA HAZELNUT

This recipe is light, creamy, and frosty, with an essence of vanilla. Vanilla extract adds the phytonutrient vanillin to support metabolism, it doesn't include any added sugars, and you probably have it hanging around with your baking supplies.

1 date
1 cup hazelnut milk
1 cup ice
1 tablespoon protein powder
1 teaspoon vanilla extract

Combine all ingredients in a high-power blender or food processor and blend until smooth. Drink immediately.

CALORIES: 210 **FAT:** 4 **CARBS:** 34 **FIBER:** 3 **PROTEIN:** 6

13. HAZELNUT DATE SHAKE

The date used in this rich, creamy, and slightly sweet shake contains fiber, which slows the release of the date's natural sugar during metabolism. So even though dates taste sweet and indulgent, their low glycemic index makes them a great ingredient for weight loss! To boost the weight-loss power of this recipe even further, add up to 3 tablespoons of protein powder, especially if you are drinking this smoothie as a meal replacement rather than a between-meal snack.

1 date
1 cup water
½ cup hazelnut milk
½ cup ice
1 tablespoon protein powder
1 teaspoon vanilla extract

Combine all ingredients in a high-power blender or food processor and blend until smooth. Drink immediately.

CALORIES: 170 **FAT:** 3 **CARBS:** 28 **FIBER:** 2 **PROTEIN:** 10

14. HAZELNUT CREAM FROSTY

This smoothie is creamy and rich, with a light hazelnut fragrance. Greek yogurt is strained and higher in protein than other types of yogurt. In fact, some Greek yogurt products are almost twice as high in protein. Dietary protein helps preserve muscle and fuels metabolism.

1 cup hazelnut milk

1 cup nonfat Greek yogurt

1 cup ice

2 tablespoons protein powder

2 teaspoons hazelnut extract

Combine all ingredients in a high-power blender or food processor and blend until smooth. Drink immediately.

CALORIES: 300 **FAT:** 6 **CARBS:** 30 **FIBER:** 4 **PROTEIN:** 32

Week 3

Grocery List

- ☐ 4 bananas
- ☐ 2 dates
- ☐ ¼ cup frozen wild blueberries
- ☐ ¼ cup frozen pineapple
- ☐ 3 cups coconut water
- ☐ 3 cups plant milk
- ☐ 1 teaspoon lemon juice
- ☐ 1½ cups nonfat Greek yogurt
- ☐ 4 tablespoons chia seed
- ☐ 1 tablespoon peanut butter
- ☐ 1 tablespoon unsweetened cocoa powder
- ☐ 1 tablespoon unsweetened fine macaroon coconut
- ☐ 3 teaspoons pure vanilla extract
- ☐ 1 teaspoon hazelnut extract
- ☐ 1 teaspoon instant coffee
- ☐ 1 teaspoon ground cinnamon

15. BERRY COBBLER

This recipe is basically a healthy wild berry cobbler in a glass, with hints of lemon and vanilla. The wild blueberries in it provide anti-inflammatory polyphenols that have the ability to reduce the appearance of body fat and cellulite.

1 date
1 cup plant milk
½ cup ice
¼ cup frozen wild blueberries
2 tablespoons chia seed
1 teaspoon vanilla extract
½ teaspoon lemon juice

Combine all ingredients in a high-power blender or food processor and blend until smooth. Drink immediately.

CALORIES: 220 **FAT:** 9 **CARBS:** 31 **FIBER:** 10 **PROTEIN:** 5

16. PIÑA COLADA

This smoothie combines coconut, pineapple, and banana in a creamy, sweet base. Bananas are an excellent source of potassium and B_6, which support weight loss by improving sleep. Proper sleep is linked to easier weight loss, while poor sleep is linked to obesity.

½ banana
1 cup coconut water
½ cup nonfat Greek yogurt
¼ cup frozen pineapple
1 tablespoon unsweetened fine macaroon coconut

Combine all ingredients in a high-power blender or food processor and blend until smooth. Drink immediately.

CALORIES: 220 **FAT:** 4 **CARBS:** 35 **FIBER:** 3 **PROTEIN:** 13

17. THE REVITALIZER

This smoothie is light and refreshing with a hint of vanilla. Think gelato with a perfect blend of sweet, cool, and aromatic vanilla. This blend is a perfect afternoon pick-me-up due to its high potassium and protein levels. To boost electrolytes after a night of drinking or a heavy workout, add a packet of electrolyte powder.

½ banana

1 cup coconut water

½ cup nonfat Greek yogurt

½ cup ice

1 teaspoon vanilla extract

Combine all ingredients in a high-power blender or food processor and blend until smooth. Drink immediately.

CALORIES: 168 **FAT:** 0 **CARBS:** 30 **FIBER:** 2 **PROTEIN:** 12

18. BANANA DATE

Greek yogurt and dates sweeten this thick, spiced smoothie. Dates are a rich source of minerals and fiber, and they serve as a whole-food sweetener for smoothies. There are hundreds of different types of dates, each with its own flavor. Sample some to find your favorite. Banana provides fructooligosaccharide, which is a prebiotic substance that encourages the growth of healthy weight-loss bacteria in the digestive system.

1 date
½ banana
½ cup plant milk
½ cup ice
¼ cup nonfat Greek yogurt
1 teaspoon vanilla extract
¼ teaspoon ground cinnamon

Combine all ingredients in a high-power blender or food processor and blend until smooth. Drink immediately.

CALORIES: 242 **FAT:** 2 **CARBS:** 30 **FIBER:** 4 **PROTEIN:** 14

19. CHOCOLATE HAZELNUT

This light and nutty smoothie is laced with hazelnut and contains cocoa, a rich source of magnesium, which helps reduce cravings for sweets. Add a few hazelnuts if you like a nuttier flavor.

1 banana
1 cup plant milk
1 tablespoon chia seed
1 tablespoon unsweetened cocoa powder
1 teaspoon hazelnut extract

Combine all ingredients in a high-power blender or food processor and blend until smooth. Drink immediately.

CALORIES: 190 **FAT:** 7 **CARBS:** 32 **FIBER:** 8 **PROTEIN:** 5

20. PEANUT BUTTER AND BANANA CREAM

This recipe has creamy banana with a little bit of comforting peanut butter flavor. Because nut butters like peanut butter add a lot of flavor, very little is needed. Nuts and nut butters provide protein and help to prevent dramatic carbohydrate-induced blood sugar spikes.

½ banana
½ cup plant milk
½ cup water
¼ cup nonfat Greek yogurt
1 tablespoon peanut butter

Combine all ingredients in a high-power blender or food processor and blend until smooth. Drink immediately.

CALORIES: 298 FAT: 9 CARBS: 30 FIBER: 5 PROTEIN: 14

21. APRÈS PLAY CAFÉ

Rehydrate yourself after playing hard and fuel up for more fun with this refreshing drink. In addition, the caffeine in coffee helps reduce inflammation triggered by intense athletic activity, which reduces pain.

½ banana
½ cup coconut water
½ cup ice
½ cup water
1 tablespoon chia seed
1 teaspoon instant coffee

Combine all ingredients in a high-power blender or food processor and blend until smooth. Drink immediately.

CALORIES: 143 FAT: 5 CARBS: 20 FIBER: 8 PROTEIN: 4

Add 1 teaspoon of unsweetened cocoa powder for a mocha flavor.

Week 4

Grocery List

- ☐ 4 bananas
- ☐ 2 figs
- ☐ ½ cup frozen peaches
- ☐ 2 tablespoons unsweetened fine macaroon coconut
- ☐ 3 cups plant milk
- ☐ 1 cup coconut water
- ☐ 1¼ cups nonfat Greek yogurt
- ☐ ¼ cup gluten-free oats
- ☐ 3 tablespoons chia seed
- ☐ 5 teaspoons unsweetened cocoa powder
- ☐ 1 tablespoon peanuts
- ☐ 1 tablespoon hulled hemp seed
- ☐ 4 teaspoons pure vanilla extract
- ☐ 1 teaspoon hazelnut extract
- ☐ 1 pinch of ground cinnamon

22. COCONUT BANANA FIG

Banana carries the flavor in this sweet and creamy blend with a hint of fig. Bananas are not only delicious, they also contain pectin, a soluble fiber that helps promote better digestion and nutrient absorption, as well as alleviating the bloating that can cause a swollen belly.

2 figs
1 banana
1 cup coconut water
1 tablespoon chia seed

Combine all ingredients in a high-power blender or food processor and blend until smooth. Drink immediately.

CALORIES: 180 **FAT:** 5 **CARBS:** 30 **FIBER:** 9 **PROTEIN:** 4

23. MORNING ENERGY BOOST

This drink is creamy and easy on the palate first thing in the morning. Having breakfast is a basic tenet for weight loss, as mentioned in Chapter 1. In addition, whole grains such as oats appear to increase the production of cholecystokinin, a hormone involved in appetite control.

½ banana
½ cup plant milk
¼ cup nonfat Greek yogurt
¼ cup ice
¼ cup gluten-free oats
1 teaspoon vanilla extract
1 pinch of ground cinnamon

Combine all ingredients in a high-power blender or food processor and blend until smooth. Drink immediately.

CALORIES: 209 **FAT:** 4 **CARBS:** 30 **FIBER:** 3 **PROTEIN:** 10

Use fresh vanilla beans and dried cinnamon stick if you like more vibrant flavors. Half of a vanilla bean and half of a cinnamon stick can be ground in a coffee grinder for about 20 seconds and then added to the smoothie before blending all the ingredients together.

24. HAZELNUT CREAM

This smoothie boasts strong hazelnut flavor in a creamy banana base. Bananas are a good source of the B vitamin folate, a key component for energy production. This helps with weight loss, as the more energy we are creating, the more calories and fat we're burning.

½ banana
½ cup plant milk
½ cup ice
¼ cup nonfat Greek yogurt
1 teaspoon hazelnut extract
1 teaspoon vanilla extract

Combine all ingredients in a high-power blender or food processor and blend until smooth. Drink immediately.

CALORIES: 220 **FAT:** 2 **CARBS:** 30 **FIBER:** 4 **PROTEIN:** 14

25. PEANUT BUTTER BANANA

Nuts are rich in calcium and B vitamins, including thiamine and B_6. B vitamins are essential for the conversion of body fat into energy.

½ banana
½ cup plant milk
¼ cup nonfat Greek yogurt
1 tablespoon peanuts

Combine all ingredients in a high-power blender or food processor and blend until smooth. Drink immediately.

CALORIES: 160 **FAT:** 6 **CARBS:** 18 **FIBER:** 2 **PROTEIN:** 10

26. CREAMY COCONUT PEACH

This delicious recipe has Hawaiian flavors with a peachy tartness. Bananas, peaches, chia, and coconut are all rich in fiber, which helps us feel full and less hungry. A meta-analysis found that increasing daily intake of fiber by 14 grams could lead to a 10 percent decrease in overall caloric intake and a weight loss of more than 1 pound a month from this one change alone.

½ banana
½ cup frozen peaches
½ cup coconut water
2 tablespoons chia seed
2 tablespoons unsweetened fine macaroon coconut

Combine all ingredients in a high-power blender or food processor and blend until smooth. Drink immediately.

CALORIES: 328 FAT: 14 CARBS: 30 FIBER: 18 PROTEIN: 8

27. CHOCOLATE FLIP

This drink is a lean chocolate dream. It's like drinking a chocolate sorbet! Cocoa contains a nutrient called epicatechin that induces lipolysis, which helps our bodies release stored fat, especially around the stomach and abdomen.

½ banana
½ cup ice
¼ cup plant milk
¼ cup nonfat Greek yogurt
1 tablespoon hulled hemp seed
1 tablespoon unsweetened cocoa powder

Combine all ingredients in a high-power blender or food processor and blend until smooth. Drink immediately.

CALORIES: 182 FAT: 5 CARBS: 24 FIBER: 3 PROTEIN: 10

Add up to 3 tablespoons of cocoa powder to increase the chocolate factor.

28. CHOCOLATE VANILLA SHAKE

Two all-American milkshake flavors—chocolate and vanilla—in a creamy base combine into one perfect smoothie! The flavonols in cocoa powder reduce our need for insulin, a hormone responsible for creating body fat.

½ banana

½ cup plant milk

¼ cup nonfat Greek yogurt

2 teaspoons unsweetened cocoa powder

2 teaspoons vanilla extract

Combine all ingredients in a high-power blender or food processor and blend until smooth. Drink immediately.

CALORIES: 254 **FAT:** 6 **CARBS:** 30 **FIBER:** 4 **PROTEIN:** 12

Week 5

Grocery List

- ☐ 2 bananas
- ☐ 2 tomatillos
- ☐ 1 apple
- ☐ 1 medium-hot pepper
- ☐ 1 inch turmeric root
- ☐ 1 cup frozen strawberries
- ☐ ½ cup frozen wild blueberries
- ☐ 3 cups carrot juice
- ☐ 1½ cups plant milk
- ☐ 1 cup brewed herbal tea
- ☐ ¾ cup nonfat Greek yogurt
- ☐ ½ cup coconut water
- ☐ 2 teaspoons lemon juice
- ☐ 6 tablespoons chia seed
- ☐ 2 tablespoons hulled hemp seed
- ☐ 1 tablespoon protein powder
- ☐ ½ teaspoon probiotic powder
- ☐ 1 teaspoon pure vanilla extract

29. VANILLA THRILLA

This smoothie is simply comfort food in a glass. Vanilla beans can be used in place of real vanilla extract, as both contain natural phytochemicals that suppress appetite and support metabolism.

½ banana
½ cup plant milk
½ cup nonfat Greek yogurt
½ cup ice
½ teaspoon vanilla extract

Combine all ingredients in a high-power blender or food processor and blend until smooth. Drink immediately.

CALORIES: 190 **FAT:** 2 **CARBS:** 30 **FIBER:** 2 **PROTEIN:** 14

Skip the flavored yogurts, as they often contain high levels of sugar, as well as synthetic color. Whole vanilla beans in place of vanilla extract will add a heady rich aroma and intense vanilla flavor.

30. SKINNY WHIP

This protein-rich smoothie is a simple daily breakfast blend. Breakfast wakes up our metabolism and gives us the energy and mental alertness we need to get our day started right. Probiotics support weight loss; in fact, the higher the level of gut flora in our digestive tracts, the easier it is to lose fat.

½ banana
½ cup coconut water
¼ cup nonfat Greek yogurt
½ cup frozen wild blueberries
1 tablespoon protein powder
½ teaspoon probiotic powder

Combine all ingredients in a high-power blender or food processor and blend until smooth. Drink immediately.

CALORIES: 272 **FAT:** 1 **CARBS:** 30 **FIBER:** 6 **PROTEIN:** 18

31. STRAWBERRY BANANA HEMP

This is a simple everyday smoothie that provides a metabolic boost in the morning. Hemp is rich in fiber, a natural appetite suppressant that helps us feel full longer and reduces cravings. Adding a few tablespoons of hulled hemp seeds to any smoothie will help curb hunger for hours. If you like a rich and creamy texture, then hemp milk is a good choice. If you prefer a lighter, frostier texture, then rice milk is a great liquid base.

½ banana
1 cup plant milk
½ cup frozen strawberries
2 tablespoons hulled hemp seed

Combine all ingredients in a high-power blender or food processor and blend until smooth. Drink immediately.

CALORIES: 270 **FAT:** 12 **CARBS:** 30 **FIBER:** 6 **PROTEIN:** 8

32. PEPPER CARROT

This smoothie is sweet and spicy with zing! Hot peppers directly affect weight loss by activating metabolically active fat cells.

1 cup carrot juice
1 cup ice
½ medium-hot pepper
2 tablespoons chia seed
1 inch fresh turmeric root

Combine all ingredients in a high-power blender or food processor and blend until smooth. Drink immediately.

CALORIES: 200 **FAT:** 7 **CARBS:** 31 **FIBER:** 9 **PROTEIN:** 6

33. MIDWINTER HARVEST

This recipe is a fresh and delicious combination of carrot juice and fruit. Strawberries contain soluble fiber that helps stabilize blood sugar and insulin, the fat storage hormone, helping to protect against weight gain.

½ apple
½ cup carrot juice
½ cup frozen strawberries
2 tablespoons chia seed
1 teaspoon lemon juice

Combine all ingredients in a high-power blender or food processor and blend until smooth. Drink immediately.

CALORIES: 220 **FAT:** 7 **CARBS:** 36 **FIBER:** 12 **PROTEIN:** 5

34. TOMATILLO CARROT

Carrot juice is a rich source of carotenoids, and this complex fruit and vegetable combination is reminiscent of a fresh field of greens. Low in calories and full of fiber, carrots are a weight-loss superfood. Due to its high fiber content, 1 cup of carrot juice will help you feel full until lunch and reduce snacking between meals.

2 tomatillos
1 cup carrot juice
½ cup ice
1 tablespoon chia seed
1 teaspoon lemon juice

Combine all ingredients in a high-power blender or food processor and blend until smooth. Drink immediately.

CALORIES: 185 **FAT:** 6 **CARBS:** 27 **FIBER:** 9 **PROTEIN:** 6

35. CARROT JUICE TISANE

This smoothie is slightly sweet, light, and fortifying! Herbal teas, such as chamomile, blend well with carrot juice. Carrot juice contains carotenoid nutrients that support the liver in fat metabolism, and thus aids weight loss.

1 cup brewed herbal tea
½ cup carrot juice
¼ cup ice
1 tablespoon chia seed

Combine all ingredients in a high-power blender or food processor and blend until smooth. Drink immediately.

CALORIES: 100 **FAT:** 4 **CARBS:** 16 **FIBER:** 5 **PROTEIN:** 3

Week 6

Grocery List

- ☐ 2 tomatillos
- ☐ 1 blood orange
- ☐ 1 garlic clove
- ☐ ¾ cup minced fresh basil leaves
- ☐ ½ cup minced baby spinach leaves
- ☐ ¼ cup fresh cilantro
- ☐ 1 inch fresh ginger root
- ☐ ½ inch fresh turmeric root
- ☐ 1 cup frozen wild blueberries
- ☐ ½ cup frozen cherries
- ☐ ¼ cup canned pumpkin
- ☐ 5½ cups carrot juice
- ☐ ½ cup sparkling water
- ☐ 5 teaspoons lemon juice
- ☐ 1 tablespoon lime juice
- ☐ 9 tablespoons chia seed
- ☐ 2 tablespoons hulled hemp seed
- ☐ 2 tablespoons pumpkin seed
- ☐ 1 teaspoon ground cinnamon
- ☐ 1 teaspoon cayenne pepper
- ☐ 1 pinch of fresh-ground black pepper

36. WILD BLUE JUICE

This luscious smoothie is fragrant and earthy. Wild blueberries have a richer flavor and twice the antioxidants of cultivated blueberries. In addition, the hulled hemp seed provides omega-3 fatty acids that support weight loss, boost mood, and reduce cravings for fats.

1 cup carrot juice
1 cup frozen wild blueberries
1 cup ice
2 tablespoons hulled hemp seed

Combine all ingredients in a high-power blender or food processor and blend until smooth. Drink immediately.

CALORIES: 290 **FAT:** 10 **CARBS:** 43 **FIBER:** 9 **PROTEIN:** 9

If you run out of carrot juice, unfiltered apple juice, which tastes great in this combination, can be used instead.

37. BLOOD ORANGE FIZZ

This recipe is the perfect blend of fruit and vegetable. The blood orange's beautiful red pigment is from its anthocyanin antioxidants. Blood oranges are also a rich source of vitamin C, calcium, folate, and thiamine, which are all nutrients that support metabolism and weight loss.

1 blood orange
½ cup carrot juice
½ cup ice
2 tablespoons chia seed
½ cup sparkling water

Combine the blood orange, carrot juice, ice, and chia seed in a high-power blender or food processor and blend until smooth. Then stir in the sparkling water and drink immediately.

CALORIES: 220 **FAT:** 8 **CARBS:** 35 **FIBER:** 11 **PROTEIN:** 6

38. MOJITO DIABLO

This smoothie is sweet and crisp, with fresh basil and lime fragrance. Sweet carrots with hot pepper create an ideal flavor combination. Hot chili peppers are a great weight-loss food as they improve control of insulin, which supports weight management and has a positive effect on treatment of obesity.

½ cup minced fresh basil leaves
1½ cups carrot juice
1 tablespoon lime juice
1 tablespoon chia seed
¼ teaspoon cayenne pepper

Combine all ingredients in a high-power blender or food processor and blend until smooth. Drink immediately.

CALORIES: 200 **FAT:** 4 **CARBS:** 39 **FIBER:** 7 **PROTEIN:** 6

39. SPICY GINGER

This smoothie is a flavorful potpourri dominated by sweet carrots, with a little ginger bite. Garlic and ginger root add some serious heat to this otherwise cool carrot concoction. Basil provides a fresh fragrance and contains phenol compounds that support weight loss by targeting metabolic stress.

1 garlic clove
1 cup carrot juice
1 cup ice
¼ cup minced fresh basil leaves
2 tablespoons chia seed
1 inch fresh ginger root
1 teaspoon lemon juice

Combine all ingredients in a high-power blender or food processor and blend until smooth. Drink immediately.

CALORIES: 210 **FAT:** 7 **CARBS:** 33 **FIBER:** 9 **PROTEIN:** 6

40. PINK POWER

Tart cherries and fresh carrot juice give this smoothie a rich, sweet flavor. Tart cherries contain anthocyanins and salicylates that reduce inflammation, helping to reduce excess water weight.

½ cup frozen cherries
½ cup carrot juice
½ cup ice
2 tablespoons chia seed
1 teaspoon lemon juice

Combine all ingredients in a high-power blender or food processor and blend until smooth. Drink immediately.

CALORIES: 284 FAT: 10 CARBS: 30 FIBER: 16 PROTEIN: 8

41. WINTER GREENS

This green drink has a rich carrot and pumpkin flavor. Pumpkin seeds are one of our richest plant sources of the mineral zinc. Zinc reduces cravings and improves the effect of insulin, as it is a cofactor that helps insulin's absorption into the cells. This reduces hyperglycemia (high blood sugar). Once sugar is in the cells, there is a feedback loop that sends messages to the endocrine system so that excess insulin isn't produce.

1 cup carrot juice
½ cup minced baby spinach leaves
¼ cup canned pumpkin
½ cup ice
2 tablespoons pumpkin seed
½ teaspoon ground cinnamon

Combine all ingredients in a high-power blender or food processor and blend until smooth. Drink immediately.

CALORIES: 206 FAT: 6 CARBS: 30 FIBER: 6 PROTEIN: 8

42. TOMATILLO COOLER

Cilantro and lemon pair well in this carrot-based smoothie. Cilantro and its seeds, known as coriander, have a citrus flavor due to linalool, a natural terpene that has been found in animal studies to cause weight loss.

2 tomatillos
½ cup carrot juice
½ cup ice
¼ cup fresh cilantro
2 tablespoons chia seed
1 tablespoon lemon juice
½ inch fresh turmeric root
1 pinch of fresh-ground black pepper

Combine all ingredients in a high-power blender or food processor and blend until smooth. Drink immediately.

CALORIES: 208 **FAT:** 10 **CARBS:** 18 **FIBER:** 14 **PROTEIN:** 6

Week 7

Grocery List

- ☐ 2 bananas
- ☐ 1 kiwi
- ☐ 1 cucumber
- ☐ ¾ cup strawberries
- ☐ ½ cup fresh greens
- ☐ 2 tablespoons minced fresh basil leaves
- ☐ ½ inch ginger root
- ☐ ½ inch fresh turmeric root
- ☐ 1 cup frozen cherries
- ☐ ¼ cup frozen mango
- ☐ 3½ cups hemp milk
- ☐ 1 cup carrot juice
- ☐ ½ cup plant milk
- ☐ ¼ cup nonfat Greek yogurt
- ☐ 4 tablespoons chia seed
- ☐ 4 cashews
- ☐ 2 tablespoons protein powder
- ☐ 2 tablespoons pumpkin seed
- ☐ 1 tablespoon hulled hemp seed
- ☐ 1 tablespoon unsweetened cocoa powder
- ☐ 2 teaspoons pure vanilla extract

43. CARROT GINGER

This is the perfect veggie smoothie, as it is sweet, fresh, and light. Additionally, the fresh ginger root supports weight loss by helping with digestion, increasing satiety, and reducing food cravings.

½ cucumber
½ cup carrot juice
2 tablespoons minced fresh basil leaves
4 cashews
½ inch fresh ginger root

Combine all ingredients in a high-power blender or food processor and blend until smooth. Drink immediately.

CALORIES: 218 **FAT:** 11 **CARBS:** 22 **FIBER:** 3 **PROTEIN:** 7

44. THE HEALER

Sweet carrot juice balances the tannic greens and earthy turmeric in this healthy blend. Turmeric contains an active compound called curcumin, a powerful anti-inflammatory agent. Turmeric is used in India as part of the daily diet to prevent edema and inflammation.

½ frozen banana
½ cup carrot juice
½ cup fresh greens
¼ cup nonfat Greek yogurt
½ inch fresh turmeric root

Combine all ingredients in a high-power blender or food processor and blend until smooth. Drink immediately.

CALORIES: 216 **FAT:** 0 **CARBS:** 30 **FIBER:** 4 **PROTEIN:** 16

45. HEMP POWER

This hemp combo is a delicious afternoon pick-me-up. Hemp supports weight loss by acting as a prebiotic and stabilizing blood sugar. Hemp is creamy, but has very little flavor, so you may want to punch it up with your favorite extracts, such as hazelnut, orange, almond, or vanilla.

1 cup hemp milk
½ cup ice
1 tablespoon hulled hemp seed
1 teaspoon vanilla extract

Combine all ingredients in a high-power blender or food processor and blend until smooth. Drink immediately.

CALORIES: 197 **FAT:** 8 **CARBS:** 22 **FIBER:** 2 **PROTEIN:** 6

46. HEMPBERRY SHAKE

This smoothie has a sweet berry flavor with a hint of tart mango. Pumpkin seeds are an excellent source of the amino acid leucine, which plays a role in preserving muscle mass during weight loss, raising the metabolism and fat-burning rate.

1 cup hemp milk
½ cup frozen strawberries
¼ cup frozen mango
¼ cup ice
2 tablespoons pumpkin seed

Combine all ingredients in a high-power blender or food processor and blend until smooth. Drink immediately.

CALORIES: 310 **FAT:** 16 **CARBS:** 30 **FIBER:** 16 **PROTEIN:** 8

This is a simple smoothie made from ingredients that can be stored in the refrigerator and freezer for months.

47. CHOCOLATE-COVERED CHERRY

This recipe was inspired by my favorite treat at my local movie house, the Rose Theatre in Port Townsend, Washington: dried cherries dipped in milk chocolate. This drink is protein rich from chia and protein power, and even small amounts of plant-based protein have been found to reduce appetite and sugar cravings.

½ frozen banana
½ cup plant milk
½ cup ice
½ cup frozen cherries
2 tablespoons chia seed
1 tablespoon protein powder
1 tablespoon unsweetened cocoa powder
1 teaspoon vanilla extract

Combine all ingredients in a high-power blender or food processor and blend until smooth. Drink immediately.

CALORIES: 175 **FAT:** 7 **CARBS:** 26 **FIBER:** 12 **PROTEIN:** 14

48. HEMP CHERRY CREAM

This classic comfort-food smoothie is as thick and creamy as the milkshakes of my childhood, thanks to hemp, one of the creamiest milk alternatives. It also gets a healthful twist from the fiber in cherries, which helps us feel full for hours.

½ frozen banana
½ cup hemp milk
½ cup frozen cherries
1 tablespoon protein powder

Combine all ingredients in a high-power blender or food processor and blend until smooth. Drink immediately.

CALORIES: 185 **FAT:** 3 **CARBS:** 30 **FIBER:** 4 **PROTEIN:** 14

49. KIWI STRAWBERRY MILKSHAKE

This refreshing smoothie includes sweet strawberry and banana with a little bright and tart kiwi flavor. If you prefer a sweeter flavor to balance the kiwi, use fruit juice in place of the hemp milk. The antioxidants in kiwi can help reduce inflammation and the appearance of cellulite.

1 kiwi

½ frozen banana

1 cup hemp milk

¼ cup frozen strawberries

2 tablespoons chia seed

Combine all ingredients in a high-power blender or food processor and blend until smooth. Drink immediately.

CALORIES: 175 **FAT:** 8 **CARBS:** 26 **FIBER:** 18 **PROTEIN:** 6

Week 8

Grocery List

- [ ] 2 bananas
- [ ] 2 dates
- [ ] 1 peach
- [ ] ½ cup frozen mango
- [ ] ¼ cup minced fresh basil leaves
- [ ] 4 cups hemp milk
- [ ] 2½ cups nonfat Greek yogurt
- [ ] 1½ cups plant milk
- [ ] 5 tablespoons protein powder
- [ ] 2 tablespoons hulled hemp seed
- [ ] 2 tablespoons instant coffee
- [ ] 3 teaspoons pure vanilla extract

50. CREAMY MANGO

The sweet mango combined with the tangy yogurt creates a perfect combination in this luscious smoothie. Mango is rich in weight-loss carotenoids and fiber. Studies have found that those who eat more fruits and vegetables have a higher level of carotenoids in their blood and lose weight more easily.

½ cup frozen mango
½ cup plant milk
½ cup nonfat Greek yogurt
¼ cup ice

Combine all ingredients in a high-power blender or food processor and blend until smooth. Drink immediately.

CALORIES: 236 **FAT:** 4 **CARBS:** 30 **FIBER:** 4 **PROTEIN:** 14

51. PEACHES AND CREAM

Plain yogurt has fewer calories and less sugar than flavored yogurt. Try adding extracts or vanilla bean to plain yogurt to boost flavor without the added calories and sugar. This smoothie is low in calories, yet sweet, creamy, and rich in flavor.

½ frozen banana
½ peach
½ cup plant milk
½ cup nonfat Greek yogurt
½ cup ice
1 teaspoon vanilla extract

Combine all ingredients in a high-power blender or food processor and blend until smooth. Drink immediately.

CALORIES: 280 **FAT:** 2 **CARBS:** 30 **FIBER:** 6 **PROTEIN:** 16

52. SWEET CREAM BREAKFAST SHAKE

Hemp milk gives smoothies a creamy and rich texture due to its natural, healthy fats and protein, whereas rice milk and nut milks are generally lighter and don't add much protein. Small amounts of protein throughout the day will support weight loss.

½ date
1 cup hemp milk
½ cup nonfat Greek yogurt
1 cup ice

Combine all ingredients in a high-power blender or food processor and blend until smooth. Drink immediately.

CALORIES: 180 **FAT:** 8 **CARBS:** 14 **FIBER:** 1 **PROTEIN:** 14

53. ICED COFFEE WHIP

This smoothie is similar in flavor to a cold white frappe, but this version is much healthier and full of protein. Instant coffee is a source of phenolic compounds that boost energy and weight loss.

1 date
1 cup hemp milk
1 cup ice
2 tablespoons protein powder
1 tablespoon instant coffee

Combine all ingredients in a high-power blender or food processor and blend until smooth. Drink immediately.

CALORIES: 190 **FAT:** 9 **CARBS:** 21 **FIBER:** 5 **PROTEIN:** 9

Instant coffee can be stored in the freezer for up to a year.

54. BANANA BASIL WHIP

This basil blend has subtle banana and hemp flavor. The hulled hemp seed tastes great and also provides gamma linolenic acid, which not only helps burn fat and promote weight loss, but also helps prevent weight gain.

½ frozen banana
½ cup plant milk
¼ cup minced fresh basil leaves
¼ cup ice
2 tablespoons hulled hemp seed

Combine all ingredients in a high-power blender or food processor and blend until smooth. Drink immediately.

CALORIES: 218 **FAT:** 8 **CARBS:** 26 **FIBER:** 4 **PROTEIN:** 8

Dried basil can be used in place of fresh leaves, in a pinch.

55. COFFEE AND CREAM

This blend tastes like cold and creamy vanilla coffee. Antioxidants in coffee inhibit free-radical damage, which leads to inflammation and sluggish metabolism.

1 cup hemp milk
1 cup ice
½ cup nonfat Greek yogurt
1 tablespoon protein powder
1 tablespoon instant coffee
1 teaspoon vanilla extract

Combine all ingredients in a high-power blender or food processor and blend until smooth. Drink immediately.

CALORIES: 180 **FAT:** 9 **CARBS:** 10 **FIBER:** 2 **PROTEIN:** 17

Instant coffee is simply freeze-dried brewed coffee.

56. HEMP WHIP

Consuming 1 to 2 grams of protein powder per 2.2 pounds of body weight per day, in conjunction with strength training, may improve muscle mass. Try this creamy and light smoothie with a subtle vanilla flavor and a boost of protein powder.

½ frozen banana

1 cup hemp milk

1 cup ice

2 tablespoons protein powder

1 teaspoon vanilla extract

Combine all ingredients in a high-power blender or food processor and blend until smooth. Drink immediately.

CALORIES: 248 **FAT:** 6 **CARBS:** 30 **FIBER:** 2 **PROTEIN:** 28

Protein powder dissolves well in smoothies and tastes delicious.

Week 9

Grocery List

- ☐ 1 fig
- ☐ 2 bananas
- ☐ 1 pear
- ☐ 1¼ cups frozen wild blueberries
- ☐ ½ cup frozen strawberries
- ☐ ¼ cup frozen wild blackberries
- ☐ 2½ cups plant milk
- ☐ 2 cups blueberry nectar
- ☐ 1¾ cups nonfat Greek yogurt
- ☐ 4 tablespoons chia seed
- ☐ 2 tablespoons hulled hemp seed
- ☐ 2 tablespoons protein powder
- ☐ 1 tablespoon instant coffee
- ☐ 1 tablespoon gluten-free oats
- ☐ 2 almonds
- ☐ 1 tablespoon unsweetened cocoa powder
- ☐ 3 teaspoons pure vanilla extract
- ☐ 1 teaspoon ground cinnamon
- ☐ 1 pinch of fresh-ground nutmeg

57. FIG COOKIE

This creamy hemp-based drink with almond and oat nibbles is comfort food in a glass. It's also healthy, as one fig provides about 27 milligrams of calcium, which helps build muscles that burn calories.

1 fig
½ cup plant milk
½ cup ice
½ cup nonfat Greek yogurt
2 almonds
1 tablespoon gluten-free oats
1 pinch of ground cinnamon
1 pinch of fresh-ground nutmeg

Combine all ingredients in a high-power blender or food processor and blend until smooth. Drink immediately.

CALORIES: 350 **FAT:** 10 **CARBS:** 30 **FIBER:** 8 **PROTEIN:** 18

58. MOCHA MORNING BOOST

This high-protein mocha smoothie is a healthier morning Frappuccino, rather than the high-fat, high-sugar, calorie-laden retail variety.

½ frozen banana
1 cup plant milk
½ cup ice
2 tablespoons chia seed
1 tablespoon instant coffee
1 tablespoon unsweetened cocoa powder

Combine all ingredients in a high-power blender or food processor and blend until smooth. Drink immediately.

CALORIES: 176 **FAT:** 8 **CARBS:** 19 **FIBER:** 8 **PROTEIN:** 5

59. CREAMY VANILLA PEAR

This smoothie combines light pear and vanilla flavors in a cream base. Greek yogurt has twice as much satisfying protein and is generally much lower in sugar than regular yogurt.

½ pear
½ cup plant milk
½ cup nonfat Greek yogurt
½ cup ice
2 tablespoons protein powder
1 teaspoon vanilla extract

Combine all ingredients in a high-power blender or food processor and blend until smooth. Drink immediately.

CALORIES: 244 **FAT:** 0 **CARBS:** 30 **FIBER:** 4 **PROTEIN:** 38

60. BLUEBERRY VANILLA

This smoothie has rich blueberry flavor and just a hint of vanilla. Blueberries reduce the inflammation that promotes insulin resistance, thus providing some protection against metabolic syndrome and its accompanying belly fat.

½ cup frozen wild blueberries
½ cup blueberry nectar
½ cup ice
½ cup plant milk
2 tablespoons chia seed
½ teaspoon vanilla extract

Combine all ingredients in a high-power blender or food processor and blend until smooth. Drink immediately.

CALORIES: 155 **FAT:** 6 **CARBS:** 20 **FIBER:** 8 **PROTEIN:** 10

61. VANILLA BERRY BANANA

The yogurt in this recipe gives this smoothie its creamy and thick texture. Greek yogurt is an excellent source of protein. Increasing protein intake by just 15 percent has been found to reduce calorie intake by as much as 400 calories per day.

½ frozen banana
¼ cup nonfat Greek yogurt
½ cup blueberry nectar
½ cup frozen strawberries
1 teaspoon vanilla extract

Combine all ingredients in a high-power blender or food processor and blend until smooth. Drink immediately.

CALORIES: 202 **FAT:** 0 **CARBS:** 30 **FIBER:** 4 **PROTEIN:** 6

62. BERRY BLAST

This blend combines complex berry flavors in a light and frosty base. The blueberries and blackberries contain antioxidant anthocyanins that help to inhibit weight gain and reduce body fat by improving metabolism at a cellular level.

½ cup blueberry nectar
½ cup frozen wild blueberries
¼ cup frozen wild blackberries
½ cup ice
2 tablespoons hulled hemp seed

Combine all ingredients in a high-power blender or food processor and blend until smooth. Drink immediately.

CALORIES: 230 **FAT:** 10 **CARBS:** 31 **FIBER:** 6 **PROTEIN:** 7

Add a teaspoon of honey if your berries are too tart.

63. PURPLE FAIRY

This elixir is rich in anthocyanins from the blueberries, which inhibit weight gain and reduce body fat through antioxidant and anti-inflammatory mechanisms.

½ frozen banana
½ cup nonfat Greek yogurt
¼ cup blueberry nectar
¼ cup frozen wild blueberries
½ teaspoon vanilla extract

Combine all ingredients in a high-power blender or food processor and blend until smooth. Drink immediately.

CALORIES: 224 **FAT:** 0 **CARBS:** 30 **FIBER:** 4 **PROTEIN:** 12

Week 10

Grocery List

- ☐ 1 apple
- ☐ 1 banana
- ☐ 1 date
- ☐ 1 cup minced fresh basil leaves
- ☐ 1 cup watermelon
- ☐ ½ cup baby kale
- ☐ ½ cup honeydew
- ☐ 1 cup frozen cherries
- ☐ 1 cup frozen wild blueberries
- ☐ 2 cups blueberry nectar
- ☐ 1 cup coconut water
- ☐ ½ cup nonfat Greek yogurt
- ☐ 2 teaspoons lemon juice
- ☐ 4 tablespoons chia seed
- ☐ 4 tablespoons protein powder
- ☐ 4 teaspoons pure vanilla extract

64. DOUBLE BLUEBERRY

Creamy, with a gorgeous purple hue, this is a quick and easy everyday smoothie. The color in blueberries comes from the anthocyanin nutrients, which quell inflammation, and each cup contains 4 grams of fiber and only 80 calories.

½ cup frozen wild blueberries

½ cup blueberry nectar

½ cup ice

2 tablespoons protein powder

2 teaspoons vanilla extract

Combine all ingredients in a high-power blender or food processor and blend until smooth. Drink immediately.

CALORIES: 142 **FAT:** 0 **CARBS:** 26 **FIBER:** 4 **PROTEIN:** 28

65. CREAMY VANILLA CHERRY

This delicious recipe is sweet and bright, and it has plenty of berry flavor. Heaven! Cherries are fiber-rich and low on the glycemic scale, so they don't trigger a spike in insulin, which is the fat-storage hormone.

½ cup blueberry nectar

½ cup frozen cherries

1 tablespoon protein powder

1 teaspoon vanilla extract

1 cup water

Combine all ingredients in a high-power blender or food processor and blend until smooth. Drink immediately.

CALORIES: 120 **FAT:** 1 **CARBS:** 25 **FIBER:** 3 **PROTEIN:** 14

66. BERRY MELON

This blend has luscious, rich berry flavor with a little lemon twist. Fresh and frozen blueberries naturally contain high concentrations of health-promoting phenolic compounds. Studies have found that those who eat wild blueberries daily have lower insulin resistance, as well as less weight gain and lower incidence of type 2 diabetes.

½ cup frozen wild blueberries
½ cup ice
½ cup honeydew
¼ cup blueberry nectar
2 tablespoons chia seed
1 teaspoon lemon juice

Combine all ingredients in a high-power blender or food processor and blend until smooth. Drink immediately.

CALORIES: 258 FAT: 10 CARBS: 30 FIBER: 16 PROTEIN: 6

67. GREEN BERRY

Enjoy your veggies in this antioxidant-rich, date-sweetened, green drink. Kale is a workout and weight-loss superfood, rich in nutrients that support metabolism and muscle development, including beta-carotene, vitamin K, vitamin C, and calcium.

1 date
½ cup baby kale
½ cup ice
¼ cup blueberry nectar
1 tablespoon chia seed

Combine all ingredients in a high-power blender or food processor and blend until smooth. Drink immediately.

CALORIES: 152 FAT: 5 CARBS: 21 FIBER: 7 PROTEIN: 4

68. BERRY MELON SLUSHY

Watermelon and blueberry create the perfect pairing in this sweet smoothie. Watermelon and blueberries are antioxidant-rich, low-calorie, and rich in flavor, making them excellent weight-loss smoothie ingredients!

1 cup watermelon
½ cup blueberry nectar
1 tablespoon protein powder
1 teaspoon vanilla extract
½ teaspoon lemon juice

Combine all ingredients in a high-power blender or food processor and blend until smooth. Drink immediately.

CALORIES: 135 **FAT:** 0 **CARBS:** 28 **FIBER:** 1 **PROTEIN:** 14

Flavorings such as vanilla, orange, or hazelnut extract add a sense of sweetness through flavor and scent without adding sugar.

69. BASIL ELIXIR

This is a simple blend of fresh herbs and apple flavor that is the perfect daily afternoon smoothie because of its medicinal support for weight loss. Basil is rich in rosmarinic acid, which improves skeletal-muscle glucose transport activity, which means muscles can more easily get the energy they need to burn calories!

1 apple
½ frozen banana
½ cup minced fresh basil leaves
1 tablespoon chia seed
1 cup water

Combine all ingredients in a high-power blender or food processor and blend until smooth. Drink immediately.

CALORIES: 148 FAT: 5 CARBS: 22 FIBER: 11 PROTEIN: 4

Add a cup of ice if you like your smoothies cold and slushy.

70. CREAMY CHERRY FREEZE

In this creamy, tart cherry freeze with a fresh herbal scent, coconut water provides the electrolytes that our muscles need for peak performance and calorie burning.

1 cup coconut water
½ cup ice
½ cup nonfat Greek yogurt
½ cup frozen cherries
½ cup minced fresh basil leaves

Combine all ingredients in a high-power blender or food processor and blend until smooth. Drink immediately.

CALORIES: 148 FAT: 0 CARBS: 26 FIBER: 2 PROTEIN: 12

Week 11

Grocery List

- [ ] 8 grapes
- [ ] 1 apple
- [ ] 1 fig
- [ ] 1 orange
- [ ] 1 banana
- [ ] 1 cucumber
- [ ] 1 avocado
- [ ] 1¾ cups minced fresh basil leaves
- [ ] ½ cup cantaloupe
- [ ] ¼ cup spinach
- [ ] 1½ inches fresh ginger root
- [ ] ½ cup frozen papaya
- [ ] ½ cup frozen peaches
- [ ] 2 cups coconut water
- [ ] ½ cup blueberry nectar
- [ ] ½ cup carrot juice
- [ ] ¼ cup nonfat Greek yogurt
- [ ] 1 teaspoon lemon juice
- [ ] 1 teaspoon lime juice
- [ ] 9 tablespoons chia seed
- [ ] 2 tablespoons hulled hemp seed
- [ ] 1 tablespoon unsweetened cocoa powder

71. BASIL PEACH

Fresh basil leaves add fragrance and flavor to this peach and citrus combo. The intense flavor and fragrance come from the essential oils in basil. These oils have powerful bioactive compounds that reduce excess water weight in our body tissues, which can help us drop extra pounds of water weight.

½ cup blueberry nectar
½ cup frozen peaches
½ cup ice
¼ cup minced fresh basil leaves
2 tablespoons chia seed
1 teaspoon lemon juice

Combine all ingredients in a high-power blender or food processor and blend until smooth. Drink immediately.

CALORIES: 236 **FAT:** 10 **CARBS:** 26 **FIBER:** 14 **PROTEIN:** 6

72. CHOCOLATE ORANGE

This blended drink is a simple and delicious chocolaty-orange weight-loss formula. Cocoa is rich in the polyphenols that reduce body weight and body fat by affecting adipocyte and lipid metabolism.

1 orange
1 cup coconut water
½ cup ice
¼ cup minced fresh basil leaves
2 tablespoons chia seed
1 tablespoon unsweetened cocoa powder

Combine all ingredients in a high-power blender or food processor and blend until smooth. Drink immediately.

CALORIES: 108 **FAT:** 6 **CARBS:** 9 **FIBER:** 11 **PROTEIN:** 4

73. GINGERED GRAPE

This smoothie tastes like a slushy grape soda with a little exotic ginger twist. Basil provides antioxidant nutrients that target metabolic stress, which results in body fat loss when ingested frequently.

8 grapes
1 cup water
½ cup ice
¼ cup minced fresh basil leaves
1 tablespoon chia seed
½ inch fresh ginger root

Combine all ingredients in a high-power blender or food processor and blend until smooth. Drink immediately.

CALORIES: 147 **FAT:** 5 **CARBS:** 20 **FIBER:** 6 **PROTEIN:** 4

74. BANANA BASIL

Enjoy the smooth coconut and banana flavors melded with fresh greens and a bit of herbal fragrance in this blend. Basil polyphenols are considered an anti-obesity agent that is able to reduce body weight and body fat by decreasing the amount and lipid content of fat-storage cells and regulating fat metabolism.

½ frozen banana
½ cup coconut water
¼ cup minced fresh basil leaves
¼ cup spinach
2 tablespoons hulled hemp seed

Combine all ingredients in a high-power blender or food processor and blend until smooth. Drink immediately.

CALORIES: 164 **FAT:** 6 **CARBS:** 22 **FIBER:** 4 **PROTEIN:** 6

75. SKINNY ELIXIR

Rosmarinic acid is a natural phenolic in basil that supports metabolism, helps to reduce the development of body fat, and eliminates extra water weight, making it an effective anti-inflammatory when eaten daily.

1 apple
1 fig
½ cucumber
¼ avocado
½ cup ice
¼ cup minced fresh basil leaves
2 tablespoons chia seed

Combine all ingredients in a high-power blender or food processor and blend until smooth. Drink immediately.

CALORIES: 307 **FAT:** 16 **CARBS:** 29 **FIBER:** 21 **PROTEIN:** 6

76. CARROT CANTALOUPE POWER ELIXIR

This elixir boasts a strange and wonderful combination, with fresh scents, loads of protein, and the weight-loss benefits of basil.

½ cup carrot juice
½ cup frozen cantaloupe
¼ cup nonfat Greek yogurt
¼ cup minced fresh basil leaves
1 tablespoon chia seed

Combine all ingredients in a high-power blender or food processor and blend until smooth. Drink immediately.

CALORIES: 178 **FAT:** 5 **CARBS:** 21 **FIBER:** 8 **PROTEIN:** 10

77. PAPAYA LIME GINGER

This spicy papaya blend is mixed in a coconut base with a little ginger and lime. Oils in limes have been found in studies to increase satiety and reduce appetite.

½ cup coconut water
½ cup frozen papaya
¼ cup minced fresh basil leaves
1 tablespoon chia seed
1 inch fresh ginger root
½ teaspoon lime juice

Combine all ingredients in a high-power blender or food processor and blend until smooth. Drink immediately.

CALORIES: 127 FAT: 5 CARBS: 16 FIBER: 7 PROTEIN: 4

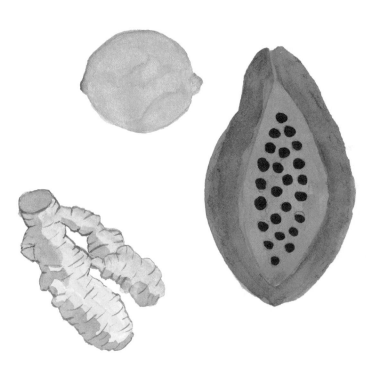

Week 12

Grocery List

- ☐ 5 fresh basil leaves
- ☐ 1 banana
- ☐ 1 date
- ☐ 1 pear
- ☐ 1 medium-hot pepper
- ☐ 1 inch fresh ginger root
- ☐ 1 inch fresh turmeric root
- ☐ 1 cup frozen strawberries
- ☐ ¼ cup frozen cherries
- ☐ 4 cups plant milk
- ☐ 1 cup nonfat Greek yogurt
- ☐ ½ cup carrot juice
- ☐ ¼ cup oat milk
- ☐ 1 vanilla bean
- ☐ 4 tablespoons chia seed
- ☐ 1 tablespoon gluten-free oats
- ☐ 2 teaspoons pure vanilla extract
- ☐ 2 pinches of ground cardamom
- ☐ 2 pinches of ground cinnamon
- ☐ 1 pinch of fresh-ground black pepper
- ☐ 1 pinch of fresh-ground nutmeg

78. SPICED CARROT

This recipe is a hot and spicy carrot-based drink. Hot peppers contain bioactive phytochemical nutrients that are appetite-suppressing and satiety-increasing.

5 fresh basil leaves
½ cup carrot juice
½ cup ice
¼ medium-hot pepper
½ inch fresh ginger root
1 pinch of fresh-ground black pepper
1 pinch of ground cardamom

Combine all ingredients in a high-power blender or food processor and blend until smooth. Drink immediately.

CALORIES: 63 FAT: 0 CARBS: 15 FIBER: 2 PROTEIN: 2

79. SWEET DATE CREAM

This creamy smoothie is comfort food in a glass. Dates are a rich source of minerals that help muscles flex efficiently, which makes our large muscle groups burn significantly more calories every minute of the day, even when we're sleeping!

1 date
½ cup plant milk
¼ cup nonfat Greek yogurt
½ cup ice
1 pinch of fresh-ground nutmeg

Combine all ingredients in a high-power blender or food processor and blend until smooth. Drink immediately.

CALORIES: 189 FAT: 2 CARBS: 30 FIBER: 2 PROTEIN: 8

80. VANILLA BEAN BLIZZARD

This creamy, high-protein, frosty drink with rich vanilla flavor is a perfect dessert or bedtime snack to keep blood sugar levels from dropping low in the night.

1 vanilla bean
1 cup plant milk
1 cup ice
½ cup nonfat Greek yogurt
½ teaspoon vanilla extract

Combine all ingredients in a high-power blender or food processor and blend until smooth. Drink immediately.

CALORIES: 135 **FAT:** 1 **CARBS:** 20 **FIBER:** 2 **PROTEIN:** 12

81. CHERRY OAT BANANA

This smoothie combines creamy, rich banana with sweet cherry goodness. Cherries are a source of melatonin and can help with insomnia. Deep sleep promotes efficient weight loss and is a critical piece of every effective weight-loss program.

½ frozen banana
½ cup ice
¼ cup frozen cherries
¼ cup oat milk
1 tablespoon chia seed
½ inch fresh turmeric root

Combine all ingredients in a high-power blender or food processor and blend until smooth. Drink immediately.

CALORIES: 179 **FAT:** 6 **CARBS:** 27 **FIBER:** 9 **PROTEIN:** 5

82. SKINNY GRANOLA

This skinny smoothie is a low-fat blend of comforting flavors with just a hint of spice. Adding ice to smoothies helps with hydration, which is important for weight loss, as even a 5 percent drop in hydration can slow metabolism.

½ frozen banana
1 cup plant milk
1 cup ice
2 tablespoons chia seed
1 tablespoon gluten-free oats
1 pinch of ground cinnamon
1 pinch of ground cardamom

Combine all ingredients in a high-power blender or food processor and blend until smooth. Drink immediately.

CALORIES: 210 **FAT:** 10 **CARBS:** 26 **FIBER:** 9 **PROTEIN:** 6

83. CINNAMON PEAR

This smoothie has a mild and delicate flavor with just a hint of sweetness and spice. Phytochemicals in cinnamon help reduce cholesterol levels and body fat composition.

½ pear
½ cup plant milk
½ cup ice
1 tablespoon chia seed
1 pinch of ground cinnamon

Combine all ingredients in a high-power blender or food processor and blend until smooth. Drink immediately.

CALORIES: 186 **FAT:** 6 **CARBS:** 27 **FIBER:** 10 **PROTEIN:** 5

If you prefer more flavor intensity, add a pinch of nutmeg or black pepper to spice it up.

84. STRAWBERRY SHAKE

The sweet strawberries, creamy yogurt, and scent of vanilla are comforting, and this smoothie is rich in protein and vitamin C. Strawberries taste sweet, but they are high in soluble fiber, which makes them a low-glycemic food and protective against weight gain.

1 cup plant milk
½ cup frozen strawberries
¼ cup nonfat Greek yogurt
1 cup ice
1 teaspoon vanilla extract

Combine all ingredients in a high-power blender or food processor and blend until smooth. Drink immediately.

CALORIES: 260 **FAT:** 2 **CARBS:** 26 **FIBER:** 6 **PROTEIN:** 8

Week 13

Grocery List

- [ ] 1 apple
- [ ] 1 banana
- [ ] 1 pear
- [ ] ¼ cup minced fresh basil leaves
- [ ] 1½ cups frozen peaches
- [ ] 1½ cups frozen strawberries
- [ ] ½ cup frozen cherries
- [ ] 3½ cups plant milk
- [ ] 1 cup nonfat Greek yogurt
- [ ] ½ cup oat milk
- [ ] 1 teaspoon lemon juice
- [ ] 1 vanilla bean
- [ ] 4 tablespoons protein powder
- [ ] 3 tablespoons chia seed
- [ ] 2 tablespoons gluten-free oats
- [ ] 1 tablespoon peanut butter
- [ ] 1 teaspoon fiber powder
- [ ] 1 tablespoon unsweetened cocoa powder
- [ ] 2 teaspoons pure vanilla extract
- [ ] 1 teaspoon ground cardamom
- [ ] 1 teaspoon ground cinnamon
- [ ] 1 pinch of fresh-ground nutmeg

85. CARDAMOM BANANA PEACH

This drink offers a taste of India in a glass. The cardamom provides exotic fragrance and flavor. Ground nutmeg is easily oxidized by exposure to light and oxygen, which depletes its flavor and weight-loss properties. To get fresh nutmeg fragrance, flavor, and nutritional potency, keep whole nutmeg on hand and grate it as needed. The protein powder, containing 10 grams of protein per tablespoon, helps stimulate the release of a hunger-fighting hormone called peptide YY, reducing appetite and helping weight loss.

1 banana
½ cup frozen peaches
½ cup ice
¼ cup plant milk
1 cup water
1 tablespoon protein powder
½ teaspoon vanilla extract
½ teaspoon ground cardamom
¼ teaspoon ground cinnamon
1 pinch of fresh-ground nutmeg

Combine all ingredients in a high-power blender or food processor and blend until smooth. Drink immediately.

CALORIES: 162 FAT: 1 CARBS: 30 FIBER: 3 PROTEIN: 10

86. PEACHES AND CREAM WITH BASIL

Basil adds a delicate herbal tone to this perfect pairing of oats and peaches. Basil also contains ursolic acid, which has been shown in laboratory studies to increase muscle and reduce body fat.

1 cup frozen peaches
½ cup plant milk
½ cup ice
¼ cup minced fresh basil leaves
2 tablespoons chia seed

Combine all ingredients in a high-power blender or food processor and blend until smooth. Drink immediately.

CALORIES: 147 FAT: 6 CARBS: 22 FIBER: 12 PROTEIN: 6

87. BEDTIME PINK DRINK

This balanced pink drink helps you wind down and enjoy a refreshing night's sleep. Uninterrupted sleep allows the endocrine system to efficiently recharge, and this means better metabolic function. Consider sipping this smoothie while you read or watch a movie at night, as part of your daily routine.

1 cup plant milk
½ cup frozen cherries
1 tablespoon protein powder
1 teaspoon fiber powder

Combine all ingredients in a high-power blender or food processor and blend until smooth. Drink immediately.

CALORIES: 145 FAT: 2 CARBS: 27 FIBER: 5 PROTEIN: 14

88. PB AND J

This drink has a classic peanut butter and jelly flavor and is packed with protein! Peanut butter is a rich source of the amino acid leucine, which plays a role in preserving muscle mass during weight loss, and also increases the rate of metabolism and fat burning.

1 cup plant milk
½ cup frozen strawberries
2 tablespoons gluten-free oats
2 tablespoons protein powder
1 tablespoon peanut butter

Combine all ingredients in a high-power blender or food processor and blend until smooth. Drink immediately.

CALORIES: 240 FAT: 12 CARBS: 27 FIBER: 8 PROTEIN: 28

89. CHOCOLATE STRAWBERRY CREAM

This recipe is decadent, like chocolate-dipped strawberries, yet it helps you lose weight! Additionally, strawberries are a good source of fiber, which helps you reach the daily recommended intake of 25 to 30 grams. A higher intake of fiber is associated with faster weight loss.

1 vanilla bean
½ cup plant milk
½ cup nonfat Greek yogurt
½ cup frozen strawberries
1 tablespoon unsweetened cocoa powder

Combine all ingredients in a high-power blender or food processor and blend until smooth. Drink immediately.

CALORIES: 178 **FAT:** 2 **CARBS:** 26 **FIBER:** 4 **PROTEIN:** 14

90. BERRY DELIGHT

The oat milk and Greek yogurt give this frosty blend a creamy base, and the vanilla lends an amazing fragrance. The probiotics in yogurt increase digestion and metabolism and help our bodies absorb the nutrients needed for weight loss.

½ cup frozen strawberries
½ cup oat milk
½ cup ice
½ cup nonfat Greek yogurt
½ teaspoon vanilla extract

Combine all ingredients in a high-power blender or food processor and blend until smooth. Drink immediately.

CALORIES: 164 **FAT:** 2 **CARBS:** 24 **FIBER:** 2 **PROTEIN:** 16

91. VANILLA PEAR

Pear, lemon, and vanilla are pure heaven in a glass! Vanilla beans and extracts provide the phytonutrient vanillin, which supports the liver in ways that improve insulin breakdown, thus preventing new body fat development.

1 apple
½ pear
1 cup water
½ cup ice
1 tablespoon chia seed
1 teaspoon lemon juice
½ teaspoon vanilla extract

Combine all ingredients in a high-power blender or food processor and blend until smooth. Drink immediately.

CALORIES: 175 FAT: 5 CARBS: 27 FIBER: 13 PROTEIN: 3

Week 14

Grocery List

- ☐ 8 grapes
- ☐ 2 apples
- ☐ 2 grapefruit
- ☐ 2 pears
- ☐ 2 tangerines
- ☐ 1 date
- ☐ 1 small tomato
- ☐ ¼ cup minced fresh basil leaves
- ☐ 1 inch ginger root
- ☐ ½ inch turmeric root
- ☐ 1 pinch of fresh oregano
- ☐ ½ cup frozen wild blueberries
- ☐ ¾ cup nonfat Greek yogurt
- ☐ ½ cup carrot juice
- ☐ ½ cup plant milk
- ☐ ½ cup tart cherry juice
- ☐ 1 tablespoon lemon juice
- ☐ 1 teaspoon coconut palm nectar
- ☐ 6 tablespoons chia seed
- ☐ 2 tablespoons hulled hemp seed
- ☐ 2 teaspoons pure vanilla extract
- ☐ 1 pinch of fresh-ground nutmeg

92. VANILLA PEAR GINGER

Ginger heats up this pear blend. Apples are an excellent source of quercetin, a very effective anti-inflammatory that affects the entire endocrine system, supporting calorie burning.

1 apple
½ pear
1 cup water
½ cup ice
1 tablespoon chia seed
½ inch fresh ginger root
½ teaspoon vanilla extract

Combine all ingredients in a high-power blender or food processor and blend until smooth. Drink immediately.

CALORIES: 171 **FAT:** 5 **CARBS:** 27 **FIBER:** 13 **PROTEIN:** 3

93. FRAGRANT GINGER PEAR

This fat-melting combination has a pear fragrance and complex flavors. Pears are a source of flavonoids and phenolic compounds that boost weight loss by acting as antioxidants that inhibit oxidation of fat cells.

1 pear
1 apple
1 cup water
½ cup ice
2 tablespoons chia seed
½ inch fresh ginger root
½ inch fresh turmeric root
1 teaspoon coconut palm nectar
½ teaspoon vanilla extract
1 pinch of fresh-ground nutmeg

Combine all ingredients in a high-power blender or food processor and blend until smooth. Drink immediately.

CALORIES: 240 **FAT:** 5 **CARBS:** 24 **FIBER:** 18 **PROTEIN:** 6

94. VANILLA PEAR CREAM

You'll find a delicate flavor with a warm vanilla base in this smoothie. High-fiber fruits are sweet treats that satisfy sugar cravings while boosting weight loss.

½ pear
1 date
1 cup ice
½ cup plant milk
¼ cup nonfat Greek yogurt
½ teaspoon vanilla extract

Combine all ingredients in a high-power blender or food processor and blend until smooth. Drink immediately.

CALORIES: 170 **FAT:** 2 **CARBS:** 26 **FIBER:** 6 **PROTEIN:** 7

95. GREEK BREAKFAST

This grapefruit juice cocktail has summer garden fragrance from the tomato and fresh basil. Tomatoes, grapefruit, and carrots all provide vitamin A precursors that are needed for healthy, youthful, and tighter skin after significant weight loss. Oregano, a popular Greek herb, contains carvacrol, which reduces inflammation and weight.

1 small tomato
½ grapefruit
½ cup carrot juice
½ cup nonfat Greek yogurt
¼ cup minced fresh basil leaves
1 pinch of fresh oregano

Combine all ingredients in a high-power blender or food processor and blend until smooth. Drink immediately.

CALORIES: 176 **FAT:** 0 **CARBS:** 30 **FIBER:** 6 **PROTEIN:** 14

96. CITRUS CHILL

The chia seed adds protein to this citrusy smoothie, which supplies the amino acids we need for efficient weight loss.

2 tangerines
½ grapefruit
1 cup water
½ cup ice
2 tablespoons chia seed

Combine all ingredients in a high-power blender or food processor and blend until smooth. Drink immediately.

CALORIES: 268 **FAT:** 10 **CARBS:** 27 **FIBER:** 20 **PROTEIN:**5

97. SWEET GRAPE AND SOUR LEMON

This smoothie has a nice balance of sweet and tart flavors. Using whole grapes in smoothies means adding grape seeds, which are powerhouses of bacteria-fighting nutrients that support metabolism.

8 grapes
½ grapefruit
1 cup water
½ cup ice
2 tablespoons hulled hemp seed
1 tablespoon lemon juice

Combine all ingredients in a high-power blender or food processor and blend until smooth. Drink immediately.

CALORIES: 130 **FAT:** 2 **CARBS:** 23 **FIBER:** 5 **PROTEIN:** 7

98. SUNRISE

This tangy and sweet smoothie has rich cherry flavor. Cherry juice contains melatonin that supports the deep sleep needed for endocrine repair at night during REM cycles. Melatonin also helps reduce the amount of cortisol (stress hormone) that affects metabolism.

½ grapefruit
½ cup frozen wild blueberries
½ cup ice
¼ cup tart cherry juice
½ cup water
1 tablespoon chia seed

Combine all ingredients in a high-power blender or food processor and blend until smooth. Drink immediately.

CALORIES: 215 **FAT:** 5 **CARBS:** 30 **FIBER:** 11 **PROTEIN:** 4

Week 15

Grocery List

- [ ] 2 apples
- [ ] 2 grapefruit
- [ ] 1 banana
- [ ] 1 orange
- [ ] 1 tangerine
- [ ] 1 cup greens
- [ ] ½ cup baby spinach
- [ ] ¼ cup minced fresh basil leaves
- [ ] ¼ cup turnip greens
- [ ] 1 tablespoon tangerine peel
- [ ] 1 inch fresh ginger root
- [ ] ½ cup frozen peaches
- [ ] ½ cup frozen wild blueberries
- [ ] ½ cup brewed green tea
- [ ] ½ cup coconut water
- [ ] ½ cup nonfat Greek yogurt
- [ ] 1 teaspoon coconut palm nectar
- [ ] 2 teaspoons lemon juice
- [ ] 5 tablespoons chia seed
- [ ] 2 tablespoons protein powder
- [ ] 1 tablespoon hulled hemp seed
- [ ] 1 tablespoon unsweetened fine macaroon coconut

99. THE GRAPEFRUIT REVITALIZER

This is a simple smoothie to make when you're busy but need a little energy boost. Keeping our energy optimal also means our metabolic functions are optimal.

½ banana
½ grapefruit
½ cup coconut water
½ cup ice
2 tablespoons protein powder

Combine all ingredients in a high-power blender or food processor and blend until smooth. Drink immediately.

CALORIES: 170 FAT: 2 CARBS: 34 FIBER: 6 PROTEIN: 8

100. GRAPEFRUIT ICY TEA

Grapefruit contains anti-inflammatory nutrients that help us shed unwanted water weight when we eat it on a regular basis. Enjoy the benefits in this light, refreshing, and slightly sweet treat.

1 grapefruit
½ cup brewed green tea
¼ cup ice
1 tablespoon hulled hemp seed
1 teaspoon coconut palm nectar

Combine all ingredients in a high-power blender or food processor and blend until smooth. Drink immediately.

CALORIES: 130 FAT: 5 CARBS: 20 FIBER: 3 PROTEIN: 5

101. GRAPEFRUIT AND GINGER

This drink is a citrus explosion with zingy ginger. Nutrients in citrus fruit and citrus peel are effective in reducing body fat in obese adults. Add a tablespoon of citrus zest directly to your smoothie to boost weight loss nutrients.

1 tangerine
½ grapefruit
½ cup ice
2 tablespoons chia seed
1 tablespoon tangerine zest
½ inch fresh ginger root

Combine all ingredients in a high-power blender or food processor and blend until smooth. Drink immediately.

CALORIES: 250 **FAT:** 12 **CARBS:** 30 **FIBER:** 12 **PROTEIN:** 5

102. GREEN AND CLEAN

Apple provides the base and greens provide the fresh-fields flavor in this recipe. Dark leafy greens are an excellent source of calcium, which helps muscles burn calories. In fact, turnip greens provide 200 milligrams of calcium per cup.

1 apple
½ cup ice
½ cup water
¼ cup turnip greens
1 tablespoon chia seed
½ teaspoon lemon juice

Combine all ingredients in a high-power blender or food processor and blend until smooth. Drink immediately.

CALORIES: 130 **FAT:** 4 **CARBS:** 21 **FIBER:** 6 **PROTEIN:** 3

103. FRESH GREENS

The sweet fruit flavors and rich texture in this simple blend of stone fruit and citrus balance the astringent nature of leafy greens. Peaches are a rich source of beta-carotene and fiber. Beta-carotene helps with reducing inflammation, which itself may facilitate weight loss, and fiber fights water retention.

1 orange
½ cup nonfat Greek yogurt
½ cup frozen peaches
½ cup greens
½ cup ice

Combine all ingredients in a high-power blender or food processor and blend until smooth. Drink immediately.

CALORIES: 156 **FAT:** 0 **CARBS:** 26 **FIBER:** 12 **PROTEIN:** 14

104. GREEN APPLE BLUEBERRY

The wild blueberries used in this smoothie are rich in flavor and contain a higher concentration of antioxidants, which reduce fat oxidation, than cultivated blueberries.

1 apple
½ cup baby spinach
½ cup frozen wild blueberries
½ cup water
¼ cup minced fresh basil leaves
1 tablespoon chia seed
1 teaspoon lemon juice

Combine all ingredients in a high-power blender or food processor and blend until smooth. Drink immediately.

CALORIES: 79 **FAT:** 2 **CARBS:** 15 **FIBER:** 9 **PROTEIN:** 3

105. GREEN HULK

You won't taste the greens, you'll only taste the tropical flavors—which makes this recipe a delicious way to incorporate dark leafy greens, an excellent nondairy source of calcium for those who prefer fruit over green smoothies.

½ frozen banana
1 cup water
½ cup ice
½ cup greens
1 tablespoon chia seed
1 tablespoon unsweetened fine macaroon coconut

Combine all ingredients in a high-power blender or food processor and blend until smooth. Drink immediately.

CALORIES: 235 **FAT:** 13 **CARBS:** 30 **FIBER:** 14 **PROTEIN:** 5

Week 16

Grocery List

- ☐ 4 tangerines
- ☐ 3 kumquats
- ☐ 2 bananas
- ☐ 1 date
- ☐ ½ cup greens
- ☐ ½ cup kale
- ☐ ¼ cup minced fresh mint leaves
- ☐ 1 inch fresh ginger root
- ☐ ½ inch fresh turmeric root
- ☐ ½ cup frozen mango
- ☐ ½ cup frozen raspberries
- ☐ 3 cups coconut water
- ☐ 1 cup brewed green tea
- ☐ 1 cup carrot juice
- ☐ ½ cup nonfat Greek yogurt
- ☐ 1 teaspoon lime juice
- ☐ 4 tablespoons chia seed
- ☐ 4 tablespoons hulled hemp seed
- ☐ 3 tablespoons protein powder
- ☐ 4 cashews
- ☐ 1 teaspoon unsweetened cocoa powder
- ☐ 3 teaspoons pure vanilla extract
- ☐ 1 pinch of ground cinnamon

106. BANANA CASHEW GREENS

This drink has delicious fresh banana and greens, with a hint of cinnamon. Cinnamon increases thermogenesis, meaning calorie burning, which supports weight loss.

½ frozen banana
½ cup coconut water
½ cup water
¼ cup greens
4 cashews
1 pinch of ground cinnamon

Combine all ingredients in a high-power blender or food processor and blend until smooth. Drink immediately.

CALORIES: 172 **FAT:** 8 **CARBS:** 24 **FIBER:** 2 **PROTEIN:** 4

107. GINGER KALE

This green drink has warming ginger and a splash of lime. Additionally, the spinach included in this recipe is a rich source of magnesium, which supports adrenal function and the deep sleep needed for efficient weight loss.

1 cup carrot juice
½ cup ice
½ cup kale
2 tablespoons chia seed
1 inch fresh ginger root
1 teaspoon lime juice

Combine all ingredients in a high-power blender or food processor and blend until smooth. Drink immediately.

CALORIES: 200 **FAT:** 7 **CARBS:** 32 **FIBER:** 9 **PROTEIN:** 6

108. GREEN BANANA SOOTHER

This soothing smoothie is creamy, sweet, and green, with a fresh banana scent. Coconut water is a great source of the potassium that is needed for proper muscle function, and the better your muscles are functioning, the more your muscles will burn glucose, which reduces the amount of glucose in the blood that is likely to become body fat when not converted to energy.

1 date
½ frozen banana
½ cup coconut water
½ cup ice
¼ cup greens
2 tablespoons protein powder
2 teaspoons vanilla extract

Combine all ingredients in a high-power blender or food processor and blend until smooth. Drink immediately.

CALORIES: 230 **FAT:** 0 **CARBS:** 30 **FIBER:** 4 **PROTEIN:** 10

109. CHOCOLATE KUMQUAT

This creamy smoothie has delicate citrus, coconut, and cocoa flavors. Cocoa polyphenols reduce metabolic syndrome belly fat. No need to peel the kumquats—just throw the whole thing right in the blender.

3 kumquats
1 tangerine
½ cup coconut water
½ cup ice
½ cup nonfat Greek yogurt
1 tablespoon protein powder
1 teaspoon unsweetened cocoa powder
1 teaspoon vanilla extract

Combine all ingredients in a high-power blender or food processor and blend until smooth. Drink immediately.

CALORIES: 211 **FAT:** 0 **CARBS:** 29 **FIBER:** 7 **PROTEIN:** 24

110. SOUR BERRY ICE

This icy blend is cool and refreshing, with a hint of sour and sweet. The chia seed gives this smoothie body. Chia seeds are tiny nutrition packets that provide 6 grams of fiber, 3 grams of omega-3 fatty acids, and 3 grams of protein in just 1 tablespoon.

1 tangerine
½ cup coconut water
½ cup frozen raspberries
½ cup ice
2 tablespoons chia seed
½ inch fresh turmeric root

Combine all ingredients in a high-power blender or food processor and blend until smooth. Drink immediately.

CALORIES: 238 **FAT:** 10 **CARBS:** 27 **FIBER:** 12 **PROTEIN:** 6

111. TANGERINE MINT COOLER

This smoothie is light, minty, and slightly sweet. Drink this tangerine mint cooler in the morning to help rev up your metabolism. Green tea has become a popular health food for its epigallocatechin gallate (EGCG) polyphenol, as this supports the production of the weight-loss hormone noradrenaline. This hormone increases fat burning and modulates dietary fat absorption and metabolism.

1 tangerine
½ cup ice
1 cup brewed green tea
¼ cup minced fresh mint leaves
2 tablespoons hulled hemp seed

Combine all ingredients in a high-power blender or food processor and blend until smooth. Drink immediately.

CALORIES: 142 **FAT:** 6 **CARBS:** 13 **FIBER:** 6 **PROTEIN:** 6

112. TROPICAL ENERGY BOOST

Enjoy this mango-banana boost with a little tangerine to sweeten.
The hulled hemp seed included in this recipe is nutritionally rich in
protein and essential fatty acids.

½ tangerine
½ frozen banana
½ cup frozen mango
1 cup coconut water
2 tablespoons hulled hemp seed

Combine all ingredients in a high-power blender or food processor
and blend until smooth. Drink immediately.

CALORIES: 280 **FAT:** 6 **CARBS:** 30 **FIBER:** 9 **PROTEIN:** 8

Week 17

Grocery List

- [ ] 10 tangerines
- [ ] 1 cucumber
- [ ] 1 peach
- [ ] ½ cup minced fresh mint leaves
- [ ] ½ cup honeydew
- [ ] ½ cup frozen pineapple
- [ ] ¼ cup minced fresh basil leaves
- [ ] ½ cup frozen wild blueberries
- [ ] 1½ inches fresh ginger root
- [ ] ½ cup carrot juice
- [ ] ½ cup coconut water
- [ ] ½ cup nonfat Greek yogurt
- [ ] ¼ cup black cherry juice
- [ ] 1 teaspoon lemon juice
- [ ] 10 tablespoons chia seed
- [ ] 1 teaspoon unsweetened cocoa powder

113. CAROTENOID CRUSH

This weird, wonderful, heady, and sweet drink is one of my favorite smoothies! The pineapple used here is a rich source of antioxidants, which help reduce inflammation.

½ tangerine
½ cup frozen pineapple
½ cup carrot juice
½ cup ice
2 tablespoons chia seed

Combine all ingredients in a high-power blender or food processor and blend until smooth. Drink immediately.

CALORIES: 230 FAT: 8 CARBS: 28 FIBER: 4 PROTEIN: 5

114. TANGERINE GINGER COCONUT

This recipe is sweet, gingery, light, and fresh. Coconut water with ice is the perfect low-calorie, nutrient-rich smoothie base. Look for coconut water that has no added sugar.

1 tangerine
½ cup coconut water
½ cup ice
½ cup nonfat Greek yogurt
1 inch fresh ginger root

Combine all ingredients in a high-power blender or food processor and blend until smooth. Drink immediately.

CALORIES: 114 FAT: 0 CARBS: 15 FIBER: 3 PROTEIN: 12

115. CHOCOLATE SUNRISE

This citrusy smoothie is tart and sweet, with antioxidant properties that help reduce inflammation.

1 tangerine
½ cup frozen wild blueberries
¼ cup black cherry juice
1 tablespoon chia seed
1 teaspoon unsweetened cocoa powder

Combine all ingredients in a high-power blender or food processor and blend until smooth. Drink immediately.

CALORIES: 185 **FAT:** 6 **CARBS:** 27 **FIBER:** 13 **PROTEIN:** 4

116. TART TANGERINE

This blended drink has a complex flavor without being too sweet. Small, low-calorie smoothies such as this are nutritious snacks that help quell cravings and keep energy up throughout the day.

1 tangerine
1 peach
½ cup ice
1 tablespoon chia seed

Combine all ingredients in a high-power blender or food processor and blend until smooth. Drink immediately.

CALORIES: 145 **FAT:** 5 **CARBS:** 18 **FIBER:** 12 **PROTEIN:** 4

117. TANGERINE MELON MINT

The fresh mint leaf fragrance is beyond wonderful in this melon and citrus smoothie. Use brightly colored melons, such as cantaloupe, watermelon, and Crenshaw, to boost the weight-loss carotenoids in smoothies.

2 tangerines
½ cup honeydew
½ cup ice
¼ cup minced fresh mint leaves
2 tablespoons chia seed

Combine all ingredients in a high-power blender or food processor and blend until smooth. Drink immediately.

CALORIES: 250 **FAT:** 10 **CARBS:** 28 **FIBER:** 20 **PROTEIN:** 7

118. GINGER CUCUMBER CITRUS

Tangerines give this smoothie a complex sweetness, and the ginger gives it a little heat. Additionally, the cucumbers provide energy-enhancing electrolytes.

2 tangerines
½ cucumber
½ cup ice
2 tablespoons chia seed
½ inch fresh ginger root
1 teaspoon lemon juice

Combine all ingredients in a high-power blender or food processor and blend until smooth. Drink immediately.

CALORIES: 218 **FAT:** 10 **CARBS:** 27 **FIBER:** 20 **PROTEIN:** 7

119. MINT CUCUMBER CITRUS

Mint plays off the citrus in this fresh and light smoothie. The polyphenols in the mint and basil are powerful antioxidants that act as anti-inflammatories.

2 tangerines
¼ cucumber
½ cup ice
¼ cup minced fresh mint leaves
¼ cup minced fresh basil leaves
2 tablespoons chia seed

Combine all ingredients in a high-power blender or food processor and blend until smooth. Drink immediately.

CALORIES: 210 **FAT:** 7 **CARBS:** 35 **FIBER:** 11 **PROTEIN:** 6

Week 18

Grocery List

- ☐ 1 tangerine
- ☐ 5 cups frozen strawberries
- ☐ 1 cup honeydew
- ☐ ½ cup watermelon
- ☐ ¼ cup minced fresh basil leaves
- ☐ 1 tablespoon minced fresh mint leaves
- ☐ ½ inch fresh ginger root
- ☐ ½ inch fresh turmeric root
- ☐ ½ cup frozen wild blueberries
- ☐ 4 cups coconut water
- ☐ 1 cup plant milk
- ☐ 1 cup sparkling water
- ☐ 1 cup brewed green tea
- ☐ 1 teaspoon lemon juice
- ☐ 7 tablespoons chia seed
- ☐ 3 tablespoons protein powder
- ☐ 2 tablespoons hulled hemp seed
- ☐ 1 teaspoon pure vanilla extract

120. HONEYDEW COOLER

This sweet and frosty drink helps reduce inflammation.

1 tangerine
1 cup honeydew
1 cup ice
1 cup brewed green tea
1 tablespoon chia seed
½ inch fresh turmeric root

Combine all ingredients in a high-power blender or food processor and blend until smooth. Drink immediately.

CALORIES: 178 **FAT:** 5 **CARBS:** 24 **FIBER:** 17 **PROTEIN:** 3

121. WATERMELON STRAWBERRY

This light smoothie is packed with summertime-fresh strawberry flavor. Add more hulled hemp seed to increase protein to fuel athletic activities.

½ cup watermelon
1 cup frozen strawberries
1 cup coconut water
2 tablespoons hulled hemp seed

Combine all ingredients in a high-power blender or food processor and blend until smooth. Drink immediately.

CALORIES: 205 **FAT:** 6 **CARBS:** 30 **FIBER:** 6 **PROTEIN:** 7

122. STRAWBERRY BASIL ICY

This icy drink is aromatic and sweet, with a light coconut flavor. The basil leaves contain an oil that is rich in weight-reducing antioxidants.

1 cup coconut water
1 cup frozen strawberries
¼ cup minced fresh basil leaves
¼ cup ice
2 tablespoons chia seed

Combine all ingredients in a high-power blender or food processor and blend until smooth. Drink immediately.

CALORIES: 236 **FAT:** 10 **CARBS:** 26 **FIBER:** 16 **PROTEIN:** 6

123. STRAWBERRY COOLER

This refreshing, sweet, and spicy version of lemonade includes ginger, a mild anti-inflammatory. Look for coconut water that is low in sugar, with no preservatives. Also avoid coconut water in plastic packaging, as plastic leaches obesogenic phthalates into coconut water.

1 cup frozen strawberries
1 cup coconut water
2 tablespoons chia seed
½ inch fresh ginger root
1 teaspoon lemon juice
1 cup sparkling water

Combine strawberries, coconut water, chia seed, ginger, and lemon juice in a high-power blender or food processor and blend until smooth. Then stir in the sparkling water and drink immediately.

CALORIES: 236 **FAT:** 10 **CARBS:** 26 **FIBER:** 16 **PROTEIN:** 5

124. STRAWBERRY MINT

This smoothie is thick and frosty, with a light mint fragrance, and is low in calories and contains no fat.

1 cup coconut water
½ cup frozen strawberries
1 tablespoon protein powder
1 tablespoon minced fresh mint leaves

Combine all ingredients in a high-power blender or food processor and blend until smooth. Drink immediately.

CALORIES: 138 **FAT:** 0 **CARBS:** 26 **FIBER:** 4 **PROTEIN:** 14

125. STRAWBERRY VANILLA BOOST

This strawberry smoothie has intense vanilla undertones. With its two tablespoons of protein powder, this smoothie has as much protein as many commercial protein bars, and for most people, the protein is easier to digest in powder form, so the nutrients get to your cells quickly.

1 cup frozen strawberries
½ cup plant milk
2 tablespoons protein powder
1 teaspoon vanilla extract

Combine all ingredients in a high-power blender or food processor and blend until smooth. Drink immediately.

CALORIES: 160 **FAT:** 6 **CARBS:** 18 **FIBER:** 2 **PROTEIN:** 10

126. RED, WHITE, AND BLUE

Strawberries contain phenolic compounds that boost immune functions and support metabolic health.

½ cup frozen strawberries
½ cup frozen wild blueberries
½ cup plant milk
½ cup ice
2 tablespoons chia seed

Combine all ingredients in a high-power blender or food processor and blend until smooth. Drink immediately.

CALORIES: 260 **FAT:** 12 **CARBS:** 30 **FIBER:** 16 **PROTEIN:** 5

Week 19

Grocery List

- ☐ 1 apple
- ☐ 1 prune
- ☐ 1 orange
- ☐ 2 cups cantaloupe
- ☐ ½ cup blackberries
- ☐ ½ cup pomegranate arils
- ☐ 1 inch fresh ginger root
- ☐ ½ inch fresh turmeric root
- ☐ 2 cups frozen strawberries
- ☐ ¾ cup frozen cherries
- ☐ ¾ cup frozen peaches
- ☐ ¼ cup frozen wild blueberries
- ☐ 3½ cups coconut water
- ☐ ½ cup nonfat Greek yogurt
- ☐ ½ cup plant milk
- ☐ 4 teaspoons lemon juice
- ☐ 6 tablespoons hulled hemp seed
- ☐ 5 tablespoons chia seed
- ☐ 1 pinch of fresh-ground black pepper

127. ORANGE CHERRY STRAWBERRY

This frosty, sweet blend includes fresh berry and citrus flavors. Increase the amount of chia to boost fiber, essential fatty acids, and protein, and follow with a tall glass of water to compensate for the chia fiber. This will provide a sustained energy boost.

½ orange
½ cup frozen strawberries
½ cup coconut water
¼ cup frozen cherries
2 tablespoons chia seed

Combine all ingredients in a high-power blender or food processor and blend until smooth. Drink immediately.

CALORIES: 280 FAT: 10 CARBS: 30 FIBER: 18 PROTEIN: 5

128. GINGER BERRY SPICE

This smoothie has a rich berry flavor, with fresh ginger and spice fragrance. Additionally, piperine, the active ingredient in black pepper, boosts turmeric's anti-inflammatory action by increasing the bioavailability of curcumin by up to 2,000 percent.

½ cup blackberries
½ cup frozen strawberries
½ cup ice
¼ cup coconut water
2 tablespoons chia seed
½ inch fresh ginger root
½ inch fresh turmeric root
1 pinch of fresh-ground black pepper

Combine all ingredients in a high-power blender or food processor and blend until smooth. Drink immediately.

CALORIES: 224 FAT: 10 CARBS: 24 FIBER: 18 PROTEIN: 5

129. CHERRY BERRY PEACH

This frosty blend of fresh fruit flavors includes hemp protein and a little citrus. Stone fruit, such as peaches and nectarines, are low calorie, have a high antioxidant capacity, and support energy production and calorie burning.

½ cup frozen cherries
½ cup coconut water
½ cup frozen peaches
¼ cup frozen strawberries
2 tablespoons hulled hemp seed
1 teaspoon lemon juice

Combine all ingredients in a high-power blender or food processor and blend until smooth. Drink immediately.

CALORIES: 234 **FAT:** 6 **CARBS:** 30 **FIBER:** 8 **PROTEIN:** 8

130. BERRY POM PEACH

This sweet and sour drink is rich in fruit flavors and a delicious way to wake up and start your day! The fruity combination in this smoothie helps sweeten and soften the intensity of the acidic tannins in the pomegranate. Punicalagins are the acidic tannins that provide free radical–scavenging health properties.

1 cup coconut water
¼ cup pomegranate arils
½ cup ice
¼ cup frozen wild blueberries
¼ cup frozen strawberries
¼ cup frozen peaches
2 tablespoons hulled hemp seed

Combine all ingredients in a high-power blender or food processor and blend until smooth. Drink immediately.

CALORIES: 222 **FAT:** 12 **CARBS:** 30 **FIBER:** 10 **PROTEIN:** 7

131. CANTALOUPE CITRUS TWIST

This lemony-fresh apple smoothie is packed with electrolytes, which drive the muscle contraction that burns glucose, or calories, and helps burn off body fat.

½ apple
1 cup cantaloupe
½ cup water
½ cup ice
1 tablespoon chia seed
1 tablespoon lemon juice

Combine all ingredients in a high-power blender or food processor and blend until smooth. Drink immediately.

CALORIES: 245 **FAT:** 5 **CARBS:** 30 **FIBER:** 12 **PROTEIN:** 4

132. CREAMY MELON

This smoothie is a blend of intricate flavors, as the prune adds a bit of sweetness and fragrance and the cantaloupe adds a fresh scent. Cantaloupe are sweet and full of fiber, so they're an excellent sweetener for weight-loss smoothies.

1 prune
½ cup plant milk
½ cup cantaloupe
½ cup nonfat Greek yogurt
¼ cup ice

Combine all ingredients in a high-power blender or food processor and blend until smooth. Drink immediately.

CALORIES: 200 **FAT:** 2 **CARBS:** 30 **FIBER:** 2 **PROTEIN:** 14

133. BERRY MELON PUNCH

This strawberry and melon combination has a trace of ginger and coconut flavors. The hemp seeds are an excellent vegan source of amino acids, which our endocrine systems need to manage energy and weight loss. Two tablespoons provide 5 grams of amino acid–rich protein.

1 cup coconut water
½ cup frozen strawberries
½ cup cantaloupe
2 tablespoons hulled hemp seed
½ inch fresh ginger root

Combine all ingredients in a high-power blender or food processor and blend until smooth. Drink immediately.

CALORIES: 240 **FAT:** 6 **CARBS:** 30 **FIBER:** 6 **PROTEIN:** 8

Week 20

Grocery List

- ☐ 3 apples
- ☐ 1 cucumber
- ☐ 2 cups minced fresh mint leaves
- ☐ 1 cup honeydew
- ☐ ½ cup pomegranate arils
- ☐ 1 cup frozen cantaloupe
- ☐ 1 cup frozen strawberries
- ☐ 1 cup frozen wild blackberries
- ☐ 1½ cups coconut water
- ☐ 1 cup brewed green tea
- ☐ ½ cup nonfat Greek yogurt
- ☐ 4 teaspoons lemon juice
- ☐ 6 tablespoons chia seed
- ☐ 3 tablespoons hulled hemp seed
- ☐ 2 tablespoons protein powder

134. MINT TEA SLUSHY

This combination has subtle tea and mint undertones. According to recent studies, just 1 to 2 cups of green tea per day is ideal for fostering weight loss.

½ cucumber
1 cup brewed green tea
1 cup frozen cantaloupe
½ cup ice
½ cup minced fresh mint leaves
2 tablespoons chia seed

Combine all ingredients in a high-power blender or food processor and blend until smooth. Drink immediately.

CALORIES: 214 FAT: 10 CARBS: 20 FIBER: 16 PROTEIN: 7

135. CUCUMBER MINT

This melon and cucumber drink has just a hint of mint, and the hemp seeds are rich in inflammation-reducing omega-3 fatty acids for proper hydration. Even a small drop in water level can affect metabolism, making it more difficult to lose weight.

½ cucumber
1 cup coconut water
1 cup honeydew
½ cup ice
½ cup minced fresh mint leaves
2 tablespoons hulled hemp seed

Combine all ingredients in a high-power blender or food processor and blend until smooth. Drink immediately.

CALORIES: 214 FAT: 6 CARBS: 30 FIBER: 6 PROTEIN: 7

136. BERRIES AND CREAM

Enjoy the hint of mint in this creamy strawberry shake. This combination is an excellent and nourishing dessert!

1 cup frozen strawberries
½ cup coconut water
½ cup nonfat Greek yogurt
½ cup ice
2 tablespoons protein powder
1 tablespoon minced fresh mint leaves

Combine all ingredients in a high-power blender or food processor and blend until smooth. Drink immediately.

CALORIES: 186 **FAT:** 0 **CARBS:** 26 **FIBER:** 4 **PROTEIN:** 22

137. BLACKBERRY JULEP

The wild blackberries in this smoothie give it a thick, sweet, and satisfying flavor, and they provide concentrated levels of polyphenols that support weight loss.

1 cup frozen wild blackberries
½ cup ice
½ cup water
¼ cup minced fresh mint leaves
2 tablespoons chia seed

Combine all ingredients in a high-power blender or food processor and blend until smooth. Drink immediately.

CALORIES: 262 **FAT:** 10 **CARBS:** 26 **FIBER:** 20 **PROTEIN:** 8

138. MINT APPLE POM

Apple takes the tartness out of the pomegranate, and the mint gives this smoothie a wonderful scent. Pomegranate arils are nutritious and provide antioxidant vitamin C and free radical–scavenging polyphenols, including ellagitannins and flavonoids that support metabolism.

1 apple
½ cup pomegranate arils
½ cup ice
½ cup water
1 tablespoon chia seed
1 tablespoon minced fresh mint leaves

Combine all ingredients in a high-power blender or food processor and blend until smooth. Drink immediately.

CALORIES: 202 **FAT:** 10 **CARBS:** 18 **FIBER:** 9 **PROTEIN:** 3

139. APPLE MINT APERITIF

The fresh mint fragrance hits the nose before the sweetness and lemon flavor hit the palate. Add water and ice to any smoothie to increase hydration and lighten the flavors as desired.

1 apple
½ cup water
½ cup ice
¼ cup minced fresh mint leaves
1 tablespoon chia seed
½ teaspoon lemon juice

Combine all ingredients in a high-power blender or food processor and blend until smooth. Drink immediately.

CALORIES: 212 **FAT:** 5 **CARBS:** 20 **FIBER:** 14 **PROTEIN:** 3

140. MINT LEMONADE REFRESHER

The fresh apple flavor with a hint of mint and citrus is a hydrating combination perfect for the late afternoon, when we're most dehydrated and tired from a busy day. The more energy we have, the more likely we'll be moving our bodies and burning calories rather than slumping into a sedentary activity.

1 apple
½ cup ice
½ cup water
¼ cup minced fresh mint leaves
1 tablespoon lemon juice
1 tablespoon hulled hemp seed

Combine all ingredients in a high-power blender or food processor and blend until smooth. Drink immediately.

CALORIES: 106 **FAT:** 3 **CARBS:** 16 **FIBER:** 6 **PROTEIN:** 3

Week 21

Grocery List

- [ ] 5 fresh mint leaves
- [ ] 3 nectarines
- [ ] 1 apple
- [ ] 1 kiwi
- [ ] 1 tomato
- [ ] ½ cup minced baby kale leaves
- [ ] ½ cup minced fresh mint leaves
- [ ] ½ inch fresh ginger root
- [ ] 1 cup frozen pineapple
- [ ] 1 cup frozen mango
- [ ] 5 frozen strawberries
- [ ] ½ cup frozen cherries
- [ ] ½ cup frozen wild blueberries
- [ ] 1½ cups coconut water
- [ ] ½ cup almond milk
- [ ] ½ cup cultured coconut milk
- [ ] ½ cup nonfat Greek yogurt
- [ ] 3 teaspoons lemon juice
- [ ] 7 tablespoons chia seed
- [ ] 3 tablespoons hulled hemp seed

141. MANGO MINT WITH CITRUS

This smoothie contains quercetin, an antioxidant flavonoid found in apples, which is a powerful anti-inflammatory to help improve energy and weight loss for those with inflammatory conditions, such as food allergies, arthritis, and autoimmune disease.

5 fresh mint leaves
1 apple
½ cup frozen mango
½ cup nonfat Greek yogurt
½ cup water
1 teaspoon lemon juice
½ inch fresh ginger root

Combine all ingredients in a high-power blender or food processor and blend until smooth. Drink immediately.

CALORIES: 200 **FAT:** 1 **CARBS:** 38 **FIBER:** 5 **PROTEIN:** 13

142. SAVORY SUMMER MIX

This combination includes cool green veggies and has a minty scent. The greens are not only earthy and flavorful, but they also provide concentrated nutrients. A half cup of kale contains 45 milligrams of calcium, which promotes weight loss by increasing muscle activity, thereby increasing calories burned.

1 tomato
½ cup fresh mint leaves
½ cup minced baby kale leaves
½ cup ice
2 tablespoons chia seed

Combine all ingredients in a high-power blender or food processor and blend until smooth. Drink immediately.

CALORIES: 186 **FAT:** 10 **CARBS:** 12 **FIBER:** 16 **PROTEIN:** 8

143. CHERRY ALMOND NECTARINE

Enjoy this nectarine and almond frosty with sweet cherries, which are rich in carotenoids that support body fat release and skin elasticity, which is needed after weight loss.

1 nectarine
½ cup almond milk
½ cup ice
½ cup frozen cherries
2 tablespoons hulled hemp seed

Combine all ingredients in a high-power blender or food processor and blend until smooth. Drink immediately.

CALORIES: 208 **FAT:** 8 **CARBS:** 28 **FIBER:** 6 **PROTEIN:** 7

144. NECTARINE AND MANGO

This smoothie is like a sorbet with delicious, fruity flavors. The mango is rich in prebiotic dietary fiber, which improves our metabolism by activating the beneficial bacteria in our digestive tracts.

1 nectarine
½ cup cultured coconut milk
½ cup frozen mango
2 tablespoons chia seed

Combine all ingredients in a high-power blender or food processor and blend until smooth. Drink immediately.

CALORIES: 300 **FAT:** 14 **CARBS:** 30 **FIBER:** 20 **PROTEIN:** 7

145. NECTARINE AND KIWI

This fresh combination is so rich in flavor that it's like a tart summer-fruit sorbet. It makes for a nutritious, fat-burning alternative to a high-calorie, sugar-laden dessert.

1 nectarine
1 kiwi
½ cup coconut water
½ cup ice
2 tablespoons chia seed

Combine all ingredients in a high-power blender or food processor and blend until smooth. Drink immediately.

CALORIES: 220 **FAT:** 10 **CARBS:** 30 **FIBER:** 18 **PROTEIN:** 6

146. THE PURPLE MERMAID

This smoothie has tropical flavors with a citrus twist. The coconut water is an excellent source of electrolytes, which conduct electrical impulses throughout our bodies, keeping our energy systems and calorie burning at peak performance.

1 cup coconut water
½ cup frozen pineapple
½ cup frozen wild blueberries
1 tablespoon chia seed
1 teaspoon lemon juice

Combine all ingredients in a high-power blender or food processor and blend until smooth. Drink immediately.

CALORIES: 225 **FAT:** 5 **CARBS:** 30 **FIBER:** 18 **PROTEIN:** 3

147. RUBY SUNRISE

This sweet, fresh combination has a light citrus flavor and fragrance. The pineapple contains the digestive enzyme bromelain, which breaks down protein and helps with digestion and metabolism.

5 frozen strawberries
1 cup water
½ cup frozen pineapple
¼ cup ice
1 tablespoon hulled hemp seed
1 teaspoon lemon juice

Combine all ingredients in a high-power blender or food processor and blend until smooth. Drink immediately.

CALORIES: 112 **FAT:** 4 **CARBS:** 20 **FIBER:** 4 **PROTEIN:** 3

Week 22

Grocery List

- [ ] 2 bananas
- [ ] 1 orange
- [ ] 1 pear
- [ ] 1½ cups frozen pineapple
- [ ] ¼ cup minced baby spinach leaves
- [ ] ¼ cup minced fresh basil leaves
- [ ] ¼ cup minced fresh mint leaves
- [ ] ¼ cup pomegranate arils
- [ ] ½ inch fresh turmeric root
- [ ] ½ cup frozen peaches
- [ ] ½ cup frozen mango
- [ ] 1½ cups apricot nectar
- [ ] 1 cup coconut water
- [ ] 1 cup nonfat Greek yogurt
- [ ] ½ cup papaya nectar
- [ ] ½ cup plant milk
- [ ] 1 teaspoon lemon juice
- [ ] 9 tablespoons chia seed
- [ ] 1 tablespoon protein powder
- [ ] 1 teaspoon pure vanilla extract
- [ ] ¼ teaspoon probiotic supplement

148. PINEAPPLE POM

This cocktail is sweet and tart, with a light coconut taste. The sweet intensity of pineapple is the perfect pairing with the tartness of the pomegranate. Polyphenols in the pomegranate arils help reduce inflammation by disrupting the inflammatory signaling pathways.

1 cup coconut water
½ cup ice
¼ cup frozen pineapple
¼ cup pomegranate arils
2 tablespoons chia seed

Combine all ingredients in a high-power blender or food processor and blend until smooth. Drink immediately.

CALORIES: 230 **FAT:** 10 **CARBS:** 30 **FIBER:** 14 **PROTEIN:** 6

149. SWEET PINEAPPLE GREENS

Pineapple helps sweeten the spinach in this green drink. This combination is so delicious that it is a stealthy way to sneak in those needed servings of vegetables to support health and weight loss.

½ frozen banana
½ cup plant milk
½ cup frozen pineapple
¼ cup minced baby spinach leaves
2 tablespoons chia seed

Combine all ingredients in a high-power blender or food processor and blend until smooth. Drink immediately.

CALORIES: 248 **FAT:** 12 **CARBS:** 26 **FIBER:** 14 **PROTEIN:** 8

150. ORANGE PINEAPPLE VANILLA

This smoothie is the perfect blend of citrus, tropical fragrance, and vanilla. Studies have found that the scent of vanilla can help to reduce appetite.

½ orange
½ cup ice
½ cup frozen pineapple
½ cup nonfat Greek yogurt
1 teaspoon vanilla extract

Combine all ingredients in a high-power blender or food processor and blend until smooth. Drink immediately.

CALORIES: 174 **FAT:** 0 **CARBS:** 30 **FIBER:** 6 **PROTEIN:** 13

151. MINT MANGO DREAM

This mango and papaya nectar blend is thick and fresh, with a bit of balmy mint. Cryptoxanthin, a carotenoid found in papaya, is a salve for the digestive tract, helping to heal and improve digestion and support metabolism.

½ cup frozen mango
½ cup papaya nectar
1 cup water
¼ cup frozen pineapple
¼ cup minced fresh mint leaves
¼ cup minced fresh basil leaves
1 tablespoon chia seed

Combine all ingredients in a high-power blender or food processor and blend until smooth. Drink immediately.

CALORIES: 230 **FAT:** 5 **CARBS:** 30 **FIBER:** 16 **PROTEIN:** 4

152. APRICOT POWER BREAKFAST

This refreshing elixir has a sweet and aromatic apricot flavor, with a frosty, creamy base. The probiotics included here help us drop weight by improving our digestion and metabolism.

½ cup apricot nectar
½ cup ice
½ cup nonfat Greek yogurt
1 tablespoon protein powder
¼ teaspoon probiotic supplement

Combine all ingredients in a high-power blender or food processor and blend until smooth. Drink immediately.

CALORIES: 154 FAT: 0 CARBS: 21 FIBER: 0 PROTEIN: 16

153. APRICOT AND PEACH

This frosty and creamy drink is rich in stone-fruit flavors and packs a wallop of anti-inflammatory carotenoids.

½ frozen banana
½ cup apricot nectar
½ cup frozen peaches
2 tablespoons chia seed
1 teaspoon lemon juice

Combine all ingredients in a high-power blender or food processor and blend until smooth. Drink immediately.

CALORIES: 280 FAT: 10 CARBS: 30 FIBER: 16 PROTEIN: 6

154. APRICOT PEAR

This apricot and pear combination is exotic, with a heady fragrance. Turmeric root supplies curcumin, a powerful anti-inflammatory that stimulates the release of excess water weight.

½ frozen banana
½ pear
¼ cup apricot nectar
½ cup ice
2 tablespoons chia seed
½ inch fresh turmeric root

Combine all ingredients in a high-power blender or food processor and blend until smooth. Drink immediately.

CALORIES: 240 FAT: 10 CARBS: 30 FIBER: 16 PROTEIN: 7

Week 23

Grocery List

- ☐ 2 avocados
- ☐ 2 bananas
- ☐ 1 date
- ☐ ½ inch fresh turmeric root
- ☐ ½ cup frozen cherries
- ☐ ¼ cup frozen blackberries
- ☐ ¼ cup frozen peaches
- ☐ ¼ cup frozen raspberries
- ☐ 2½ cups apricot nectar
- ☐ 1 cup almond milk
- ☐ ½ cup coconut water
- ☐ ½ cup nonfat Greek yogurt
- ☐ ½ cup papaya nectar
- ☐ 2 teaspoons lime juice
- ☐ 1 teaspoon lemon juice
- ☐ 10 tablespoons chia seed
- ☐ 2 teaspoons pure vanilla extract
- ☐ 1 teaspoon unsweetened cocoa powder
- ☐ 2 pinches of ground cardamom
- ☐ 2 pinches of fresh-ground black pepper
- ☐ 1 pinch of ground cinnamon

155. APRICOT CHERRY SWIRL

Sweet cherry and tart apricot are a divine pairing with a little citrus and vanilla finish. Cherries have natural phytochemicals that trigger a calming effect, helping to reduce stress hormones, which have a negative impact on fat metabolism.

½ cup apricot nectar
½ cup frozen cherries
1 tablespoon chia seed
1 teaspoon lemon juice
½ teaspoon vanilla extract

Combine all ingredients in a high-power blender or food processor and blend until smooth. Drink immediately.

CALORIES: 189 FAT: 5 CARBS: 29 FIBER: 8 PROTEIN: 4

156. SPICED APRICOT

This medicinal elixir is a powerful blend of spices that trigger weight loss. The black pepper is rich in potassium and works synergistically with turmeric to help stimulate the release of extra water weight.

1 cup apricot nectar
1 cup ice
1 tablespoon chia seed
½ inch fresh turmeric root
1 pinch of ground cardamom
1 pinch of fresh-ground black pepper

Combine all ingredients in a high-power blender or food processor and blend until smooth. Drink immediately.

CALORIES: 190 FAT: 4 CARBS: 41 FIBER: 5 PROTEIN: 3

157. APRICOT FROSTY

This frosty blend is tart and spicy, with a sweet hint of date. The piperine in the freshly ground black pepper reduces inflammation in the gut, which helps flatten swollen bellies.

1 date
½ cup apricot nectar
¼ cup frozen blackberries
¼ cup frozen peaches
2 tablespoons chia seed
1 pinch of fresh-ground black pepper
1 pinch of ground cardamom

Combine all ingredients in a high-power blender or food processor and blend until smooth. Drink immediately.

CALORIES: 310 **FAT:** 10 **CARBS:** 30 **FIBER:** 18 **PROTEIN:** 8

158. APRICOT CINNAMON CREAM

This frosty fruit blend is slightly sweet, with a hint of cinnamon. Raspberries contain raspberry ketone, a natural plant nutrient that may promote lipolysis, which is the technical term for body fat breakdown and release.

½ frozen banana
½ cup apricot nectar
1 cup water
¼ cup frozen raspberries
½ cup ice
2 tablespoons chia seed
1 pinch of ground cinnamon

Combine all ingredients in a high-power blender or food processor and blend until smooth. Drink immediately.

CALORIES: 238 **FAT:** 10 **CARBS:** 30 **FIBER:** 18 **PROTEIN:** 8

159. COCOA ALMOND CRUSH

This super creamy concoction has a little charge of chocolate. The unsweetened cocoa contains flavonoids, which help reduce weight gain by improving the way our bodies utilize insulin.

½ avocado
½ frozen banana
1 cup almond milk
½ cup ice
2 tablespoons chia seed
1 teaspoon unsweetened cocoa powder
1 teaspoon vanilla extract

Combine all ingredients in a high-power blender or food processor and blend until smooth. Drink immediately.

CALORIES: 378 **FAT:** 24 **CARBS:** 26 **FIBER:** 20 **PROTEIN:** 8

160. THE ISLANDER

This drink has papaya flavor in a fresh avocado base. Lime juice is the perfect pairing with papaya. Avocados contain monounsaturated fatty acids, which are healthy fats that improve fat burning, especially in the abdominal area.

½ avocado
½ cup papaya nectar
½ cup ice
2 tablespoons chia seed
½ teaspoon lime juice

Combine all ingredients in a high-power blender or food processor and blend until smooth. Drink immediately.

CALORIES: 342 **FAT:** 20 **CARBS:** 26 **FIBER:** 18 **PROTEIN:** 7

161. COCONUT AVOCADO LIME

This smoothie is rich and thick with just a hint of lime. Avocados contain healthful fats that help reduce cholesterol levels and satisfy cravings for unhealthy fats.

¼ avocado
½ frozen banana
½ cup coconut water
½ cup nonfat Greek yogurt
1 teaspoon lime juice

Combine all ingredients in a high-power blender or food processor and blend until smooth. Drink immediately.

CALORIES: 250 **FAT:** 12 **CARBS:** 28 **FIBER:** 6 **PROTEIN:** 14

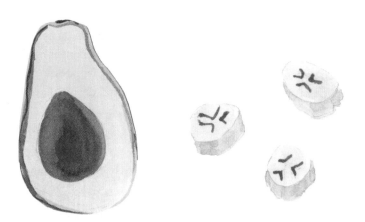

Week 24

Grocery List

- ☐ 1 date
- ☐ 1 small tomato
- ☐ 1 apple
- ☐ 1 banana
- ☐ 1 avocado
- ☐ 1 cucumber
- ☐ ¼ cup minced fresh basil leaves
- ☐ 3½ cups frozen cherries
- ☐ 2 cups plant milk
- ☐ 1 cup coconut water
- ☐ 1 cup nonfat Greek yogurt
- ☐ ½ cup black cherry juice
- ☐ ½ cup hazelnut milk
- ☐ 1 teaspoon lemon juice
- ☐ 6 tablespoons protein powder
- ☐ 5 tablespoons chia seed
- ☐ 6 teaspoons pure vanilla extract
- ☐ 1 pinch of fresh-ground black pepper

162. GREEN LUSHY

This blend is silky and sweet and so good for you! Avocados provide 35 percent more potassium than a banana, plus energizing vitamins, including K, B_6, B_5, C, and E. They are high in calories, so use just one-quarter of an avocado per smoothie.

½ banana
¼ avocado
½ cup coconut water
¼ cup frozen cherries
2 tablespoons chia seed

Combine all ingredients in a high-power blender or food processor and blend until smooth. Drink immediately.

CALORIES: 250 FAT: 12 CARBS: 35 FIBER: 12 PROTEIN: 5

163. FAUX PEACH

This medley is satisfying and energizing while providing appetite-suppressing and health-supporting fats.

1 small tomato
½ apple
½ date
¼ avocado
½ cup water
½ cup ice
1 tablespoon chia seed

Combine all ingredients in a high-power blender or food processor and blend until smooth. Drink immediately.

CALORIES: 210 FAT: 9 CARBS: 33 FIBER: 10 PROTEIN: 4

164. BASIL AVOCADO CREAM

This is a savory herbal blend with just a touch of sweetness from the date. The fats in the avocado and chia seed support the nervous system, which helps regulate many bodily functions that affect weight loss.

½ date
¼ avocado
1 cup diced cucumber
1 cup plant milk
½ cup ice
¼ cup minced fresh basil leaves
1 tablespoon chia seed

Combine all ingredients in a high-power blender or food processor and blend until smooth. Drink immediately.

CALORIES: 220 FAT: 14 CARBS: 21 FIBER: 9 PROTEIN: 6

165. HAZELNUT CHERRY

Cherry, hazelnut, and vanilla mingle beautifully in this cool, frosty concoction. If you tend to skip breakfast, whip this little smoothie up and get your metabolism moving first thing in the morning to increase weight loss.

½ cup hazelnut milk
½ cup ice
½ cup frozen cherries
2 tablespoons protein powder
2 teaspoons vanilla extract

Combine all ingredients in a high-power blender or food processor and blend until smooth. Drink immediately.

CALORIES: 148 FAT: 2 CARBS: 23 FIBER: 2 PROTEIN: 10

166. VANILLA CHERRY FREEZE

This frosty, sweet cherry freeze has rich fruity flavor and vanilla fragrance. Very low in calories and high in protein, this super nutritious mix is the perfect after-dinner dessert to calm nerves and improve sleep for a boost to fat burning during the night.

1½ cups frozen cherries
½ cup coconut water
½ cup nonfat Greek yogurt
2 tablespoons protein powder
2 teaspoons vanilla extract

Combine all ingredients in a high-power blender or food processor and blend until smooth. Drink immediately.

CALORIES: 186 **FAT:** 1 **CARBS:** 30 **FIBER:** 5 **PROTEIN:** 18

167. CHERRY CITRUS SPICE

This rich cherry smoothie has a little citrus and spice. This calming blend can help with the transition from a stimulating day to a restful, weight-loss supportive sleep, due to the melatonin in the cherries and cherry juice.

½ cup black cherry juice
1 cup water
½ cup frozen cherries
1 tablespoon chia seed
1 teaspoon lemon juice
1 pinch of fresh-ground black pepper

Combine all ingredients in a high-power blender or food processor and blend until smooth. Drink immediately.

CALORIES: 183 **FAT:** 5 **CARBS:** 29 **FIBER:** 8 **PROTEIN:** 4

168. SOUR CHERRY VANILLA

This creamy and rich combination is only slightly sweet, with a little sour-cherry edge. Cherries contain antioxidant anthocyanins that help reduce the pain from inflammation, and less pain means a reduction of cortisol in the blood. This is beneficial, as cortisol can increase body fat.

½ cup plant milk
½ cup ice
½ cup nonfat Greek yogurt
½ cup frozen cherries
2 tablespoons protein powder
2 teaspoons vanilla extract

Combine all ingredients in a high-power blender or food processor and blend until smooth. Drink immediately.

CALORIES: 115 **FAT:** 2 **CARBS:** 14 **FIBER:** 1 **PROTEIN:** 20

Week 25

Grocery List

- [ ] 8 grapes
- [ ] 6 cherries
- [ ] 2 peaches
- [ ] ½ cup frozen pineapple
- [ ] ½ inch fresh ginger root
- [ ] 1 banana
- [ ] 2 cups frozen cherries
- [ ] ½ cup frozen peaches
- [ ] ½ cup frozen wild blackberries
- [ ] 2½ cups coconut water
- [ ] 1 cup plant milk
- [ ] ¼ cup nonfat Greek yogurt
- [ ] 3 teaspoons lemon juice
- [ ] 6 tablespoons protein powder
- [ ] 5 tablespoons chia seed
- [ ] 7 teaspoons pure vanilla extract
- [ ] 1 pinch of fresh-ground black pepper
- [ ] 1 pinch of ground cardamom

169. GRAPE CHERRY DREAM

This dreamy drink is sweet and fruity with layers of flavor. The sweetness of grape juice complements the tartness of fruits like tart cherries and pomegranate. Red grapes contain resveratrol, which, research indicates, may help us lose weight by increasing our sensitivity to insulin.

8 grapes
½ cup water
½ cup ice
½ cup frozen cherries
2 tablespoons protein powder
2 teaspoons vanilla extract
1 teaspoon lemon juice

Combine all ingredients in a high-power blender or food processor and blend until smooth. Drink immediately.

CALORIES: 210 **FAT:** 0 **CARBS:** 30 **FIBER:** 12 **PROTEIN:** 9

170. CHERRY PINEAPPLE

The flavor elements in pineapple and cherries balance perfectly with a little vanilla and enough protein to help us feel full longer.

½ cup coconut water
½ cup frozen cherries
½ cup frozen pineapple
½ cup ice
2 tablespoons protein powder
2 teaspoons vanilla extract

Combine all ingredients in a high-power blender or food processor and blend until smooth. Drink immediately.

CALORIES: 154 **FAT:** 0 **CARBS:** 30 **FIBER:** 2 **PROTEIN:** 9

171. SPICED CHERRY REFRESHER

Hot and heady spices complement the sweet cherries and citrus in this refreshing blend. The phenolics in cherries help modulate fat metabolism as well as reduce inflammation in the belly area.

6 cherries
½ cup coconut water
1 tablespoon chia seed
1 teaspoon lemon juice
1 pinch of ground cardamom
1 pinch of fresh-ground black pepper

Combine all ingredients in a high-power blender or food processor and blend until smooth. Drink immediately.

CALORIES: 127 **FAT:** 5 **CARBS:** 22 **FIBER:** 8 **PROTEIN:** 4

172. PEACH BERRY

This peachy drink is light and fresh with a hint of citrus. The coconut water is an ideal smoothie base because it doesn't have added sugar or food colorings, and it's low in calories and rich in electrolytes.

1 peach
½ cup coconut water
½ cup frozen wild blackberries
2 tablespoons protein powder
2 teaspoons vanilla extract
1 teaspoon lemon juice

Combine all ingredients in a high-power blender or food processor and blend until smooth. Drink immediately.

CALORIES: 174 **FAT:** 0 **CARBS:** 30 **FIBER:** 6 **PROTEIN:** 10

173. GINGERED PEACH

Enjoy peach flavor that is not too sweet thanks to a little heat from the ginger, which improves digestion. When nutrients from our food are absorbed into the bloodstream, they are then carried through our blood vessels to the cells that need them, and this diminishes food cravings.

½ peach
½ frozen banana
½ cup coconut water
½ cup ice
2 tablespoons chia seed
½ inch fresh ginger root

Combine all ingredients in a high-power blender or food processor and blend until smooth. Drink immediately.

CALORIES: 214 **FAT:** 10 **CARBS:** 30 **FIBER:** 16 **PROTEIN:** 6

174. PEACHY BANANA

This enticing combination is creamy with layers of flavor and fragrance, as more than 80 natural compounds contribute to a peach's aroma. Peaches contain ellagic acid, a potent antioxidant that reduces the belly fat caused by metabolic syndrome.

½ peach
½ frozen banana
½ cup coconut water
½ cup plant milk
¼ cup frozen cherries
¼ cup ice
2 tablespoons chia seed

Combine all ingredients in a high-power blender or food processor and blend until smooth.

CALORIES: 356 **FAT:** 12 **CARBS:** 30 **FIBER:** 16 **PROTEIN:** 6

175. CHERRY VANILLA PEACH

This delicious combination is creamy and sweet and has layers of flavors. The yogurt provides protein, which reduces cravings, helps stabilize blood sugar, and provides the amino acids needed for long-lasting energy. Sweet, tart, dark, and sour cherries all contain anthocyanins and proanthocyanidins that help reduce inflammation and water weight.

½ cup plant milk
½ cup frozen cherries
½ cup frozen peaches
¼ cup nonfat Greek yogurt
1 teaspoon vanilla extract

Combine all ingredients in a high-power blender or food processor and blend until smooth. Drink immediately.

CALORIES: 212 FAT: 2 CARBS: 30 FIBER: 4 PROTEIN: 12

Week 26

Grocery List

- ☐ 9 donut peaches
- ☐ 2 oranges
- ☐ 1 banana
- ☐ ¼ cup minced fresh basil leaves
- ☐ ¼ cup minced fresh cilantro leaves
- ☐ ¼ cup pomegranate arils
- ☐ ½ inch fresh ginger root
- ☐ ½ inch fresh turmeric root
- ☐ ½ cup frozen wild blueberries
- ☐ ¼ cup frozen cherries
- ☐ 2 cups coconut water
- ☐ 1 cup brewed hibiscus tea
- ☐ ½ cup nonfat Greek yogurt
- ☐ ¼ cup black cherry juice
- ☐ 1 teaspoon lime juice
- ☐ 5 tablespoons protein powder
- ☐ 4 tablespoons hulled hemp seed
- ☐ 3 tablespoons chia seed
- ☐ 1 tablespoon unsweetened cocoa powder
- ☐ 5 teaspoons pure vanilla extract
- ☐ 1 teaspoon ground cinnamon
- ☐ 1 pinch of fresh-ground black pepper

176. GINGERED DONUT PEACH

Try this delightful combination of sweet peaches with a little heat and citrus. The ginger root has a warming effect, which stimulates and supports digestion.

2 donut peaches
½ cup coconut water
½ cup ice
2 tablespoons chia seed
½ inch fresh ginger root

Combine all ingredients in a high-power blender or food processor and blend until smooth. Drink immediately.

CALORIES: 266 FAT: 10 CARBS: 14 FIBER: 16 PROTEIN: 6

177. CINNAMON PEACH

Donut peaches are luscious, and this smoothie has a little vanilla and a hint of cinnamon. Even a small amount of spice provides medicinal benefits. According to one study, just half a teaspoon of cinnamon per day is enough to control cholesterol and triglyceride levels for many people.

2 donut peaches
½ cup coconut water
½ cup ice
½ cup nonfat Greek yogurt
1 tablespoon protein powder
1 teaspoon vanilla extract
¼ teaspoon ground cinnamon

Combine all ingredients in a high-power blender or food processor and blend until smooth. Drink immediately.

CALORIES: 210 FAT: 0 CARBS: 30 FIBER: 4 PROTEIN: 16

178. CILANTRO PEACH ORANGE

This smoothie has fresh cilantro fragrance in a sweet orange juice and fresh peach base. Cilantro leaves and their seeds, known as coriander, help reduce the belly fat that is so common with metabolic syndromes.

2 donut peaches
½ orange
½ cup ice
½ cup water
¼ cup minced fresh cilantro leaves
2 tablespoons hulled hemp seed

Combine all ingredients in a high-power blender or food processor and blend until smooth. Drink immediately.

CALORIES: 214 **FAT:** 6 **CARBS:** 30 **FIBER:** 10 **PROTEIN:** 6

179. ORANGE PEACH

This smoothie has a citrus base with a hint of vanilla. Peaches and citrus provide vitamin C, which reduces oxidation and improves energy.

1 donut peach
1 orange
½ cup water
½ cup ice
2 tablespoons protein powder
2 teaspoons vanilla extract

Combine all ingredients in a high-power blender or food processor and blend until smooth. Drink immediately.

CALORIES: 200 **FAT:** 2 **CARBS:** 30 **FIBER:** 12 **PROTEIN:** 8

180. BASIL ORANGE PEACH

This basil orange smoothie with a little lime packs a lot of fat-burning and inflammation-reducing power nutrients.

1 donut peach

½ orange

½ cup coconut water

½ cup ice

¼ cup minced fresh basil leaves

2 tablespoons hulled hemp seed

½ inch fresh turmeric root

1 teaspoon lime juice

Combine all ingredients in a high-power blender or food processor and blend until smooth. Drink immediately.

CALORIES: 248 FAT: 6 CARBS: 30 FIBER: 6 PROTEIN: 7

181. SPICED HIBISCUS BERRY

This mix provides a refreshing blend of tea tannins and berry flavors. Black pepper helps stimulate healthy immune function and tastes amazing in smoothies!

1 donut peach
1 cup brewed hibiscus tea
¼ cup pomegranate arils
½ cup frozen wild blueberries
½ cup ice
1 tablespoon chia seed
1 pinch of fresh-ground black pepper

Combine all ingredients in a high-power blender or food processor and blend until smooth. Drink immediately.

CALORIES: 184 FAT: 5 CARBS: 30 FIBER: 10 PROTEIN: 4

182. CHOCOLATE CHERRY

This sweet cherry blend includes coconut and rich vanilla flavor. Bananas are rich in prebiotics that feed the good microbes in the digestive tract that increase weight loss.

½ frozen banana
½ cup coconut water
¼ cup frozen cherries
¼ cup black cherry juice
2 tablespoons protein powder
1 tablespoon unsweetened cocoa powder
2 teaspoons vanilla extract

Combine all ingredients in a high-power blender or food processor and blend until smooth. Drink immediately.

CALORIES: 184 FAT: 0 CARBS: 30 FIBER: 6 PROTEIN: 10

Week 27

Grocery List

- ☐ 1 apple
- ☐ 1 banana
- ☐ 1 celery stalk
- ☐ 1 fig
- ☐ 1 date
- ☐ 1 cucumber
- ☐ 1 medium-hot pepper
- ☐ ½ inch fresh turmeric root
- ☐ 2½ cups cherry tomatoes
- ☐ ½ cup minced fresh basil leaves
- ☐ 1 cup frozen cherries
- ☐ ½ cup frozen wild blueberries
- ☐ ½ cup frozen mango
- ☐ 2 cups nonfat Greek yogurt
- ☐ ½ cup carrot juice
- ☐ 1 cup black cherry juice
- ☐ 4 teaspoons lemon juice
- ☐ 1 vanilla bean
- ☐ 4 tablespoons chia seed
- ☐ 2 tablespoons hulled hemp seed
- ☐ 1 teaspoon horseradish
- ☐ 1 teaspoon hot sauce
- ☐ 1 pinch of cayenne pepper
- ☐ 1 pinch of celery salt
- ☐ 1 pinch of fresh-ground black pepper

183. BERRY MANGO TART

This creamy, blueberry-rich drink offers a tart citrus flavor to the palate. Mangiferin in mango helps control white adipose tissue accumulation, which reduces obesity.

½ cup frozen wild blueberries
½ cup frozen mango
1 cup water
¼ cup nonfat Greek yogurt
¼ cup black cherry juice
1 teaspoon lemon juice

Combine all ingredients in a high-power blender or food processor and blend until smooth. Drink immediately.

CALORIES: 160 **FAT:** 1 **CARBS:** 34 **FIBER:** 4 **PROTEIN:** 7

184. DOUBLE CHERRY

This recipe calls for black cherry juice, which is rich in anti-inflammatory anthocyanins. Inflammation can be reduced by natural anti-inflammatories from foods, such as cherries and cherry juice, helping to reduce the need for pharmaceutical anti-inflammatories that can have adverse effects.

½ frozen banana
½ cup black cherry juice
½ cup frozen cherries
1 cup water
2 tablespoons hulled hemp seed

Combine all ingredients in a high-power blender or food processor and blend until smooth. Drink immediately.

CALORIES: 255 **FAT:** 6 **CARBS:** 30 **FIBER:** 5 **PROTEIN:** 7

185. APPLE TOMATO DATE

This drink tastes like a tomato-yogurt bisque sweetened with a date. Yogurt provides protein, which supports the enzymes in fat cells that release stored body fat, so it's a great smoothie addition for those who aim to lose stubborn body fat.

1 date
½ apple
½ cup ice
½ cup water
½ cup cherry tomatoes
½ cup nonfat Greek yogurt

Combine all ingredients in a high-power blender or food processor and blend until smooth. Drink immediately.

CALORIES: 200 **FAT:** 0 **CARBS:** 30 **FIBER:** 10 **PROTEIN:** 12

186. TOMATO KICKER

When available, use garden-fresh tomatoes in this cool mix with a touch of heat. Carotenoid antioxidants in hot peppers protect healthy cells from oxidative stress, and a daily dose can help release stubborn body fat.

½ cucumber
½ cup cherry tomatoes
½ cup ice
½ cup water
¼ medium-hot pepper
2 tablespoons chia seed

Combine all ingredients in a high-power blender or food processor and blend until smooth. Drink immediately.

CALORIES: 180 **FAT:** 10 **CARBS:** 10 **FIBER:** 14 **PROTEIN:** 7

187. FRESH BLOODY MARY

Entertaining is a snap with this healthy version of the classic drink, and it has almost no calories so you can drink this one all day long. Celery is a rich source of phenolic phytonutrients, including caffeic acid, caffeoylquinic acid, cinnamic acid, coumaric acid, ferulic acid, apigenin, luteolin, quercetin, kaempferol, lunularin, beta-sitosterol, and furanocoumarins. These antioxidants help body fat get active and release, which increases weight loss.

1 celery stalk
1 cup cherry tomatoes
½ cup ice
½ cup water
1 tablespoon lemon juice
½ teaspoon horseradish
½ teaspoon hot sauce
1 pinch of fresh-ground black pepper
1 pinch of celery salt
1 pinch of cayenne pepper

Combine all ingredients in a high-power blender or food processor and blend until smooth. Drink immediately.

CALORIES: 29 **FAT:** 0 **CARBS:** 7 **FIBER:** 2 **PROTEIN:** 1

188. SUMMERTIME SLIMMER

Enjoy fresh-from-the-garden summertime flavor in this smoothie, which is rich in the nutrients needed to convert food into energy.

½ cup carrot juice
½ cup ice
½ cup minced fresh basil leaves
½ cup cherry tomatoes
2 tablespoons chia seed

Combine all ingredients in a high-power blender or food processor and blend until smooth. Drink immediately.

CALORIES: 202 **FAT:** 10 **CARBS:** 16 **FIBER:** 14 **PROTEIN:** 7

189. APPLE CHERRY FIG

This drink is intensely sweet with warm vanilla and fig undertones. Fruit that is frozen at the peak of ripeness has concentrated nutrients that are released when thawed. Drink immediately after blending for maximum nutrient-potency.

1 fig
1 vanilla bean
½ apple
½ cup nonfat Greek yogurt
½ cup frozen cherries
½ cup water
½ inch fresh turmeric root

Combine all ingredients in a high-power blender or food processor and blend until smooth. Drink immediately.

CALORIES: 220 **FAT:** 0 **CARBS:** 30 **FIBER:** 9 **PROTEIN:** 13

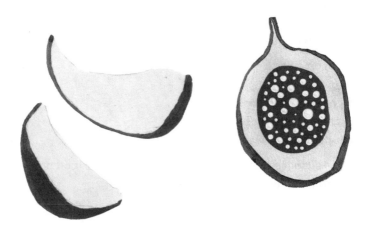

Week 28

Grocery List

- ☐ 2 figs
- ☐ 1 kiwi
- ☐ 1 banana
- ☐ 3 cups honeydew
- ☐ 1 cup cantaloupe
- ☐ 1 cup watermelon
- ☐ ½ inch fresh turmeric root
- ☐ 2½ cups brewed green tea
- ☐ 1 cup coconut water
- ☐ ½ cup almond milk
- ☐ ½ cup hazelnut milk
- ☐ ½ cup nonfat Greek yogurt
- ☐ 1 teaspoon lime juice
- ☐ 1 teaspoon lemon juice
- ☐ 6 tablespoons chia seed
- ☐ 6 tablespoons hulled hemp seed
- ☐ 1 teaspoon pure vanilla extract
- ☐ 1 pinch of fresh-ground black pepper
- ☐ 1 pinch of ground cinnamon

190. HAZELNUT FIG WHIP

This smoothie combines a creamy banana flavor with a little fig. Bananas and banana peel are packed with melatonin, which helps improve sleep and reduce stress hormones. Add a tablespoon of banana peel to get the extra melatonin, if the banana is organic and if using a high-power blender that can easily grind a fibrous peel.

1 fig
½ frozen banana
½ cup hazelnut milk
½ cup ice
2 tablespoons hulled hemp seed

Combine all ingredients in a high-power blender or food processor and blend until smooth. Drink immediately.

CALORIES: 234 **FAT:** 8 **CARBS:** 30 **FIBER:** 5 **PROTEIN:** 7

191. SPICED ALMOND CREAM

This creamy, vanilla-based smoothie is gratifying, with a hint of fig and spices. This combination is low in calories and rich in protein so it's a great option for those with blood sugar issues, such as hypoglycemia or diabetes.

1 fig
½ cup almond milk
½ cup ice
½ cup water
½ cup nonfat Greek yogurt
½ teaspoon vanilla extract
1 pinch of ground cinnamon
1 pinch of fresh-ground black pepper

Combine all ingredients in a high-power blender or food processor and blend until smooth. Drink immediately.

CALORIES: 125 **FAT:** 1 **CARBS:** 15 **FIBER:** 1 **PROTEIN:** 13

192. SWEET TEA

Lightly brewed green tea provides a nutrient-dense base for this melon smoothie. Green tea contains antioxidant compounds that are powerful weight-loss nutrients.

½ frozen banana

1 cup brewed green tea

½ cup honeydew

2 tablespoons chia seed

Combine all ingredients in a high-power blender or food processor and blend until smooth. Drink immediately.

CALORIES: 222 **FAT:** 10 **CARBS:** 24 **FIBER:** 14 **PROTEIN:** 6

193. MELON CITRUS

This citrus smoothie combines a sweet watermelon flavor with tangy lime.

1 cup watermelon

½ cup honeydew

½ cup ice

2 tablespoons chia seed

½ inch fresh turmeric root

1 teaspoon lime juice

Combine all ingredients in a high-power blender or food processor and blend until smooth. Drink immediately.

CALORIES: 214 **FAT:** 10 **CARBS:** 22 **FIBER:** 14 **PROTEIN:** 6

194. MELON TEA FREEZE

This is a light, revitalizing smoothie and a weight-loss promoting alternative to a sweet alcoholic drink like a margarita!

1 cup honeydew
1 cup brewed green tea
½ cup ice
2 tablespoons hulled hemp seed

Combine all ingredients in a high-power blender or food processor and blend until smooth.

CALORIES: 160 **FAT:** 6 **CARBS:** 30 **FIBER:** 4 **PROTEIN:** 6

195. SVELTE SYNERGY

This frosty coconut and melon power blend will kickstart your energy. The minerals in the coconut water and the protein in the hemp seed may be just what you need when your energy starts to lag during the day.

1 cup honeydew
1 cup coconut water
½ cup brewed green tea
½ cup ice
2 tablespoons hulled hemp seed

Combine all ingredients in a high-power blender or food processor and blend until smooth. Drink immediately.

CALORIES: 194 **FAT:** 6 **CARBS:** 30 **FIBER:** 4 **PROTEIN:** 6

196. KIWI QUENCHER

This fresh kiwi smoothie combines sweet melon with intense kiwi flavor and a bit of citrus.

1 kiwi

1 cup cantaloupe

½ cup water

½ cup ice

2 tablespoons chia seed

½ teaspoon lemon juice

Combine all ingredients in a high-power blender or food processor and blend until smooth. Drink immediately.

CALORIES: 236 **FAT:** 10 **CARBS:** 26 **FIBER:** 16 **PROTEIN:** 6

Week 29

Grocery List

- ☐ 3 apples
- ☐ 3 tomatoes
- ☐ 3 kiwis
- ☐ 1 avocado
- ☐ 1 banana
- ☐ 1 cucumber
- ☐ 5 tablespoons minced fresh mint leaves
- ☐ ¼ cup minced fresh basil leaves
- ☐ ½ inch fresh ginger root
- ☐ ½ inch fresh turmeric root
- ☐ 1 cup frozen strawberries
- ☐ 1½ cups coconut water
- ☐ ½ cup carrot juice
- ☐ 5 teaspoons lemon juice
- ☐ 9 tablespoons chia seed
- ☐ 1 tablespoon protein powder

197. STRAWBERRY AND COCONUT ICY

This berry and kiwi blend is the perfect balance of sweet and tart. If you like a tarter flavor, use two kiwis in this recipe to boost the chlorophyll, which is a green plant membrane that increases weight loss.

1 kiwi
1 cup frozen strawberries
½ cup coconut water
½ cup ice
2 tablespoons chia seed

Combine all ingredients in a high-power blender or food processor and blend until smooth. Drink immediately.

CALORIES: 224 FAT: 10 CARBS: 30 FIBER: 18 PROTEIN: 6

198. KIWI APPLE

This refreshing treat is tart and sweet with citrus undertones. Kiwis contain the carotenoids beta-carotene, lutein, and xanthophylls, which have an affinity for fat tissue where these nutrients help body fat become more bioactive so it can be released during exercise.

1 kiwi
1 apple
½ cup ice
½ cup water
1 tablespoon protein powder
½ inch fresh turmeric root
1 teaspoon lemon juice

Combine all ingredients in a high-power blender or food processor and blend until smooth. Drink immediately.

CALORIES: 150 FAT: 2 CARBS: 33 FIBER: 7 PROTEIN: 4

199. KIWI BANANA

In this drink, you'll find an intense blend of tart and creamy, with chia protein. Kiwi provides flavonoids, which decrease the absorption of fat and may also increase calorie expenditure.

½ kiwi
½ frozen banana
½ cup coconut water
½ cup ice
2 tablespoons chia seed

Combine all ingredients in a high-power blender or food processor and blend until smooth. Drink immediately.

CALORIES: 200 **FAT:** 7 **CARBS:** 33 **FIBER:** 10 **PROTEIN:** 5

200. SKINNY GINGER

This vegetable-based drink comes alive with the flavors of mint and ginger. The cucumbers contain phytonutrients called cucurbitacins, which support immune function and metabolism while reducing inflammation.

1 tomato
½ cucumber
½ cup coconut water
½ cup ice
2 tablespoons chia seed
1 tablespoon minced fresh mint leaves
½ inch fresh ginger root

Combine all ingredients in a high-power blender or food processor and blend until smooth. Drink immediately.

CALORIES: 198 **FAT:** 10 **CARBS:** 16 **FIBER:** 14 **PROTEIN:** 6

201. PARADISE IN A GLASS

The ingredients here create a creamy drink with fresh avocado flavor. Phytochemicals found in tomatoes, such as phytoene, phytofluene, beta-carotene, flavonoids, carotenoids, lycopene, quercetin, polyphenols, and kaempferol, act as nutrient-messengers that communicate with DNA and keep metabolism working optimally.

½ tomato
1 apple
½ cup ice
½ cup water
¼ avocado
1 tablespoon chia seed
1 tablespoon lemon juice

Combine all ingredients in a high-power blender or food processor and blend until smooth. Drink immediately.

CALORIES: 207 FAT: 5 CARBS: 22 FIBER: 12 PROTEIN: 3

202. MINTY V-3

This is a simple vegetable combination perfect for those easing their way into green smoothies. Additionally, the terpenes and polyphenols in tomato juice can help the body clear unhealthy fat.

¼ tomato
½ cup carrot juice
½ cup water
½ cup ice
¼ cup minced fresh mint leaves
1 tablespoon chia seed

Combine all ingredients in a high-power blender or food processor and blend until smooth. Drink immediately.

CALORIES: 129 FAT: 5 CARBS: 15 FIBER: 8 PROTEIN: 4

SMOOTHIE RECIPES

203. LOVE APPLE

This drink has a fresh, light, and earthy flavor. The fiber in apples, tomatoes, basil, and chia all help body cells use insulin more effectively, thus balancing blood sugar and reducing body fat development.

1 apple
½ tomato
½ cup ice
½ cup water
¼ cup minced fresh basil leaves
1 tablespoon chia seed
1 teaspoon lemon juice

Combine all ingredients in a high-power blender or food processor and blend until smooth. Drink immediately.

CALORIES: 176 **FAT:** 5 **CARBS:** 14 **FIBER:** 12 **PROTEIN:** 3

Week 30

Grocery List

- ☐ 6 apricots
- ☐ 2 black velvet apricots
- ☐ 2 bananas
- ☐ 1 apple
- ☐ 1 orange
- ☐ 1 cup watermelon
- ☐ 1½ cups minced fresh basil leaves
- ☐ ¼ cup minced fresh mint leaves
- ☐ 1½ cups coconut water
- ☐ 1 cup blueberry nectar
- ☐ ½ cup nonfat Greek yogurt
- ☐ 4 teaspoons lemon juice
- ☐ 1 tablespoon lime juice
- ☐ 9 tablespoons chia seed
- ☐ 4 cashews
- ☐ 1 tablespoon hulled hemp seed

204. TART BANANA

This smoothie's fresh fruit flavor combines well with the creaminess of the frozen banana, and the apricot has a slight tartness that complements the sweetness of the rich blueberry nectar. Apricots supply provitamin A, which turns into vitamin A when needed and supports metabolism in indirect yet essential ways to increase weight loss.

2 apricots
½ frozen banana
½ cup water
¼ cup blueberry nectar
2 tablespoons chia seed

Combine all ingredients in a high-power blender or food processor and blend until smooth. Drink immediately.

CALORIES: 230 **FAT:** 10 **CARBS:** 30 **FIBER:** 14 **PROTEIN:** 6

205. BLACK VELVET APRICOT

This tart and complex drink has a deep apricot flavor. Black velvet apricots are particularly rich in beta-carotene, an antioxidant that helps detoxify the liver, which supports its ability to manage insulin, thus reducing body fat storage.

2 black velvet apricots
½ cup coconut water
½ cup ice
½ cup blueberry nectar
2 tablespoons chia seed

Combine all ingredients in a high-power blender or food processor and blend until smooth. Drink immediately.

CALORIES: 210 **FAT:** 10 **CARBS:** 30 **FIBER:** 14 **PROTEIN:** 6

206. APRICOT APPLE

Apple, apricot, and banana flavors create a not-too-sweet, rich, and frosty blend. The quercetin in apples assists in mobilizing fat so our bodies can burn it for energy.

1 apple
1 apricot
½ frozen banana
½ cup water
½ cup ice
1 tablespoon chia seed

Combine all ingredients in a high-power blender or food processor and blend until smooth. Drink immediately.

CALORIES: 220 **FAT:** 5 **CARBS:** 24 **FIBER:** 20 **PROTEIN:** 4

207. FRESH APRICOT

The light fruit flavor of this combination has a nutty bite with a twist of citrus. Cashews are a rich source of bioactive proanthocyanidins, which are known to affect weight loss by increasing energy expenditure. In other words, cashews can increase energy and weight loss.

1½ cups water
1 apricot
½ cup ice
4 cashews
1 teaspoon lemon juice

Combine all ingredients in a high-power blender or food processor and blend until smooth. Drink immediately.

CALORIES: 165 **FAT:** 11 **CARBS:** 11 **FIBER:** 1 **PROTEIN:** 5

208. BASIL ORANGE

You'll taste orange infused with herbs in this cool and creamy blend. Basil helps lower blood sugar levels, which reduces the production of insulin, the fat storage hormone.

1 orange
2 apricots
½ cup ice
½ cup water
½ cup nonfat Greek yogurt
¼ cup minced fresh basil leaves
1 tablespoon hulled hemp seed

Combine all ingredients in a high-power blender or food processor and blend until smooth. Drink immediately.

CALORIES: 210 **FAT:** 3 **CARBS:** 25 **FIBER:** 9 **PROTEIN:** 15

209. WATERMELON LEMONADE

Watermelon takes center stage in this refreshing blend. Watermelon provides lutein and zeaxanthin, and the levels of these carotenoids in the body correlate with ease of weight loss, meaning the higher the level, the easier we lose body fat.

½ frozen banana
1 cup ice
½ cup watermelon
½ cup coconut water
½ cup water
2 tablespoons chia seed
1 tablespoon lemon juice

Combine all ingredients in a high-power blender or food processor and blend until smooth. Drink immediately.

CALORIES: 200 **FAT:** 10 **CARBS:** 30 **FIBER:** 14 **PROTEIN:** 6

210. MINT MELON MOJITO

Watermelon and mint are the perfect pairing and give this smoothie its luxurious flavor. Watermelon is rich in lycopene, an antioxidant that reduces oxidative stress on fat cells and improves fat-weight loss.

½ cup coconut water
½ cup water
½ cup watermelon
½ cup ice
¼ cup minced fresh mint leaves
2 tablespoons chia seed
1 tablespoon lime juice

Combine all ingredients in a high-power blender or food processor and blend until smooth. Drink immediately.

CALORIES: 187 **FAT:** 10 **CARBS:** 14 **FIBER:** 13 **PROTEIN:** 7

Week 31

Grocery List

- ☐ 5 fresh basil leaves
- ☐ 1 apple
- ☐ 1 banana
- ☐ 1½ cups watermelon
- ☐ ¼ cup minced fresh mint leaves
- ☐ 2½ cups frozen wild blueberries
- ☐ ½ cup frozen cherries
- ☐ 2 cups coconut water
- ☐ 1½ cups blueberry nectar
- ☐ 1 cup nonfat Greek yogurt
- ☐ 1 teaspoon lime juice
- ☐ 6 tablespoons chia seed
- ☐ 2 tablespoons protein powder
- ☐ 1 tablespoon hulled hemp seed
- ☐ 1 tablespoon unsweetened fine macaroon coconut
- ☐ 2 teaspoons pure vanilla extract

211. MINT WATERMELON

This blend is surprisingly sweet, tasty, and refreshing, with a strong watermelon flavor. Lycopene is a carotene phytochemical found in watermelon proven to significantly reduce body weight, body fat, and waist circumference when ingested daily.

1 apple
5 fresh basil leaves
1 cup watermelon
½ cup ice
½ cup water
¼ cup minced fresh mint leaves
1 tablespoon chia seed

Combine all ingredients in a high-power blender or food processor and blend until smooth. Drink immediately.

CALORIES: 226 **FAT:** 5 **CARBS:** 28 **FIBER:** 9 **PROTEIN:** 3

212. COCONUT WATERMELON BANANA

This refreshing treat offers an indulgent and healthy taste of the tropics. Watermelons are a rich source of lycopene, which reduces oxidative stress and supports bioactive fat cells to induce lipolysis.

½ frozen banana
½ cup coconut water
½ cup watermelon
½ cup ice
½ cup nonfat Greek yogurt
1 tablespoon unsweetened fine macaroon coconut

Combine all ingredients in a high-power blender or food processor and blend until smooth. Drink immediately.

CALORIES: 194 **FAT:** 4 **CARBS:** 30 **FIBER:** 2 **PROTEIN:** 14

213. BLUEBERRY CHERRY TART

This drink combines tart, bright fruit flavors in a frosty blend. Add a little pineapple or apple juice if this combination is too tart for your taste. Blueberries are rich in anthocyanins, which provide anti-inflammatory properties that help reduce water weight.

½ cup blueberry nectar
½ cup ice
½ cup water
½ cup frozen cherries
¼ cup frozen wild blueberries
2 tablespoons chia seed

Combine all ingredients in a high-power blender or food processor and blend until smooth. Drink immediately.

CALORIES: 210 FAT: 7 CARBS: 33 FIBER: 10 PROTEIN: 4

214. BLUEBERRY FAIRY

This tart, slightly sweet, and refreshing smoothie is dense in antioxidant polyphenols, which give this drink its rich purple color and reduce belly fat by modulating metabolic imbalances.

½ cup frozen wild blueberries
½ cup ice
½ cup water
½ cup blueberry nectar
1 tablespoon chia seed

Combine all ingredients in a high-power blender or food processor and blend until smooth. Drink immediately.

CALORIES: 177 FAT: 5 CARBS: 27 FIBER: 6 PROTEIN: 3

215. WILD BLUEBERRY QUENCHER

This smoothie is filled with tart, fresh, clear blueberry flavor, and the nutrients in blueberries have been found to influence genes that regulate fat burning and storage.

½ cup coconut water
½ cup frozen wild blueberries
½ cup ice
½ cup water
1 tablespoon hulled hemp seed

Combine all ingredients in a high-power blender or food processor and blend until smooth. Drink immediately.

CALORIES: 108 FAT: 3 CARBS: 17 FIBER: 1 PROTEIN: 3

216. KUL KAH HAN GARDEN

The pairing of fresh wild blueberries or huckleberries with vanilla is perfection in this recipe! It was inspired by the native Pacific Northwest evergreen huckleberries growing at Kul Kah Han Native Plant Garden in Chimacum, Washington.

½ cup coconut water
½ cup frozen wild blueberries or huckleberries
½ cup nonfat Greek yogurt
½ cup ice
½ cup water
2 tablespoons protein powder
2 teaspoons vanilla extract

Combine all ingredients in a high-power blender or food processor and blend until smooth. Drink immediately.

CALORIES: 168 FAT: 0 CARBS: 22 FIBER: 4 PROTEIN: 20

217. WILD BLUEBERRY LIME

Wild berries have about twice the nutrient level of cultivated berries and give this smoothie its antioxidant power and intense blueberry flavor.

½ cup coconut water
½ cup frozen wild blueberries
¼ cup blueberry nectar
½ cup water
2 tablespoons chia seed
1 teaspoon lime juice

Combine all ingredients in a high-power blender or food processor and blend until smooth. Drink immediately.

CALORIES: 261 **FAT:** 10 **CARBS:** 30 **FIBER:** 15 **PROTEIN:** 5

Week 32

Grocery List

- ☐ 2 papayas
- ☐ 1 banana
- ☐ 1 orange
- ☐ ¼ cup minced fresh basil leaves
- ☐ 1 tablespoon lime peel
- ☐ ½ inch fresh turmeric root
- ☐ ½ cup frozen mango
- ☐ ¼ cup frozen cherries
- ☐ ¼ cup frozen raspberries
- ☐ 2 cups mango nectar
- ☐ 1 cup sparkling water
- ☐ ½ cup coconut water
- ☐ 5 teaspoons lime juice
- ☐ 1 teaspoon lemon juice
- ☐ 5 tablespoons chia seed
- ☐ 5 tablespoons hulled hemp seed
- ☐ 2 tablespoons protein powder
- ☐ 2 teaspoons pure vanilla extract

218. BASIL MANGO

This recipe is a gentle blend of mango and basil. Mango is rich in beta-cryptoxanthin, a xanthophyll carotenoid, which can significantly reduce visceral fat when ingested daily.

½ cup mango nectar

½ cup ice

½ cup water

½ cup frozen mango

¼ cup minced fresh basil leaves

2 tablespoons hulled hemp seed

Combine all ingredients in a high-power blender or food processor and blend until smooth. Drink immediately.

CALORIES: 205 FAT: 6 CARBS: 30 FIBER: 3 PROTEIN: 7

219. TROPICAL ORANGE

This frosty blend is slightly tropical, with a little orange and vanilla flavor. That heady fragrance from vanilla extract and vanilla beans is vanillic acid, which studies are finding suppresses inflammation.

1 orange

½ cup mango nectar

½ cup ice

2 tablespoons protein powder

2 teaspoons vanilla extract

Combine all ingredients in a high-power blender or food processor and blend until smooth. Drink immediately.

CALORIES: 184 FAT: 1 CARBS: 30 FIBER: 3 PROTEIN: 9

220. AFTERNOON OASIS

This drink has bright flavors that each get their moment on the palate. Hulled hemp seed provides the protein, with 5 grams in just 2 tablespoons. Cherries provide glucaric acid, a toxin scavenger that improves liver function and promotes a heathy metabolism.

1 cup mango nectar
½ cup ice
½ cup water
¼ cup frozen raspberries
¼ cup frozen cherries
2 tablespoons hulled hemp seed

Combine all ingredients in a high-power blender or food processor and blend until smooth. Drink immediately.

CALORIES: 228 **FAT:** 6 **CARBS:** 30 **FIBER:** 4 **PROTEIN:** 7

221. PAPAYA CITRUS SOOTHER

This smoothie is light, fresh, and easy to digest. Papaya is an excellent source of beta-carotene, which is stored in adipose tissue where it can help moderate obesity as it controls body fat production.

½ papaya
¼ cup water
¼ cup ice
1 tablespoon chia seed
1 teaspoon lemon juice

Combine all ingredients in a high-power blender or food processor and blend until smooth. Drink immediately.

CALORIES: 132 **FAT:** 5 **CARBS:** 17 **FIBER:** 8 **PROTEIN:** 3

222. PAPAYA LIME CRUSH

Papaya and lime make a heavenly combination. Carotenoids from the papaya affect the biology of fat cells and control hunger signaling as well as inflammation.

½ papaya
¼ cup water
¼ cup ice
1 tablespoon hulled hemp seed
1 teaspoon lime juice

Combine all ingredients in a high-power blender or food processor and blend until smooth. Drink immediately.

CALORIES: 107 FAT: 3 CARBS: 17 FIBER: 3 PROTEIN: 4

223. PAPAYA LIME FIZZ

This perfect blend of papaya and lime is hydrating and makes for a nice little afternoon energizer. Citrus fruit, and especially citrus peel, are showing promise in altering fat tissue and reducing body fat when eaten daily.

½ papaya
2 tablespoons chia seed
1 tablespoon lime juice
1 tablespoon lime zest
1 cup sparkling water

Combine papaya, chia seed, lime juice, and lime zest, in a high-power blender or food processor and blend until smooth. Then stir in the sparkling water and drink immediately.

CALORIES: 202 FAT: 10 CARBS: 18 FIBER: 14 PROTEIN: 7

Filtered (flat) tap water can be used instead of sparkling water and can be blended together with the other ingredients at the same time. If you do use sparkling water, be sure to add it after blending the rest of the ingredients, as blending pops all the bubbles.

224. MAUI MORNING

This smoothie has an intense papaya and lime flavor. Curcumin, a bioactive agent in turmeric, reduces excess water and inflammation when ingested regularly.

½ frozen banana

¼ papaya

½ cup coconut water

½ cup ice

2 tablespoons chia seed

½ inch fresh turmeric root

1 teaspoon lime juice

Combine all ingredients in a high-power blender or food processor and blend until smooth. Drink immediately.

CALORIES: 225 **FAT:** 10 **CARBS:** 30 **FIBER:** 16 **PROTEIN:** 6

Week 33

Grocery List

- ☐ 2 mandarin oranges
- ☐ 2 papayas
- ☐ 1 medium-hot pepper
- ☐ 2 cups watermelon
- ☐ ½ cup frozen mango
- ☐ 1 tablespoon papaya peel
- ☐ ½ inch fresh turmeric root
- ☐ 1 cup frozen strawberries
- ☐ ½ cup frozen cherries
- ☐ ½ cup frozen pineapple
- ☐ ½ cup frozen wild blueberries
- ☐ 1½ cups coconut water
- ☐ 1 cup blueberry nectar
- ☐ ½ cup brewed green tea
- ☐ 1 tablespoon lemon juice
- ☐ 2 teaspoons lime juice
- ☐ 5 tablespoons chia seed
- ☐ 5 tablespoons protein powder
- ☐ 2 tablespoons hulled hemp seed
- ☐ 6 teaspoons pure vanilla extract

225. HAWAIIAN DREAM

This refreshing drink tastes like a sunny day on a Hawaiian beach. Papaya is a rich source of the carotenoids that regulate leptin, the hormone that controls hunger and fat storage.

¼ papaya
½ cup frozen pineapple
½ cup coconut water
½ cup ice
2 tablespoons protein powder
2 teaspoons vanilla extract

Combine all ingredients in a high-power blender or food processor and blend until smooth. Drink immediately.

CALORIES: 168 **FAT:** 0 **CARBS:** 30 **FIBER:** 4 **PROTEIN:** 10

226. VANILLA MANDARIN

This blend has sweet mandarin citrus and rich exotic papaya flavors, with blueberry high notes. Vanilla contains a simple phenolic compound known as vanillin that may help obese people lose significant amounts of weight. Real vanilla extract and vanilla beans are excellent sources of vanillin.

1 mandarin orange
¼ papaya
½ cup frozen wild blueberries
½ cup ice
½ cup water
2 tablespoons chia seed
1 tablespoon lemon juice
1 teaspoon vanilla extract

Combine all ingredients in a high-power blender or food processor and blend until smooth. Drink immediately.

CALORIES: 252 **FAT:** 10 **CARBS:** 30 **FIBER:** 18 **PROTEIN:** 6

227. PAPAYA MANGO LIME

The tropical flavors are complemented by the fresh lime, while the protein and essential fatty acids from the hemp seed satisfy hunger. Both papaya and mango are rich in carotenoids, which support weight loss by affecting our genes.

¼ papaya
½ cup coconut water
½ cup frozen mango
½ cup ice
2 tablespoons hulled hemp seed
1 teaspoon lime juice

Combine all ingredients in a high-power blender or food processor and blend until smooth. Drink immediately.

CALORIES: 190 FAT: 6 CARBS: 28 FIBER: 4 PROTEIN: 6

228. CHERRY BLUE PAPAYA

Enjoy this sweet cherry base with just a little papaya and vanilla flavor. Cherries are rich in carotenoids and polyphenols, which reduce the belly fat that is commonly caused by metabolic syndrome.

¼ papaya
½ cup frozen cherries
½ cup coconut water
½ cup water
¼ cup blueberry nectar
2 tablespoons protein powder
½ inch fresh turmeric root
2 teaspoons vanilla extract

Combine all ingredients in a high-power blender or food processor and blend until smooth. Drink immediately.

CALORIES: 264 FAT: 0 CARBS: 30 FIBER: 4 PROTEIN: 10

229. HOT PEPPER PAPAYA

This pink beauty has a fragrant pepper scent and a sweet strawberry flavor, as well as a slight heat. One active substance in hot peppers called capsaicin, activates receptors, causing an increase in intracellular calcium levels and triggering the sympathetic nervous system to improve weight loss.

⅙ papaya
1 cup frozen strawberries
½ cup brewed green tea
½ cup water
¼ medium-hot pepper
2 tablespoons chia seed
1 tablespoon papaya peel

Combine all ingredients in a high-power blender or food processor and blend until smooth. Drink immediately.

CALORIES: 222 **FAT:** 10 **CARBS:** 22 **FIBER:** 16 **PROTEIN:** 7

230. ORANGE PAPAYA LIME

This smoothie has a light and tropical citrus flavor. The flesh of papaya is rich in lycopene, which helps reduce body fat storage via the hormone insulin, due to its ability to regulate glycolipids.

1 mandarin orange
½ papaya
½ cup ice
½ cup water
1 tablespoon chia seed
1 teaspoon lime juice

Combine all ingredients in a high-power blender or food processor and blend until smooth. Drink immediately.

CALORIES: 205 **FAT:** 5 **CARBS:** 24 **FIBER:** 16 **PROTEIN:** 4

231. WATERMELON BLUEBERRY

This delicious smoothie tastes like a sweet blueberry dessert. Exquisite! Watermelon nutrients trigger the satiety response, helping us feel less hungry and improving body-weight management.

2 cups watermelon
½ cup blueberry nectar
1 tablespoon protein powder
1 teaspoon vanilla extract

Combine all ingredients in a high-power blender or food processor and blend until smooth. Drink immediately.

CALORIES: 190 **FAT:** 1 **CARBS:** 37 **FIBER:** 1 **PROTEIN:** 14

Week 34

Grocery List

- [ ] 6 cups watermelon
- [ ] 1 banana
- [ ] 1 grapefruit
- [ ] 1 medium-hot pepper
- [ ] ½ cup minced baby kale leaves
- [ ] 1 inch fresh ginger root
- [ ] ½ inch fresh turmeric root
- [ ] ½ cup frozen wild blueberries
- [ ] ½ cup brewed green tea
- [ ] ½ cup carrot juice
- [ ] ½ cup nonfat Greek yogurt
- [ ] ½ cup rice milk
- [ ] ¼ cup papaya nectar
- [ ] 4 teaspoons lime juice
- [ ] 11 tablespoons chia seed

232. GINGER BERRY MELON

This blend is a simple yet perfect combination of sweet and spicy. Additionally, ginger may elevate mood, as it stimulates neurotransmitters in the gastrointestinal tract that make us feel happy.

1 cup watermelon
½ cup frozen wild blueberries
½ cup ice
1 tablespoon chia seed
½ inch fresh ginger root

Combine all ingredients in a high-power blender or food processor and blend until smooth. Drink immediately.

CALORIES: 153 **FAT:** 5 **CARBS:** 23 **FIBER:** 10 **PROTEIN:** 2

233. WATERMELON BANANA CREAM

This blended drink is sweet and rich in fruit flavor. Watermelon and papaya nectar are rich in the carotenoids that affect obesity and associated pathophysiological disorders, including metabolic inflammation, insulin resistance, and hepatic steatosis.

½ frozen banana
½ cup watermelon
¼ cup papaya nectar
½ cup water
2 tablespoons chia seed

Combine all ingredients in a high-power blender or food processor and blend until smooth. Drink immediately.

CALORIES: 302 **FAT:** 10 **CARBS:** 30 **FIBER:** 14 **PROTEIN:** 4

234. HOT WATERMELON

Hot peppers give this smoothie a little heat on the palate. Choose chile peppers that have the level of heat intensity that you prefer. I like mild heat, and I love this combination of cool and hot. Peppers are rich in carotene, a fat-soluble vitamin that reduces body fat development.

1 cup watermelon
1 cup ice
¼ medium-hot pepper
2 tablespoons chia seed

Combine all ingredients in a high-power blender or food processor and blend until smooth. Drink immediately.

CALORIES: 200 **FAT:** 10 **CARBS:** 16 **FIBER:** 14 **PROTEIN:** 4

235. MELON FREEZE

If you like tart and sweet, you'll love this citrusy fresh smoothie. The natural polyphenols in grapefruit and grapefruit juice enhance the effects of nutrients in watermelon, energizing their potential to reduce inflammation and improve metabolism.

1 cup watermelon
¼ grapefruit
½ cup ice
2 tablespoons chia seed
1 tablespoon lime juice

Combine all ingredients in a high-power blender or food processor and blend until smooth. Drink immediately.

CALORIES: 232 **FAT:** 10 **CARBS:** 26 **FIBER:** 14 **PROTEIN:** 4

236. GINGER MELON TEA

The ginger root and green tea in this recipe may give you a flatter belly, as they both reduce intestinal inflammation.

1 cup watermelon
½ cup brewed green tea
½ cup ice
2 tablespoons chia seed
½ inch fresh ginger root
1 teaspoon lime juice

Combine all ingredients in a high-power blender or food processor and blend until smooth. Drink immediately.

CALORIES: 150 **FAT:** 7 **CARBS:** 21 **FIBER:** 8 **PROTEIN:** 5

237. WATERMELON SHAKE

This delicious drink is creamy, pink, and sweet. The children who tested this recipe said it is "kid approved." Greek yogurt contains probiotics that aid in digestion of the anti-obesity nutrients in fruits and vegetables.

1 cup watermelon
½ cup rice milk
½ cup nonfat Greek yogurt
½ inch fresh turmeric root

Combine all ingredients in a high-power blender or food processor and blend until smooth. Drink immediately.

CALORIES: 172 **FAT:** 2 **CARBS:** 28 **FIBER:** 0 **PROTEIN:** 12

238. WATERMELON SMASH

This smoothie is surprisingly sweet, tasty, and refreshing, with a prominent watermelon flavor. Baby greens are tender and mild and blend more easily than mature greens. Kale is a rich source of calcium, a mineral that works with vitamin D to help us build muscle and shed body fat.

½ cup watermelon
½ cup ice
½ cup minced baby kale leaves
½ cup carrot juice
2 tablespoons chia seed

Combine all ingredients in a high-power blender or food processor and blend until smooth. Drink immediately.

CALORIES: 180 **FAT:** 7 **CARBS:** 26 **FIBER:** 9 **PROTEIN:** 5

Week 35

Grocery List

- ☐ 1 apricot
- ☐ 1 nectarine
- ☐ 1 orange
- ☐ 4½ cups watermelon
- ☐ ¼ cup minced fresh mint leaves
- ☐ 1 inch fresh turmeric root
- ☐ 1½ cups frozen strawberries
- ☐ 1 cup frozen peaches
- ☐ 1½ cups coconut water
- ☐ 1 cup nonfat Greek yogurt
- ☐ 1 cup peach nectar
- ☐ ½ cup rice milk
- ☐ 2 tablespoons lime juice
- ☐ ½ cup lemon juice
- ☐ 8 tablespoons chia seed
- ☐ 2 tablespoons protein powder
- ☐ 1 pinch of ground cinnamon

239. STRAWBERRY WATERMELON ICY

Berries and melon pair well in this recipe, and a little citrus addition is sublime! Use frozen watermelon and eliminate the ice for even richer flavor. Both the strawberries and watermelon are rich in anti-inflammatory and anti-obesity nutrients, including vitamin C and carotenoids.

½ cup frozen strawberries
½ cup watermelon
½ cup water
¼ cup ice
2 tablespoons chia seed
1 teaspoon lemon juice

Combine all ingredients in a high-power blender or food processor and blend until smooth. Drink immediately.

CALORIES: 150 **FAT:** 7 **CARBS:** 22 **FIBER:** 9 **PROTEIN:** 4

240. WATERMELON MINT

Watermelon and mint pair perfectly together in this smoothie, which contains water and ice to counter the damaging effects of dehydration, which is the most common cause of fatigue and can lead to a sedentary lifestyle.

1 cup watermelon
½ cup water
½ cup ice
½ cup frozen peaches
¼ cup minced fresh mint leaves
2 tablespoons chia seed

Combine all ingredients in a high-power blender or food processor and blend until smooth. Drink immediately.

CALORIES: 180 **FAT:** 7 **CARBS:** 29 **FIBER:** 9 **PROTEIN:** 5

241. WATERMELON LEMON COOLER

This smoothie has a predominantly watermelon flavor, with berry and light coconut notes. Add a tiny pinch of salt to bring out the strawberry and basil flavors. Coconut water is rich in potassium, which is so essential for weight loss that low levels are a predictor for obesity.

1 cup watermelon

1 cup coconut water

½ cup frozen strawberries

¼ cup lemon juice

2 tablespoons chia seed

2 tablespoons lime juice

Combine all ingredients in a high-power blender or food processor and blend until smooth. Drink immediately.

CALORIES: 238 **FAT:** 10 **CARBS:** 30 **FIBER:** 16 **PROTEIN:** 5

242. WATERMELON WITH TURMERIC

Sweet melon and berries flavor this drink, and bright yellow turmeric adds color and fragrance. Watermelon is a weight-loss power food! Watermelon is so rich in carotenoids that daily intake supports body fat reduction.

1 cup watermelon

½ cup frozen strawberries

½ cup coconut water

2 tablespoons chia seed

½ inch fresh turmeric root

Combine all ingredients in a high-power blender or food processor and blend until smooth. Drink immediately.

CALORIES: 232 **FAT:** 10 **CARBS:** 26 **FIBER:** 14 **PROTEIN:** 4

243. WATERMELON ORANGE POWER

This fresh and juicy combination is sweet with a golden glow from the turmeric, and it delivers a significant dose of carotenoids, including lycopene and beta-carotene. Carotenoids support weight loss by speeding up metabolism and stimulating the body's ability to burn fat.

½ orange
1 cup watermelon
½ cup ice
2 tablespoons chia seed
2 tablespoons protein powder
½ inch fresh turmeric root

Combine all ingredients in a high-power blender or food processor and blend until smooth. Drink immediately.

CALORIES: 310 **FAT:** 10 **CARBS:** 30 **FIBER:** 16 **PROTEIN:** 12

244. PEACH APRICOT NECTARINE

This recipe is a creamy blend that is rich in tart stone-fruit flavor, with a bit of citrus. Stone fruits are loaded with carotenoids, such as beta-carotene, lycopene, lutein, cryptoxanthin, and zeaxanthin. These critical nutrients modulate neuroinflammation and reduce pain and stiffness, which supports effective workouts.

1 apricot
1 nectarine
¼ cup peach nectar
½ cup frozen peaches
½ cup ice
½ cup nonfat Greek yogurt
1 teaspoon lemon juice

Combine all ingredients in a high-power blender or food processor and blend until smooth. Drink immediately.

CALORIES: 254 **FAT:** 0 **CARBS:** 30 **FIBER:** 4 **PROTEIN:** 13

245. SOUTHERN BELLE

This variation on the classic peaches-and-cream dish is so delicious that you may want to have it every day! Cinnamon adds depth of flavor and an aromatic complement to the peach nectar. Cinnamon has been found to reduce the negative effects of unhealthy dietary fats, which is supportive of an overall weight-loss plan.

½ cup peach nectar
½ cup ice
½ cup rice milk
½ cup nonfat Greek yogurt
1 pinch of ground cinnamon

Combine all ingredients in a high-power blender or food processor and blend until smooth. Drink immediately.

CALORIES: 196 **FAT:** 2 **CARBS:** 30 **FIBER:** 0 **PROTEIN:** 12

Week 36

Grocery List

- [ ] 2 dates
- [ ] 3 bananas
- [ ] 1 cup frozen cherries
- [ ] ½ cup frozen wild blueberries
- [ ] 4½ cups almond milk
- [ ] 2 cups nonfat Greek yogurt
- [ ] 1 teaspoon lemon juice
- [ ] 3 tablespoons chia seed
- [ ] 4 almonds
- [ ] 2 cashews
- [ ] 1 tablespoon unsweetened cocoa powder
- [ ] 2 teaspoons pure vanilla extract
- [ ] 1 teaspoon instant coffee
- [ ] 4 pinches of fresh-ground nutmeg

246. COCOA CASHEW DREAM

This drink is creamy, rich, and chocolaty. Cocoa's polyphenolic compounds support vascular function, which optimizes blood flow to muscles, thereby increasing calories burned.

1 frozen banana
1 cup almond milk
2 cashews
1 tablespoon unsweetened cocoa powder

Combine all ingredients in a high-power blender or food processor and blend until smooth. Drink immediately.

CALORIES: 233 **FAT:** 9 **CARBS:** 30 **FIBER:** 5 **PROTEIN:** 6

247. BLUEBERRY NUTMEG

Creamy, subtle blueberry flavor shines in this smoothie, with a hint of nutmeg. Yogurt provides amino acids that the body needs for production of enzymes and hormones used to regulate metabolism.

½ frozen banana
½ cup almond milk
½ cup nonfat Greek yogurt
½ cup frozen wild blueberries
1 pinch of fresh-ground nutmeg

Combine all ingredients in a high-power blender or food processor and blend until smooth. Drink immediately.

CALORIES: 168 **FAT:** 2 **CARBS:** 28 **FIBER:** 4 **PROTEIN:** 14

248. ALMOND DATE COFFEE

This is a light and refreshing pick-me-up for the morning, or for an afternoon wake-up from a nap. It also provides a low-calorie way to get a caffeine kick. An energy boost used as momentum for physical activity can be just the push needed when starting a new exercise routine.

1 date

1 cup almond milk

1 cup ice

1 tablespoon chia seed

1 teaspoon instant coffee

1 pinch of fresh-ground nutmeg

Combine all ingredients in a high-power blender or food processor and blend until smooth. Drink immediately.

CALORIES: 150 **FAT:** 6 **CARBS:** 22 **FIBER:** 5 **PROTEIN:** 4

249. SWEET ALMOND CREAM

This creamy treat is smooth, with a little nutmeg fragrance. This combination is low in calories, yet high in protein and antioxidants. It's the perfect smoothie for energizing the metabolism.

½ cup almond milk

½ cup frozen cherries

½ cup nonfat Greek yogurt

1 teaspoon vanilla extract

1 pinch of fresh-ground nutmeg

Combine all ingredients in a high-power blender or food processor and blend until smooth. Drink immediately.

CALORIES: 142 **FAT:** 1 **CARBS:** 18 **FIBER:** 2 **PROTEIN:** 14

250. CREAMY ALMOND NUTMEG

A toasted almond flavor combines with creamy yogurt in this protein-rich drink that is just a little sweet. Studies have found that a higher-protein diet equates to a higher rate of weight loss.

4 almonds
1 date
½ cup almond milk
1 cup water
½ cup ice
½ cup nonfat Greek yogurt
1 pinch of fresh-ground nutmeg

Combine all ingredients in a high-power blender or food processor and blend until smooth. Drink immediately.

CALORIES: 308 **FAT:** 16 **CARBS:** 26 **FIBER:** 6 **PROTEIN:** 14

251. SWEET CHERRY CREAM

This blend with sweet cherries is frosty and rich. Chia seeds are perfect little fuel packets because they contain fiber that helps the carbohydrates to release slowly, giving your body energy longer and allowing time for the body to burn the calories, rather than storing them away as fat.

½ frozen banana
½ cup almond milk
½ cup ice
½ cup frozen cherries
2 tablespoons chia seed

Combine all ingredients in a high-power blender or food processor and blend until smooth. Drink immediately.

CALORIES: 254 **FAT:** 12 **CARBS:** 28 **FIBER:** 16 **PROTEIN:** 6

252. LEMON VANILLA CREAM

Light lemon and vanilla flavors shine in this protein-rich smoothie. Bananas provide potassium, which has been proven to increase weight loss.

½ frozen banana
½ cup almond milk
½ cup ice
½ cup nonfat Greek yogurt
1 teaspoon lemon juice
½ teaspoon vanilla extract

Combine all ingredients in a high-power blender or food processor and blend until smooth. Drink immediately.

CALORIES: 140 **FAT:** 2 **CARBS:** 18 **FIBER:** 2 **PROTEIN:** 14

Week 37

Grocery List

- ☐ 3 bananas
- ☐ 2 dates
- ☐ ½ cup frozen cherries
- ☐ 6½ cups almond milk
- ☐ 1½ cups nonfat Greek yogurt
- ☐ 1 vanilla bean
- ☐ 20 almonds
- ☐ 6 cashews
- ☐ 3 tablespoons unsweetened cocoa powder
- ☐ 1 tablespoon hulled hemp seed
- ☐ 1 tablespoon unsweetened fine macaroon coconut
- ☐ 2 teaspoons pure vanilla extract
- ☐ 1 pinch of fresh-ground nutmeg

253. ALMOND CRUNCH

This combination has a sweet and creamy base with crunchy bits of almonds. Almonds are a rich source of metabolism-enhancing nutrients, including vitamin E, protein, fiber, B vitamins, minerals, and healthful fats. They also provide phytosterols that improve vascular function, which enhances athletic activity.

8 almonds
1 date
½ cup almond milk
½ cup ice
¼ cup nonfat Greek yogurt
1 tablespoon hulled hemp seed

Combine all ingredients in a high-power blender or food processor and blend until smooth. Drink immediately.

CALORIES: 312 **FAT:** 32 **CARBS:** 25 **FIBER:** 6 **PROTEIN:** 15

Chopped almonds are available in the bulk foods section of many grocery stores.

254. COCONUT ALMOND COCOA

Chocolaty with a bit of coconut, this smoothie tastes similar to an almond-coconut chocolate bar, but not too sweet. Cocoa contains flavanols, which have been shown to lower blood pressure by relaxing blood vessels.

2 cups almond milk
½ cup ice
2 almonds
1 tablespoon unsweetened fine macaroon coconut
1 tablespoon unsweetened cocoa powder

Combine all ingredients in a high-power blender or food processor and blend until smooth. Drink immediately.

CALORIES: 140 **FAT:** 11 **CARBS:** 8 **FIBER:** 3 **PROTEIN:** 5

255. VANILLA CHERRY ALMOND

The vanilla fragrance in this recipe hits your nose before the cherry flavor pops in your mouth! Cherries are an excellent source of fiber, which provides longer-lasting energy from this smoothie.

4 almonds
½ cup almond milk
½ cup ice
½ cup frozen cherries
½ teaspoon vanilla extract

Combine all ingredients in a high-power blender or food processor and blend until smooth. Drink immediately.

CALORIES: 228 **FAT:** 16 **CARBS:** 16 **FIBER:** 6 **PROTEIN:** 8

256. CHOCOLATE ALMOND MILKSHAKE

Enjoy this rich and sweet milkshake, which has almond and vanilla flavor without all the guilt. Almonds help us take in the 25 grams of fiber per day shown to lower the risk for hypertension and high cholesterol.

2 almonds
½ frozen banana
½ cup almond milk
½ cup ice
½ cup nonfat Greek yogurt
1 tablespoon unsweetened cocoa powder
1 teaspoon vanilla extract

Combine all ingredients in a high-power blender or food processor and blend until smooth. Drink immediately.

CALORIES: 246 **FAT:** 10 **CARBS:** 22 **FIBER:** 4 **PROTEIN:** 16

257. CREAMY ALMOND DATE

This smoothie is creamy, nutty, and reminiscent of eggnog. Studies show that increasing protein intake from dietary sources, such as yogurt and nuts, reduces the appetite and sugar cravings.

½ date

2 cashews

½ frozen banana

1 cup almond milk

¼ cup nonfat Greek yogurt

1 pinch of fresh-ground nutmeg

Combine all ingredients in a high-power blender or food processor and blend until smooth. Drink immediately.

CALORIES: 150 FAT: 4 CARBS: 23 FIBER: 2 PROTEIN: 8

258. VANILLA CASHEW DREAM

I could drink this every day. The ground cashews give this smoothie a pudding-like quality that's so delicious, it could be served as a dessert! Replacing high-sugar, high-fat desserts with nutritious smoothies is a fast-track strategy to weight loss.

1 vanilla bean

4 cashews

½ frozen banana

1 cup almond milk

¼ cup nonfat Greek yogurt

1 tablespoon unsweetened cocoa powder

Combine all ingredients in a high-power blender or food processor and blend until smooth. Drink immediately.

CALORIES: 210 FAT: 10 CARBS: 22 FIBER: 4 PROTEIN: 11

259. BANANA ALMOND SHAKE

Almonds provide protein, fiber, and healthful fats in this creamy, nutty, and dessert-like recipe. This simple combination can be made every day, providing a sustainable way to make smoothies a part of your life for the long haul, to help you maintain weight loss your entire life.

1 frozen banana
1 cup almond milk
4 almonds

Combine all ingredients in a high-power blender or food processor and blend until smooth. Drink immediately.

CALORIES: 160 **FAT:** 6 **CARBS:** 26 **FIBER:** 3 **PROTEIN:** 4

Add a few drops of almond extract for an even deeper flavor.

Week 38

Grocery List

- ☐ 2 bananas
- ☐ 1 apple
- ☐ 1 date
- ☐ 1 avocado
- ☐ 2½ cups frozen wild blueberries
- ☐ ½ cup pomegranate arils
- ☐ ½ cup frozen raspberries
- ☐ 1 cup blueberry nectar
- ☐ 1 cup coconut water
- ☐ 1 cup brewed green tea
- ☐ ½ cup almond milk
- ☐ ½ cup nonfat Greek yogurt
- ☐ ½ cup plant milk
- ☐ 2 tablespoons lime juice
- ☐ 3 tablespoons chia seed
- ☐ 2 tablespoons hulled hemp seed
- ☐ 4 almonds
- ☐ 2 tablespoons protein powder
- ☐ 2 teaspoons pure vanilla extract
- ☐ 1 teaspoon ground cinnamon

260. BERRY BLUES

Frozen raspberries provide rich texture and color but can often be a bit tart. Adding some fruit juice nectar will sweeten up a smoothie. The color in the berries of this antioxidant-rich smoothie comes from health-promoting polyphenols, so the richer the color, the more antioxidants there are in the smoothie. Polyphenol antioxidants reduce inflammation and improve energy, which is often needed to help those who are sedentary due to fatigue and pain.

½ cup blueberry nectar
½ cup water
½ cup frozen wild blueberries
½ cup frozen raspberries
½ cup ice
1 tablespoon chia seed

Combine all ingredients in a high-power blender or food processor and blend until smooth. Drink immediately.

CALORIES: 180 FAT: 4 CARBS: 36 FIBER: 11 PROTEIN: 3

261. ANTIOXIDANT MAXIMIZER

In this smoothie, you'll find sweet blueberry flavor with tart pomegranate undertones, as well as antioxidant polyphenols that give this smoothie its deep red-purple coloring. Pomegranate polyphenols increase body fat metabolism.

½ cup blueberry nectar
½ cup pomegranate arils
¼ cup frozen wild blueberries
½ cup ice
1 tablespoon chia seed

Combine all ingredients in a high-power blender or food processor and blend until smooth. Drink immediately.

CALORIES: 200 FAT: 5 CARBS: 40 FIBER: 9 PROTEIN: 3

262. BLUEBERRY ALMOND

This smoothie is a thick and exotic blend with rich almond and date flavors. Daily consumption of whole blueberries has been proven in numerous studies to reduce the risk for type 2 diabetes, as blueberries increase cellular insulin sensitivity.

4 almonds
1 date
½ cup frozen wild blueberries
1 cup brewed green tea

Combine all ingredients in a high-power blender or food processor and blend until smooth. Drink immediately.

CALORIES: 261 **FAT:** 14 **CARBS:** 30 **FIBER:** 9 **PROTEIN:** 6

263. THE VIOLET TUTU

The ingredients in this drink make it creamy, rich, and full of fresh flavor. Blueberry phytochemicals have been found to alleviate hyperglycemia and boost energy.

¼ avocado
½ frozen banana
½ cup coconut water
½ cup ice
½ cup frozen wild blueberries
1 tablespoon chia seed

Combine all ingredients in a high-power blender or food processor and blend until smooth. Drink immediately.

CALORIES: 220 **FAT:** 10 **CARBS:** 28 **FIBER:** 16 **PROTEIN:** 5

264. BLUEBERRY BANANA

This is a tasty and creamy smoothie, with a rich blueberry flavor and a hit of protein for energy and muscle development. The more muscle, the greater the number of calories burned every minute of the day and night.

½ frozen banana
½ cup almond milk
½ cup frozen wild blueberries
1 cup water
2 tablespoons protein powder
2 teaspoons vanilla extract

Combine all ingredients in a high-power blender or food processor and blend until smooth. Drink immediately.

CALORIES: 200 FAT: 2 CARBS: 30 FIBER: 6 PROTEIN: 10

265. CINNAMON APPLE CREAM

A luscious fresh apple flavor is the base in this cinnamon treat! Apples provide quercetin, which quells histamine-mediated inflammation and supports metabolism.

½ apple
½ cup plant milk
½ cup ice
½ cup nonfat Greek yogurt
¼ teaspoon ground cinnamon

Combine all ingredients in a high-power blender or food processor and blend until smooth. Drink immediately.

CALORIES: 178 FAT: 2 CARBS: 28 FIBER: 4 PROTEIN: 14

266. KEY LIME PIE

Fresh lime and banana flavors come through in this recipe, with a hint of sweet, crisp Fuji apple. Hemp seed is rich in fiber, which slows the digestion of carbohydrates, allowing time for their calories to be burned, rather than stored as body fat.

½ frozen banana
½ apple
½ cup coconut water
½ cup water
2 tablespoons lime juice
2 tablespoons hulled hemp seed

Combine all ingredients in a high-power blender or food processor and blend until smooth. Drink immediately.

CALORIES: 210 **FAT:** 6 **CARBS:** 30 **FIBER:** 6 **PROTEIN:** 8

Week 39

Grocery List

- ☐ 5 apples
- ☐ 3 star fruits
- ☐ 1 grapefruit
- ☐ 1 papaya
- ☐ ½ cup minced fresh mint leaves
- ☐ ½ cup watermelon
- ☐ ¼ cup minced fresh basil leaves
- ☐ 1 cup brewed green tea
- ☐ 1 cup nonfat Greek yogurt
- ☐ ½ cup black cherry juice
- ☐ ½ cup coconut water
- ☐ 1 teaspoon lemon juice
- ☐ 7 tablespoons chia seed
- ☐ 1 teaspoon pure vanilla extract
- ☐ 1 pinch of fresh-ground black pepper
- ☐ 1 pinch of ground cardamom
- ☐ 1 pinch of ground cinnamon

267. CHERRY BASIL

This recipe combines a sweet apple flavor with herbaceous basil fragrance. Basil oils help reduce stress hormone production, which in turn reduces cortisol-mediated inflammation and fatigue.

½ apple
½ cup black cherry juice
½ cup ice
¼ cup minced fresh basil leaves
2 tablespoons chia seed

Combine all ingredients in a high-power blender or food processor and blend until smooth. Drink immediately.

CALORIES: 252 **FAT:** 10 **CARBS:** 30 **FIBER:** 14 **PROTEIN:** 5

268. APPLE MINT CRUSH

Apples provide flavonols, which promote healthy hormones that control metabolism.

1 apple
½ cup ice
½ cup nonfat Greek yogurt
¼ cup water
¼ cup minced fresh mint leaves

Combine all ingredients in a high-power blender or food processor and blend until smooth. Drink immediately.

CALORIES: 174 **FAT:** 0 **CARBS:** 26 **FIBER:** 6 **PROTEIN:** 12

269. SPICED APPLE CIDER

Apples are an excellent source of soluble fiber, which holds onto water in our digestive tracts, allowing the water to hydrate us over many hours. This reduces false hunger signals.

1 apple
½ cup ice
1 cup water
1 tablespoon chia seed
1 pinch of ground cinnamon
1 pinch of ground cardamom
1 pinch of fresh-ground black pepper

Combine all ingredients in a high-power blender or food processor and blend until smooth. Drink immediately.

CALORIES: 174 FAT: 5 CARBS: 28 FIBER: 8 PROTEIN: 3

270. MOUNTAIN BREEZE

This drink is bitter and tart, yet also sweet with apple flavor. Fresh juices from apples and grapefruit contain antioxidants that can protect cells from oxidative stress, thus reducing inflammation.

1 apple
½ grapefruit
½ cup ice
¼ cup water
1 tablespoon chia seed

Combine all ingredients in a high-power blender or food processor and blend until smooth. Drink immediately.

CALORIES: 168 FAT: 5 CARBS: 26 FIBER: 10 PROTEIN: 4

271. STAR FRUIT TEA

This delicate combination has a light mint fragrance and sweet, astringent star fruit flavor. Additionally, star fruit is a potent source of inflammation-reducing polyphenolic antioxidants.

1 star fruit
1 cup brewed green tea
½ cup ice
¼ cup minced fresh mint leaves
2 tablespoons chia seed

Combine all ingredients in a high-power blender or food processor and blend until smooth. Drink immediately.

CALORIES: 130 **FAT:** 7 **CARBS:** 15 **FIBER:** 10 **PROTEIN:** 5

272. STAR FRUIT AND CREAM

This smoothie is tannic and perfumed with the delightful scent of fresh star fruit. Star fruit fiber supports weight loss and insulin function.

1 star fruit
1 apple
½ cup water
½ cup ice
½ cup nonfat Greek yogurt

Combine all ingredients in a high-power blender or food processor and blend until smooth. Drink immediately.

CALORIES: 145 **FAT:** 0 **CARBS:** 18 **FIBER:** 6 **PROTEIN:** 14

273. STAR FRUIT AND PAPAYA

Vanilla balances lemon and adds depth of flavor to this smoothie.
Papaya peel contains concentrated amounts of carotenoids, such
as lutein and beta-carotene.

1 star fruit
¼ organic papaya with peel
½ cup watermelon
½ cup coconut water
½ cup ice
1 teaspoon lemon juice
1 teaspoon vanilla extract
1 tablespoon chia seed

Combine all ingredients in a high-power blender or food processor
and blend until smooth. Drink immediately.

CALORIES: 138 **FAT:** 0 **CARBS:** 30 **FIBER:** 6 **PROTEIN:** 5

Week 40

Grocery List

- ☐ 3 bananas
- ☐ 1 cucumber
- ☐ ½ inch fresh turmeric root
- ☐ ½ cup frozen wild blueberries
- ☐ ¼ cup frozen blackberries
- ☐ 5 cups coconut water
- ☐ 1 tablespoon lemon juice
- ☐ 1 teaspoon coconut palm nectar
- ☐ 4 tablespoons chia seed
- ☐ 3 tablespoons hulled hemp seed
- ☐ 3 tablespoons unsweetened cocoa powder
- ☐ 2 almonds
- ☐ 2 cashews
- ☐ 1 tablespoon unsweetened fine macaroon coconut
- ☐ 1 tablespoon protein powder
- ☐ 2 teaspoons instant coffee
- ☐ 3 teaspoons pure vanilla extract
- ☐ 1 pinch of fresh-ground black pepper

274. COCONUT BLACKBERRY ICY

This drink is slightly sweet with rich berry flavor. The bananas provide an excellent source of vitamin B_6. Also, blackberries are loaded with about 8 grams of fiber per cup, and their polyphenol antioxidants help us lose weight as they fuel metabolic processes.

½ frozen banana

½ cup coconut water

½ cup water

¼ cup frozen blackberries

1 tablespoon chia seed

Combine all ingredients in a high-power blender or food processor and blend until smooth. Drink immediately.

CALORIES: 150 FAT: 4 CARBS: 29 FIBER: 7 PROTEIN: 3

275. CHOCOLATE BANANA CASHEW

This recipe has creamy banana and cashew flavors, with subtle cocoa tones laced throughout. The cashews are a good source of calcium, which helps fat cells release stored body fat.

½ frozen banana

½ cup coconut water

½ cup ice

2 cashews

1 tablespoon hulled hemp seed

1 tablespoon unsweetened cocoa powder

Combine all ingredients in a high-power blender or food processor and blend until smooth. Drink immediately.

CALORIES: 178 FAT: 7 CARBS: 24 FIBER: 3 PROTEIN: 5

276. LEMON VANILLA DROP

In this smoothie, you'll taste a sour lemon flavor with a tinge of sweetness. Coconut water is low in calories and rich in electrolytes, which is good for hydration and muscle movement.

½ cucumber

1 cup coconut water

1 cup ice

2 tablespoons chia seed

1 tablespoon lemon juice

1 teaspoon coconut palm nectar

1 teaspoon vanilla extract

Combine all ingredients in a high-power blender or food processor and blend until smooth. Drink immediately.

CALORIES: 190 FAT: 7 CARBS: 27 FIBER: 8 PROTEIN: 5

277. COCONUT COFFEE

This smoothie is as frosty and rich as a blended caffè latte and just as satisfying. Coffee contains polyphenol antioxidant compounds that improve metabolic syndrome, a condition that affects an estimated 25 percent of the US population, by improving the way our bodies use insulin.

½ frozen banana

½ cup coconut water

1 cup water

¼ cup ice

1 tablespoon protein powder

1 teaspoon instant coffee

1 teaspoon vanilla extract

Combine all ingredients in a high-power blender or food processor and blend until smooth. Drink immediately.

CALORIES: 196 FAT: 0 CARBS: 30 FIBER: 4 PROTEIN: 5

278. THE GOLDEN BERRY

This is a simple and refreshing blend. The coconut water is an excellent source of potassium, and in lab studies, phytochemicals in wild blueberries helped alleviate high blood sugar.

½ cup coconut water

½ cup water

½ cup ice

½ cup frozen wild blueberries

1 tablespoon chia seed

½ inch fresh turmeric root

1 pinch of fresh-ground black pepper

Combine all ingredients in a high-power blender or food processor and blend until smooth. Drink immediately.

CALORIES: 126 FAT: 5 CARBS: 16 FIBER: 9 PROTEIN: 3

279. COCONUT COFFEE MOCHA

Wake up with this drink, which includes your favorite coffee flavors and a solid dose of vegan protein, for abundant nutrient-supported energy.

½ frozen banana

½ cup coconut water

1 cup water

2 tablespoons hulled hemp seed

1 tablespoon unsweetened cocoa powder

1 teaspoon instant coffee

¼ teaspoon vanilla extract

Combine all ingredients in a high-power blender or food processor and blend until smooth. Drink immediately.

CALORIES: 186 FAT: 7 CARBS: 24 FIBER: 5 PROTEIN: 7

280. ALMOND COCOA COCONUT CRUNCH

This smoothie is rich in healthful fats that help cells hold on to water longer, thus supporting hydration and energy.

½ frozen banana

1 cup coconut water

½ cup water

2 almonds

1 tablespoon unsweetened fine macaroon coconut

1 tablespoon unsweetened cocoa powder

Combine all ingredients in a high-power blender or food processor and blend until smooth. Drink immediately.

CALORIES: 227 FAT: 11 CARBS: 29 FIBER: 6 PROTEIN: 5

Week 41

Grocery List

- ☐ 2 dates
- ☐ 1 blood orange
- ☐ 1 kiwi
- ☐ 1 apple
- ☐ 1 banana
- ☐ 1½ inches fresh ginger root
- ☐ 1½ cups frozen wild blueberries
- ☐ ½ cup frozen pineapple
- ☐ ½ cup frozen raspberries
- ☐ 5 cups brewed green tea
- ☐ 1½ cups coconut water
- ☐ 1 cup sparkling water
- ☐ 1 teaspoon lemon juice
- ☐ 12 tablespoons chia seed
- ☐ 1 tablespoon protein powder
- ☐ 2 almonds
- ☐ 2 teaspoons unsweetened cocoa powder
- ☐ 1 teaspoon acacia fiber
- ☐ 1 teaspoon pure vanilla extract
- ☐ 1 teaspoon ground cinnamon

281. BLUEBERRY VANILLA REFRESHER

This is a very low-calorie and hydrating smoothie that is chock-full of energizing electrolytes!

½ cup coconut water

½ cup water

½ cup ice

½ cup frozen wild blueberries

2 tablespoons chia seed

1 teaspoon lemon juice

½ teaspoon vanilla extract

Combine all ingredients in a high-power blender or food processor and blend until smooth. Drink immediately.

CALORIES: 170 FAT: 7 CARBS: 24 FIBER: 10 PROTEIN: 4

282. CHOCOLATE ALMOND DATE COCONUT

Unsweetened cocoa powder contains compounds that help reduce inflammation in the intestine, which lets you show off your six-pack!

1 date

1 cup coconut water

1 cup ice

2 almonds

1 tablespoon protein powder

2 teaspoons unsweetened cocoa powder

Combine all ingredients in a high-power blender or food processor and blend until smooth. Drink immediately.

CALORIES: 160 FAT: 3 CARBS: 28 FIBER: 3 PROTEIN: 14

283. GINGER AND BLOOD ORANGE

This smoothie is cool and fresh with a strong ginger hit. Green tea polyphenols are powerful anti-inflammatories that support muscle function and development.

1 blood orange
1 cup brewed green tea
¼ cup ice
2 tablespoons chia seed
½ inch fresh ginger root
1 cup sparkling water

Combine blood orange, green tea, ice, chia seed, and ginger root in a high-power blender or food processor and blend until smooth. Then stir in the sparkling water and drink immediately.

CALORIES: 212 FAT: 10 CARBS: 20 FIBER: 16 PROTEIN: 6

284. TANGY AND SWEET

Intensely sweet fruits, such as pineapple and wild blueberries, pair well with the herbal flavor of green tea. Green tea polyphenols are proven weight-loss nutrients. Simply adding a cup of green tea to your daily smoothie is a powerful weight-loss strategy.

1 kiwi
1 cup brewed green tea
½ cup frozen wild blueberries
½ cup frozen pineapple
2 tablespoons chia seed

Combine all ingredients in a high-power blender or food processor and blend until smooth. Drink immediately.

CALORIES: 258 FAT: 10 CARBS: 30 FIBER: 18 PROTEIN: 6

285. VIOLET TEA ELIXIR

Fresh ginger is the highlight of this sweet, tea-based smoothie. This combo provides a triple hit of antioxidants, as the apple contains quercetin, the wild blueberries are a rich source of polyphenols, and the green tea is infused with energy-supporting flavonoids.

½ apple
1 cup brewed green tea
½ cup frozen wild blueberries
¼ cup ice
2 tablespoons chia seed
½ inch fresh ginger root

Combine all ingredients in a high-power blender or food processor and blend until smooth. Drink immediately.

CALORIES: 226 **FAT:** 10 **CARBS:** 26 **FIBER:** 18 **PROTEIN:** 6

286. SPICED ICED TEA

This smoothie provides quick hydration, with light cinnamon and ginger flavors.

½ frozen banana
1 cup brewed green tea
½ cup ice
2 tablespoons chia seed
½ inch fresh ginger root
½ teaspoon ground cinnamon

Combine all ingredients in a high-power blender or food processor and blend until smooth. Drink immediately.

CALORIES: 196 FAT: 10 CARBS: 16 FIBER: 14 PROTEIN: 6

287. CHIA ENERGY BOOSTER

This recipe combines raspberry and vanilla flavors sweetened with a date. Using whole fruits such as dates, rather than refined sugar, is an effective weight-loss strategy. The fruits' natural fiber slows the digestion of the simple sugars, allowing the calories to be used for energy rather than stored away as body fat.

1 date
1 cup brewed green tea
½ cup frozen raspberries
½ cup ice
2 tablespoons chia seed
1 teaspoon acacia fiber
½ teaspoon vanilla extract

Combine all ingredients in a high-power blender or food processor and blend until smooth. Drink immediately.

CALORIES: 220 FAT: 7 CARBS: 33 FIBER: 13 PROTEIN: 5

Week 42

Grocery List

- [ ] 20 cherries
- [ ] 6 oranges
- [ ] 5 strawberries
- [ ] 1 tangerine
- [ ] 1 grapefruit
- [ ] ½ cup honeydew
- [ ] ½ inch fresh ginger root
- [ ] 1 inch fresh turmeric root
- [ ] ½ cup frozen raspberries
- [ ] 1 cup brewed green tea
- [ ] 1 cup nonfat Greek yogurt
- [ ] 3 teaspoons lemon juice
- [ ] 1 teaspoon lime juice
- [ ] 3 tablespoons chia seed
- [ ] 2 tablespoons hulled hemp seed
- [ ] 1 teaspoon pure vanilla extract
- [ ] 1 pinch of fresh-ground black pepper
- [ ] 1 pinch of ground cinnamon

288. SOUR BERRY BREW

Raspberries pair well with the earthy flavor of green tea in this smoothie. Raspberries are naturally rich in phenolic compounds that may stimulate weight loss.

1 cup brewed green tea
½ cup ice
½ cup frozen raspberries
2 tablespoons chia seed

Combine all ingredients in a high-power blender or food processor and blend until smooth. Drink immediately.

CALORIES: 170 **FAT:** 10 **CARBS:** 10 **FIBER:** 16 **PROTEIN:** 6

289. VANILLA BEAN CREAM CITRUS

This smoothie tastes like an orange cream frozen dessert with a little tart grapefruit. Essential oils in citrus fruit increase fat metabolism. Add a tablespoon of the peel, which contains concentrated amounts of these nutrient-packed oils to power boost the weight-loss effect of your smoothie.

1 orange
½ grapefruit
½ cup ice
½ cup water
½ cup nonfat Greek yogurt
1 teaspoon vanilla extract

Combine all ingredients in a high-power blender or food processor and blend until smooth. Drink immediately.

CALORIES: 150 **FAT:** 0 **CARBS:** 20 **FIBER:** 8 **PROTEIN:** 12

290. ÜBER ORANGE CITRUS

You'll taste layers of orange flavor in this smoothie, with golden turmeric color and tangy tangerine. Turmeric provides curcumin, which modifies insulin and metabolism to improve weight loss.

1 tangerine
½ orange
½ cup ice
1 tablespoon chia seed
1 teaspoon lime juice
½ inch fresh turmeric root

Combine all ingredients in a high-power blender or food processor and blend until smooth. Drink immediately.

CALORIES: 165 **FAT:** 5 **CARBS:** 21 **FIBER:** 11 **PROTEIN:** 2

291. CINNAMON CHERRY

This citrus-based fat burner is cool and invigorating, with a bit of warm spice. Freshly ground black pepper is an excellent source of potassium that's needed for cardiovascular health and exercise.

10 cherries
1 orange
½ cup water
1 teaspoon lemon juice
1 pinch of ground cinnamon
1 pinch of fresh-ground black pepper

Combine all ingredients in a high-power blender or food processor and blend until smooth. Drink immediately.

CALORIES: 125 **FAT:** 0 **CARBS:** 22 **FIBER:** 10 **PROTEIN:** 2

292. SPICY ORANGE CHERRY

This smoothie features orange and cherry flavors with the heat of ginger. Fresh ginger root provides essential oils that increase weight loss by enhancing digestion and metabolism.

10 cherries
1 orange
½ cup water
½ cup ice
½ cup nonfat Greek yogurt
½ inch fresh ginger root
½ inch fresh turmeric root

Combine all ingredients in a high-power blender or food processor and blend until smooth. Drink immediately.

CALORIES: 170 **FAT:** 0 **CARBS:** 30 **FIBER:** 8 **PROTEIN:** 13

293. STRAWBERRY CITRUS

Sweet strawberries and tart citrus flavors are featured in this recipe. Strawberries contain powerful polyphenol compounds that reduce inflammation and water weight.

5 strawberries
1 orange
½ cup water
1 tablespoon hulled hemp seed
1 teaspoon lemon juice

Combine all ingredients in a high-power blender or food processor and blend until smooth. Drink immediately.

CALORIES: 126 **FAT:** 3 **CARBS:** 17 **FIBER:** 8 **PROTEIN:** 4

294. CITRUS MELON

The lemon carries this smoothie and brightens the orange and melon flavors. This combination is packed with vitamin C, which supports weight loss, as it is essential for proper cellular and endocrine function.

1 orange
½ cup honeydew
½ cup ice
1 tablespoon hulled hemp seed
1 teaspoon lemon juice

Combine all ingredients in a high-power blender or food processor and blend until smooth. Drink immediately.

CALORIES: 130 **FAT:** 3 **CARBS:** 22 **FIBER:** 8 **PROTEIN:** 4

Week 43

Grocery List

- [ ] 8 mandarin oranges
- [ ] 1 cucumber
- [ ] 1 banana
- [ ] 1 medium-hot pepper
- [ ] 1 cup cooked squash
- [ ] ½ inch fresh turmeric root
- [ ] ½ cup frozen wild blueberries
- [ ] 2 cups nonfat Greek yogurt
- [ ] 1 cup brewed chai tea
- [ ] ½ cup brewed green tea
- [ ] ½ cup plant milk
- [ ] 1 tablespoon lime juice
- [ ] 1 teaspoon lemon juice
- [ ] 1 vanilla bean
- [ ] 2 tablespoons chia seed
- [ ] 2 tablespoons hulled hemp seed
- [ ] 1 tablespoon protein powder
- [ ] 1 tablespoon unsweetened cocoa powder
- [ ] 1 teaspoon ground cinnamon
- [ ] 1 teaspoon pure vanilla extract
- [ ] 1 teaspoon ground star anise
- [ ] 1 pinch of fresh-ground nutmeg

295. VANILLA ORANGE CREAM

This bright orange smoothie is creamy with a trace of vanilla. Protein powders provide an array of amino acids, which are the building blocks for hormones, enzymes, and muscle development. Adding small doses of protein into the diet throughout the day is an effective weight-loss strategy.

2 mandarin oranges
½ cup ice
½ cup nonfat Greek yogurt
¼ cup water
1 tablespoon protein powder
½ inch fresh turmeric root
1 teaspoon vanilla extract

Combine all ingredients in a high-power blender or food processor and blend until smooth. Drink immediately.

CALORIES: 120 **FAT:** 2 **CARBS:** 18 **FIBER:** 6 **PROTEIN:** 16

296. ANISE MANDARIN

This sweet mandarin orange smoothie has a touch of licorice spice. Warming spices help stimulate digestion, waking up your metabolism. Adding water and ice to smoothies supports weight loss, as it is a simple and sustainable hydration strategy.

2 mandarin oranges
½ cup water
½ cup ice
1 tablespoon hulled hemp seed
¼ teaspoon ground star anise

Combine all ingredients in a high-power blender or food processor and blend until smooth. Drink immediately.

CALORIES: 144 **FAT:** 3 **CARBS:** 26 **FIBER:** 4 **PROTEIN:** 4

297. ORANGE VANILLA LIME

The flavor of this smoothie is reminiscent of creamy orange ice cream. Organisms in yogurt, such as *Lactobacillus acidophilus*, increase the absorption of metabolism-supporting nutrients, such as polyphenols, carotenoids, and B vitamins.

2 mandarin oranges
1 vanilla bean
½ cup ice
½ cup nonfat Greek yogurt
¼ cup water
1 tablespoon lime juice

Combine all ingredients in a high-power blender or food processor and blend until smooth. Drink immediately.

CALORIES: 112 **FAT:** 0 **CARBS:** 18 **FIBER:** 4 **PROTEIN:** 13

298. CHOCOLATE ORANGE CREAM

Try this creamy orange whip with a little cocoa undertone as a snack or a dessert. Cocoa polyphenols support weight loss, as they modulate fats and reduce cholesterol.

2 mandarin oranges
½ cup plant milk
½ cup ice
½ cup nonfat Greek yogurt
1 tablespoon unsweetened cocoa powder

Combine all ingredients in a high-power blender or food processor and blend until smooth. Drink immediately.

CALORIES: 192 **FAT:** 4 **CARBS:** 24 **FIBER:** 4 **PROTEIN:** 13

299. BENGAL TIGER

Move over, chai! Cinnamon accents this yogurt-and-spiced-tea blend. Teas provide flavor without calories as the liquid base for smoothies. The spices in chai tea, including black pepper and cardamom, are highly effective anti-inflammatories that help reduce water weight and the appearance of cellulite.

1 frozen banana
1 cup brewed chai tea
½ cup nonfat Greek yogurt
½ cup ice
1 pinch of ground cinnamon
1 pinch of fresh-ground nutmeg

Combine all ingredients in a high-power blender or food processor and blend until smooth. Drink immediately.

CALORIES: 172 **FAT:** 0 **CARBS:** 30 **FIBER:** 4 **PROTEIN:** 12

300. HOTACADA

Squash is an excellent source of fiber and mixed carotenoids. Hot chili peppers target fat metabolism, energy expenditure, and thermogenesis.

½ cucumber
½ medium-hot pepper
½ cup brewed green tea
½ cup cooked squash
2 tablespoons chia seed

Combine all ingredients in a high-power blender or food processor and blend until smooth. Drink immediately.

CALORIES: 150 **FAT:** 7 **CARBS:** 20 **FIBER:** 10 **PROTEIN:** 6

301. BLUEBERRY PIE

Taste real blueberry pie flavor in this satisfying and hearty smoothie. Squash is rich in alpha-carotene, which has powerful effects on body weight. Researchers found that in women, the higher the blood level of alpha-carotene, the lower the body fat mass.

½ cup water
½ cup frozen wild blueberries
½ cup cooked squash
2 tablespoons hulled hemp seed
½ teaspoon ground cinnamon
1 teaspoon lemon juice

Combine all ingredients in a high-power blender or food processor and blend until smooth. Drink immediately.

CALORIES: 170 **FAT:** 10 **CARBS:** 17 **FIBER:** 6 **PROTEIN:** 7

Week 44

Grocery List

- [ ] 8 strawberries
- [ ] 2 apples
- [ ] 1 banana
- [ ] 1 date
- [ ] 1 tangerine
- [ ] 1 tomato
- [ ] 1 apple
- [ ] 1 cucumber
- [ ] 1 orange
- [ ] 1 cup cooked squash
- [ ] ½ cup watermelon
- [ ] 3 inches fresh ginger root
- [ ] 2 inches fresh turmeric root
- [ ] 1 cup brewed green tea
- [ ] 1 cup cranberry juice
- [ ] ½ cup coconut water
- [ ] ½ cup black cherry juice
- [ ] 4 teaspoons lime juice
- [ ] 2 teaspoons lemon juice
- [ ] 6 tablespoons chia seed
- [ ] 1 tablespoon hulled hemp seed
- [ ] 1 teaspoon orange extract
- [ ] 1 teaspoon xylitol
- [ ] 1 pinch of ground cinnamon

302. SWEET SQUASH

This smoothie is a squash lover's simple pleasure. Squash doesn't contain any fat or cholesterol, and it's rich in electrolytes and low in calories.

1 date
½ cup coconut water
1 cup water
½ cup cooked squash
1 tablespoon chia seed
1 inch fresh turmeric root

Combine all ingredients in a high-power blender or food processor and blend until smooth. Drink immediately.

CALORIES: 150 **FAT:** 4 **CARBS:** 28 **FIBER:** 6 **PROTEIN:** 3

303. TANGERINE SQUASH

This sweet and savory squash smoothie has a little citrus character. Squash is a low-calorie food and a rich source of weight-reducing carotenoids, and it's also high in a type of fiber that makes cells more receptive to insulin.

1 tangerine
½ cup cooked squash
½ cup water
½ cup ice
1 tablespoon chia seed
1 teaspoon lemon juice
1 pinch of ground cinnamon

Combine all ingredients in a high-power blender or food processor and blend until smooth. Drink immediately.

CALORIES: 140 **FAT:** 6 **CARBS:** 18 **FIBER:** 11 **PROTEIN:** 6

304. WINTER GARDEN

Tomato and ginger flavors dominate this recipe, with a little hint of lime. Adding chia seed to smoothies that contain carotenoid-rich foods increases the absorption of these fat-soluble vitamins.

1 tomato
½ cucumber
½ cup water
1 tablespoon lime juice
1 tablespoon chia seed
1 inch fresh turmeric root
1 inch fresh ginger root

Combine all ingredients in a high-power blender or food processor and blend until smooth. Drink immediately.

CALORIES: 112 FAT: 6 CARBS: 10 FIBER: 9 PROTEIN: 6

305. APPLE CRANBERRY FREEZE

This jazzy, tart, spicy, and sour combo has intense cranberry flavor! Xylitol is sweet and inhibits the growth of a common bacteria that causes ear infections and tooth cavities. Bacteria deplete our B vitamins, which are needed for metabolic functions and energy. Therefore, xylitol is considered a weight-loss-promoting sweetener.

1 apple
½ cup ice
¼ cup cranberry juice
¼ cup water
1 tablespoon chia seed
1 inch fresh ginger root
1 teaspoon lemon juice
1 teaspoon xylitol

Combine all ingredients in a high-power blender or food processor and blend until smooth. Drink immediately.

CALORIES: 182 FAT: 5 CARBS: 24 FIBER: 17 PROTEIN: 3

306. WATERMELON SLUSHY

This smoothie is cool, fresh, tart, and flavorful. The orange extract adds flavor without adding sugar or calories. Cranberries contain proanthocyanidins that keep bacteria, such as *E. coli*, from sticking to the urinary tract, thus their benefit in reducing urinary tract infections. Reducing pathogenic bacteria helps reduce systemic inflammation that causes fatigue and sluggish metabolism.

½ cup watermelon
¼ cup cranberry juice
¼ cup black cherry juice
1 tablespoon chia seed
1 teaspoon orange extract

Combine all ingredients in a high-power blender or food processor and blend until smooth. Drink immediately.

CALORIES: 154 FAT: 5 CARBS: 22 FIBER: 6 PROTEIN: 3

307. APPLE CRANBERRY ORANGE

The tartness of cranberry juice is balanced with sweet fruit flavors in this classic blend. Cranberries and cranberry juice are both rich in proanthocyanidins that help tighten skin, which gives a more youthful appearance after significant weight loss.

½ orange
½ apple
½ frozen banana
¼ cup cranberry juice
1 tablespoon hulled hemp seed

Combine all ingredients in a high-power blender or food processor and blend until smooth. Drink immediately.

CALORIES: 186 FAT: 3 CARBS: 30 FIBER: 5 PROTEIN: 4

308. STRAWBERRY LIME GINGER

This smoothie has a lightly sweet green-tea base with a little citrus and ginger flavor. Strawberries contain both soluble and insoluble fiber, which both support weight loss by increasing the efficacy of insulin and also by keeping the gastrointestinal tract clean and supporting liver function.

8 strawberries
1 cup brewed green tea
½ cup ice
1 inch fresh ginger root
1 tablespoon chia seed
1 teaspoon lime juice

Combine all ingredients in a high-power blender or food processor and blend until smooth. Drink immediately.

CALORIES: 72 **FAT:** 5 **CARBS:** 9 **FIBER:** 8 **PROTEIN:** 3

Week 45

Grocery List

- ☐ 1 lime
- ☐ 1 banana
- ☐ 1 papaya
- ☐ ¼ cup minced fresh mint leaves
- ☐ 5 inches fresh ginger root
- ☐ ½ inch fresh turmeric root
- ☐ ¾ cup frozen mango
- ☐ ½ cup frozen pomegranate arils
- ☐ ¼ cup frozen strawberries
- ☐ 6 cups brewed green tea
- ☐ 3 cups sparkling water
- ☐ 1½ cups coconut water
- ☐ 1½ cups papaya nectar
- ☐ ½ cup nonfat Greek yogurt
- ☐ ½ cup rice milk
- ☐ 1 teaspoon coconut palm nectar
- ☐ 4 tablespoons chia seed
- ☐ 1 pinch of five-spice powder

309. GINGER POM

Enjoy this minty smoothie, rich in weight-loss nutrients. Also included in this smoothie are pomegranate arils, a potent source of antioxidants.

1 cup coconut water
1 cup brewed green tea
½ cup frozen pomegranate arils
¼ cup minced fresh mint leaves
1 inch fresh ginger root

Combine all ingredients in a high-power blender or food processor and blend until smooth. Drink immediately.

CALORIES: 120 **FAT:** 1 **CARBS:** 28 **FIBER:** 4 **PROTEIN:** 2

310. GINGER LIME COOLER

This spicy version of limeade is ultra-refreshing with sparkling water. The ginger is a mild anti-inflammatory and provides antioxidants that support the immune system.

1 cup sparkling water, plus 1 cup to be added after blending
1 cup ice
1 cup brewed green tea
½ lime
1 inch fresh ginger root
1 teaspoon coconut palm nectar

Combine 1 cup of sparkling water with ice, green tea, lime, ginger, and coconut palm nectar in a high-power blender or food processor and blend until smooth. Then stir in the second cup of sparkling water and drink immediately.

CALORIES: 48 **FAT:** 0 **CARBS:** 14 **FIBER:** 4 **PROTEIN:** 2

311. GINGER TEA SPRITZER

This drink is slushy, light, and bubbly, with a tang of ginger heat.

1 cup brewed green tea
½ cup ice
2 inches fresh ginger root
1 cup sparkling water

Combine the green tea, ice, and ginger in a high-power blender or food processor and blend until smooth. Then stir in the sparkling water and drink immediately.

CALORIES: 8 FAT: 0 CARBS: 2 FIBER: 0 PROTEIN: 0

312. STRAWBERRY MANGO FROSTY

Cold and thirst quenching, this simple smoothie is equally appropriate as an afternoon pick-me-up or a light dessert. Strawberries are sweet but low in glycemic load, as they are rich in soluble fiber.

1 cup brewed green tea
½ cup papaya nectar
¼ cup frozen strawberries
¼ cup frozen mango
¼ cup ice
1 tablespoon chia seed

Combine all ingredients in a high-power blender or food processor and blend until smooth. Drink immediately.

CALORIES: 172 FAT: 5 CARBS: 26 FIBER: 7 PROTEIN: 2

313. TROPICAL WHIP

The ingredients in this smoothie provide a protein-rich, creamy, tropical blend.

1 cup brewed green tea
½ frozen banana
½ cup papaya nectar
½ cup frozen mango
½ cup ice
½ cup nonfat Greek yogurt
1 inch fresh ginger root

Combine all ingredients in a high-power blender or food processor and blend until smooth. Drink immediately.

CALORIES: 232 **FAT:** 0 **CARBS:** 30 **FIBER:** 2 **PROTEIN:** 14

314. PAPAYA COOLER

This simple blend is sweet and light and has a tropical fragrance. The phytochemical epigallocatechin gallate (EGCG) in green tea is linked to significant weight loss and reduction of body fat.

1 cup brewed green tea
½ cup ice
½ cup papaya nectar
¼ papaya
2 tablespoons chia seed
½ inch fresh turmeric root

Combine all ingredients in a high-power blender or food processor and blend until smooth. Drink immediately.

CALORIES: 190 **FAT:** 7 **CARBS:** 31 **FIBER:** 9 **PROTEIN:** 4

315. FIVE-SPICE COCONUT

You'll taste a frosty blend of spice and sweetness in this smoothie. Five-spice powder is a combination of spices that generally includes cloves, fenugreek, cinnamon, star anise, cayenne pepper, and ginger. Cloves contain antioxidant polyphenols that appear to feed the intestinal bacteria that support weight loss.

½ frozen banana
½ cup rice milk
½ cup coconut water
½ cup ice
1 tablespoon chia seed
1 pinch of five-spice powder

Combine all ingredients in a high-power blender or food processor and blend until smooth. Drink immediately.

CALORIES: 180 **FAT:** 10 **CARBS:** 16 **FIBER:** 7 **PROTEIN:** 2

Week 46

Grocery List

- ☐ 2 bananas
- ☐ 1 date
- ☐ ½ inch fresh ginger root
- ☐ ½ inch fresh turmeric root
- ☐ ½ cup frozen cherries
- ☐ 1½ cups nonfat Greek yogurt
- ☐ 3½ cups rice milk
- ☐ 4 tablespoons protein powder
- ☐ 10 teaspoons unsweetened cocoa powder
- ☐ 2 tablespoons chia seed
- ☐ 6 teaspoons pure vanilla extract
- ☐ 1 teaspoon ground cinnamon
- ☐ 1 pinch of cayenne pepper

316. CHERRY VANILLA CREAM

This fragrant vanilla combination works equally well as a breakfast drink or a dessert. Vanilla bean and vanilla extract provide a surprising benefit: in preliminary studies, researchers found that just the smell of vanilla helps with weight loss by creating a sense of satiety rather than deprivation.

1 cup rice milk
½ cup frozen cherries
½ cup nonfat Greek yogurt
½ cup ice
½ teaspoon vanilla extract

Combine all ingredients in a high-power blender or food processor and blend until smooth. Drink immediately.

CALORIES: 240 **FAT:** 2 **CARBS:** 30 **FIBER:** 2 **PROTEIN:** 12

317. MEXICAN CHOCOLATE

This rich and spicy chocolate shake has a cool bite and hot undertones. Add 2 teaspoons of instant coffee granules if you want a caffeine kick in this Mexican chocolate treat. Cayenne pepper stimulates fat cells to activate the release of stored fat.

½ cup rice milk
½ cup ice
½ cup nonfat Greek yogurt
1 tablespoon protein powder
1 teaspoon unsweetened cocoa powder
1 teaspoon vanilla extract
1 pinch of cayenne pepper
1 pinch of ground cinnamon

Combine all ingredients in a high-power blender or food processor and blend until smooth. Drink immediately.

CALORIES: 155 **FAT:** 2 **CARBS:** 17 **FIBER:** 0 **PROTEIN:** 12

318. GINGER BANANA CREAM

Enjoy this creamy banana blend with warm ginger undertones and bright golden turmeric color and fragrance. One of the ways that turmeric helps with weight loss is by its anti-inflammatory action, which increases excretion of obesogenic toxins through sweat glands.

½ frozen banana
½ cup rice milk
½ cup ice
1 tablespoon chia seed
½ inch fresh ginger root
½ inch fresh turmeric root

Combine all ingredients in a high-power blender or food processor and blend until smooth. Drink immediately.

CALORIES: 185 FAT: 6 CARBS: 27 FIBER: 8 PROTEIN: 3

319. CINNAMON SWIRL

This smoothie is simple and sweet with a pleasant tinge of cinnamon spice. Add extra cinnamon if you want to spice it up even more. Cinnamon helps lower cholesterol and triglyceride levels.

1 cup rice milk
½ cup ice
1 tablespoon protein powder
1 teaspoon vanilla extract
¼ teaspoon ground cinnamon

Combine all ingredients in a high-power blender or food processor and blend until smooth. Drink immediately.

CALORIES: 170 FAT: 3 CARBS: 23 FIBER: 0 PROTEIN: 14

320. VANILLA RICE CREAM

This rice milk drink is creamy with subdued vanilla and banana flavors. Bananas are a good source of tryptophan, a precursor to serotonin, a brain chemical that helps regulate mood.

½ frozen banana
½ cup water
1 cup ice
¼ cup rice milk
1 tablespoon chia seed
1 teaspoon vanilla extract

Combine all ingredients in a high-power blender or food processor and blend until smooth. Drink immediately.

CALORIES: 160 **FAT:** 5 **CARBS:** 27 **FIBER:** 5 **PROTEIN:** 3

321. CREAMY SWEET COCOA

This smoothie offers chocolaty goodness with just a little kick of sweetness. Dates are nutritional powerhouses rich in fiber, potassium, B vitamins, calcium, magnesium, lutein, and beta-carotene.

1 date
½ frozen banana
¼ cup rice milk
½ cup ice
2 tablespoons protein powder
2 tablespoons unsweetened cocoa powder
2 teaspoons vanilla extract

Combine all ingredients in a high-power blender or food processor and blend until smooth. Drink immediately.

CALORIES: 191 **FAT:** 2 **CARBS:** 30 **FIBER:** 4 **PROTEIN:** 9

322. VANILLA CREAM COCOA

This comforting smoothie tastes like a creamy chocolate milkshake. Most Greek yogurt products contain two anti-obesity probiotic strains, *Lactobacillus acidophilus and Lactobacillus casei*, that help us absorb nutrients that convert body fat into energy.

½ frozen banana
½ cup rice milk
½ cup nonfat Greek yogurt
1 tablespoon unsweetened cocoa powder
½ teaspoon vanilla extract

Combine all ingredients in a high-power blender or food processor and blend until smooth. Drink immediately.

CALORIES: 204 **FAT:** 2 **CARBS:** 30 **FIBER:** 2 **PROTEIN:** 13

Week 47

Grocery List

- ☐ 2 prunes
- ☐ 1 orange
- ☐ 3 bananas
- ☐ ½ cup frozen cherries
- ☐ ½ cup frozen wild blueberries
- ☐ 3 cups nonfat Greek yogurt
- ☐ 3 cups rice milk
- ☐ ½ cup coconut water
- ☐ ½ cup plant milk
- ☐ 1 teaspoon coconut palm nectar
- ☐ 5 tablespoons protein powder
- ☐ 8 teaspoons pure vanilla extract
- ☐ 1 teaspoon ground cinnamon
- ☐ 2 pinches of fresh-ground nutmeg

323. CARAMEL CREAM

This smoothie tastes like a vanilla wafer cookie. Add a pinch or two of cinnamon or nutmeg if you like a little spice. Coconut palm nectar is a low-glycemic sweetener that comes in the form of syrup or crystals. Its glycemic index is only 35, compared to honey (which is around 70) and sugar (which is close to 100). Coconut palm nectar also has less than 20 percent fructose, compared to agave at around 75 percent and high-fructose corn syrup at 55 percent. Still, only use about a teaspoon of coconut palm nectar in a smoothie.

½ frozen banana
½ cup rice milk
½ cup nonfat Greek yogurt
1 tablespoon protein powder
1 teaspoon vanilla extract
1 teaspoon coconut palm nectar

Combine all ingredients in a high-power blender or food processor and blend until smooth. Drink immediately.

CALORIES: 231 **FAT:** 2 **CARBS:** 30 **FIBER:** 2 **PROTEIN:** 13

324. BLUE WHIP

This light and fruity drink is energizing and won't weigh you down. Oligofructose (also known as oligosaccharides) are a form of fiber naturally found in bananas that acts as a prebiotic to help foster the growth of healthful, weight-loss-inducing bacteria in the gut.

½ frozen banana
1 cup rice milk
½ cup frozen wild blueberries
½ cup nonfat Greek yogurt

Combine all ingredients in a high-power blender or food processor and blend until smooth. Drink immediately.

CALORIES: 274 **FAT:** 2 **CARBS:** 30 **FIBER:** 2 **PROTEIN:** 12

325. VANILLA POWER

This light drink is subtly sweet with a heady vanilla aroma. Vanillin, a phytochemical produced by the vanilla bean, has been well studied for its ability to reduce adipose tissue weight.

½ frozen banana
½ cup plant milk
½ cup nonfat Greek yogurt
1 tablespoon vanilla extract

Combine all ingredients in a high-power blender or food processor and blend until smooth. Drink immediately.

CALORIES: 184 **FAT:** 2 **CARBS:** 30 **FIBER:** 2 **PROTEIN:** 12

326. SPICED CREAM

This smoothie is creamy and rich like a dessert. You get double hits of protein from the yogurt and the protein powder.

2 prunes
½ cup rice milk
½ cup ice
½ cup nonfat Greek yogurt
1 tablespoon protein powder
1 teaspoon vanilla extract
1 pinch of ground cinnamon
1 pinch of fresh-ground nutmeg

Combine all ingredients in a high-power blender or food processor and blend until smooth. Drink immediately.

CALORIES: 194 **FAT:** 2 **CARBS:** 30 **FIBER:** 2 **PROTEIN:** 12

327. VANILLA ORANGE

This smoothie combines creamy vanilla with a touch of orange flavor. Vanilla bean can add a whole new flavor dimension to this combination. Use one whole vanilla bean in place of the vanilla extract for a more complex, tasty treat.

1 orange
½ cup coconut water
½ cup ice
½ cup nonfat Greek yogurt
¼ cup water
1 teaspoon vanilla extract

Combine all ingredients in a high-power blender or food processor and blend until smooth. Drink immediately.

CALORIES: 194 **FAT:** 2 **CARBS:** 25 **FIBER:** 3 **PROTEIN:** 12

328. CHERRY CLOUD

This shake is creamy, delicious, and supports restful sleep. The cherries provide melatonin and tryptophan, which induce restorative sleep. Add half an inch of fresh turmeric root for an earthy flavor and to boost the anti-inflammatory action of the ingredients in this blend.

½ cup rice milk
½ cup frozen cherries
½ cup nonfat Greek yogurt
1 tablespoon protein powder
1 teaspoon vanilla extract

Combine all ingredients in a high-power blender or food processor and blend until smooth. Drink immediately.

CALORIES: 196 **FAT:** 2 **CARBS:** 30 **FIBER:** 2 **PROTEIN:** 16

329. VANILLA RICE DREAM

I love this rich, nutmeg-spiced smoothie, which tastes a lot like eggnog! The American diet overuses fat, sugar, and salt to flavor food, while healthier cuisines depend on herbs and spices—like the ones used in this recipe—that also provide nutritional benefits.

1 frozen banana

1 cup ice

½ cup rice milk

2 tablespoons protein powder

3 teaspoons vanilla extract

1 pinch of fresh-ground nutmeg

Combine all ingredients in a high-power blender or food processor and blend until smooth. Drink immediately.

CALORIES: 222 **FAT:** 2 **CARBS:** 30 **FIBER:** 4 **PROTEIN:** 8

Week 48

Grocery List

- ☐ 1 banana
- ☐ 1 date
- ☐ 3 cups frozen wild blueberries
- ☐ 2½ cups pomegranate arils
- ☐ ½ inch fresh turmeric root
- ☐ ½ cup frozen cherries
- ☐ 1 cup brewed green tea
- ☐ 1 cup cultured coconut milk
- ☐ ¾ cup nonfat Greek yogurt
- ☐ ½ cup coconut water
- ☐ ½ cup rice milk
- ☐ 1 teaspoon lemon juice
- ☐ 3 tablespoons chia seed
- ☐ 2 tablespoons hulled hemp seed
- ☐ 2 teaspoons instant coffee
- ☐ 1 teaspoon fiber supplement
- ☐ 1 teaspoon pure vanilla extract
- ☐ ½ teaspoon probiotic supplement
- ☐ 1 teaspoon ground cardamom
- ☐ 1 pinch of ground cinnamon

330. LOTUS SPICE

This spiced smoothie is addictive! Full of fiber, probiotics, and warming spices, this combo is a great daily digestive that also heats up metabolism.

1 date
½ cup rice milk
1 cup water
½ cup nonfat Greek yogurt
¼ teaspoon ground cardamom
1 pinch of ground cinnamon

Combine all ingredients in a high-power blender or food processor and blend until smooth. Drink immediately.

CALORIES: 180 **FAT:** 2 **CARBS:** 30 **FIBER:** 1 **PROTEIN:** 12

331. DETOX SMOOTHIE

This juicy and fresh smoothie provides detoxifying nutrients that help maintain a healthy metabolism. Hemp provides a rich array of minerals, including zinc, calcium, phosphorous, magnesium, and iron. Adding soluble fiber to a smoothie helps reduce the overall glycemic load.

1 cup frozen wild blueberries
½ cup pomegranate arils
½ cup ice
¼ cup water
1 tablespoon hulled hemp seed
1 teaspoon fiber supplement
½ teaspoon probiotic supplement

Combine all ingredients in a high-power blender or food processor and blend until smooth. Drink immediately.

CALORIES: 108 **FAT:** 3 **CARBS:** 30 **FIBER:** 7 **PROTEIN:** 3

332. POMEGRANATE BREEZE

This super-antioxidant mix is sweet, with the scent of vanilla and lemon. Just three ounces of pomegranate juice or arils per day reduces the oxidation process of fats in our bodies, which helps limit the accumulation of unhealthy fats in our arteries.

1 cup ice
1 cup water
½ cup pomegranate arils
½ cup frozen wild blueberries
1 tablespoon chia seed
1 teaspoon lemon juice
1 teaspoon vanilla extract

Combine all ingredients in a high-power blender or food processor and blend until smooth. Drink immediately.

CALORIES:180 **FAT:** 5 **CARBS:** 31 **FIBER:** 10 **PROTEIN:** 3

333. COOL BLUE MORNING

This blend is a magic combination of flavors and nutrients, making it the perfect daily smoothie for hedonism and health. Pomegranates are rich in antioxidant polyphenols and conjugated linolenic acid, which increase fat metabolism and boost overall metabolism.

1 cup brewed green tea
½ cup frozen wild blueberries
½ cup pomegranate arils
¼ cup ice
1 tablespoon chia seed
½ inch fresh turmeric root

Combine all ingredients in a high-power blender or food processor and blend until smooth. Drink immediately.

CALORIES: 170 **FAT:** 5 **CARBS:** 30 **FIBER:** 10 **PROTEIN:** 4

334. ANTIOXIDANT ICY

This drink is the perfect blend, as the blueberries sweeten up the astringent pomegranate. Pomegranate and wild blueberries are two of the richest food sources of antioxidants discovered to date, and blueberries are a great way to add flavor, anthocyanin color, 4 grams of fiber, and only 80 calories per cup.

1 cup pomegranate arils
½ cup ice
½ cup frozen wild blueberries
1 tablespoon chia seed

Combine all ingredients in a high-power blender or food processor and blend until smooth. Add a few tablespoons of water, if needed, to blend. Drink immediately.

CALORIES: 226 **FAT:** 5 **CARBS:** 28 **FIBER:** 24 **PROTEIN:** 3

335. CHERRY REFRESHER

This rich and replenishing smoothie is a powerhouse of potassium. The caffeine in coffee can function as a pain reliever, hence its use in over-the-counter pain medications to reduce headaches and muscle pain.

½ frozen banana
½ cup cultured coconut milk
½ cup ice
½ cup frozen cherries
2 teaspoons instant coffee

Combine all ingredients in a high-power blender or food processor and blend until smooth. Drink immediately.

CALORIES: 135 **FAT:** 3 **CARBS:** 29 **FIBER:** 5 **PROTEIN:** 2

336. BLUEBERRIES AND COCONUT CREAM

This creamy, sweet, high-energy combination is rich in protein from the yogurt and hemp seed. Cultured coconut milks often contain weight loss–inducing strains of probiotics, such as *Lactobacillus thermophilus*, *Lactobacillus acidophilus*, and *Lactobacillus bulgaricus*. One study indicated that these organisms can help reduce total body fat within weeks, when taken daily.

¼ frozen banana
½ cup coconut water
¼ cup cultured coconut milk
¼ cup frozen wild blueberries
¼ cup nonfat Greek yogurt
1 tablespoon hulled hemp seed

Combine all ingredients in a high-power blender or food processor and blend until smooth. Drink immediately.

CALORIES: 150 **FAT:** 5 **CARBS:** 20 **FIBER:** 4 **PROTEIN:** 9

Week 49

Grocery List

- ☐ 1 date
- ☐ 1 banana
- ☐ 1½ cups frozen wild blueberries
- ☐ 1 cup frozen cherries
- ☐ ½ cup frozen blackberries
- ☐ ½ cup frozen mango
- ☐ ½ cup frozen peaches
- ☐ ½ cup frozen pineapple
- ☐ 5 cups cultured coconut milk
- ☐ 3 cups nonfat Greek yogurt
- ☐ 1 vanilla bean
- ☐ ½ cup unsweetened fine macaroon coconut
- ☐ 3 tablespoons hulled hemp seed
- ☐ 6½ teaspoons unsweetened cocoa powder

337. CHERRY BIOTIC BLAST

Indulge yourself with this creamy delight while it soothes the digestive tract with its probiotic culture.

½ frozen banana
½ cup cultured coconut milk
¼ cup frozen cherries
½ cup ice
½ cup nonfat Greek yogurt

Combine all ingredients in a high-power blender or food processor and blend until smooth. Drink immediately.

CALORIES: 202 **FAT:** 4 **CARBS:** 30 **FIBER:** 4 **PROTEIN:** 14

338. MILK CHOCOLATE FROSTY

This smoothie is creamy and rich in chocolate flavor, and the cultured coconut milk provides probiotics that support muscle development.

½ frozen banana
¼ cup cultured coconut milk
½ cup ice
¼ cup nonfat Greek yogurt
1 tablespoon hulled hemp seed
3 teaspoons unsweetened cocoa powder

Combine all ingredients in a high-power blender or food processor and blend until smooth. Drink immediately.

CALORIES: 168 **FAT:** 6 **CARBS:** 21 **FIBER:** 4 **PROTEIN:** 10

339. CHOCOLATE CHERRY ICY

Drink away your chocolate cravings with this tart and sweet coconut smoothie. Unsweetened cocoa powder is very nutritious and adds metabolism-improving antioxidants to any smoothie.

1 cup cultured coconut milk
½ cup frozen cherries
½ cup ice
2 tablespoons hulled hemp seed
3 teaspoons unsweetened cocoa powder

Combine all ingredients in a high-power blender or food processor and blend until smooth. Drink immediately.

CALORIES: 228 **FAT:** 14 **CARBS:** 24 **FIBER:** 8 **PROTEIN:** 8

340. PEACHY COLADA

This smoothie is a tropical treat available year-round. Cultured coconut milk contains healthful probiotics, just like those in yogurt and kefir, and it's delicious too! Probiotics are healthy bacteria that adhere to our intestinal lining, where they help us with detoxification and support the absorption of plant nutrients in our digestive tract.

1 cup cultured coconut milk
¼ cup frozen peaches
¼ cup frozen mango
½ cup unsweetened fine macaroon coconut
¼ cup ice

Combine all ingredients in a high-power blender or food processor and blend until smooth. Drink immediately.

CALORIES: 236 **FAT:** 18 **CARBS:** 20 **FIBER:** 8 **PROTEIN:** 2

341. PURPLE PINEAPPLE

This energy-boosting combination is creamy, tart, and tangy. Blackberries are a good source of fiber, vitamins C and E, and the minerals selenium and calcium, and have only around 40 calories in a half cup.

1 cup cultured coconut milk
½ cup frozen blackberries
½ cup frozen pineapple
½ cup nonfat Greek yogurt

Combine all ingredients in a high-power blender or food processor and blend until smooth. Drink immediately.

CALORIES: 226 **FAT:** 6 **CARBS:** 30 **FIBER:** 8 **PROTEIN:** 14

342. CREAMY WILD BLUEBERRY

This smoothie is like an old-fashioned blueberry milkshake. The cultured coconut milk provides probiotics, and the wild blueberries are one of our richest sources of antioxidant polyphenols.

1 cup cultured coconut milk
1 cup frozen wild blueberries
½ cup nonfat Greek yogurt

Combine all ingredients in a high-power blender or food processor and blend until smooth. Drink immediately.

CALORIES: 208 **FAT:** 6 **CARBS:** 30 **FIBER:** 10 **PROTEIN:** 14

343. VANILLA DREAM SHAKE

The heady vanilla bean flavor is brilliant in this creamy and cool blend. Dates provide a sweet flavor, and they're rich in fiber.

½ date
1 vanilla bean
½ cup frozen wild blueberries
½ cup water
1 cup nonfat Greek yogurt

Combine all ingredients in a high-power blender or food processor and blend until smooth. Drink immediately.

CALORIES: 200 **FAT:** 1 **CARBS:** 25 **FIBER:** 4 **PROTEIN:** 23

Week 50

Grocery List

- ☐ 2 bananas
- ☐ ½ inch fresh turmeric root
- ☐ 1 cup frozen cherries
- ☐ ½ cup frozen raspberries
- ☐ 1 date
- ☐ 1 cup frozen pineapple
- ☐ 4½ cups nonfat Greek yogurt
- ☐ 2 cups coconut water
- ☐ 2 cups plant milk
- ☐ 1 cup cultured coconut milk
- ☐ 1 teaspoon lemon juice
- ☐ 1 vanilla bean
- ☐ 8 almonds
- ☐ 2 tablespoons unsweetened cocoa powder
- ☐ 2 teaspoons pure vanilla extract
- ☐ 1 pinch of fresh-ground black pepper
- ☐ 1 pinch of ground cardamom

344. COCONUT DATE

Enjoy this creamy and comforting ambrosia blend! Cultured coconut milk tastes like yogurt with a tinge of tartness, which pairs well with the sweet, earthy flavor of dates. Probiotics in cultured coconut milk increase weight loss. One study indicated that *Lactobacillus rhamnosus*, a strain often found in yogurt and cultured coconut milk, may reduce white adipose tissue in a matter of weeks when taken daily.

1 date
1 cup water
½ cup cultured coconut milk
½ cup nonfat Greek yogurt
¼ cup ice

Combine all ingredients in a high-power blender or food processor and blend until smooth. Drink immediately.

CALORIES: 234 **FAT:** 3 **CARBS:** 30 **FIBER:** 5 **PROTEIN:** 13

345. TROPICAL POWER SMOOTHIE

This blend is light but full-bodied with coconut and cream. Studies on the weight-loss effects of probiotics indicated that adding these organisms to the diet, without even reducing caloric intake, triggered fat loss.

1 cup frozen pineapple
½ cup cultured coconut milk
½ cup coconut water
½ cup nonfat Greek yogurt

Combine all ingredients in a high-power blender or food processor and blend until smooth. Drink immediately.

CALORIES: 204 **FAT:** 4 **CARBS:** 30 **FIBER:** 4 **PROTEIN:** 13

346. TART RASPBERRY VANILLA

Vanilla beans provide intense flavor to this creamy berry smoothie. Vanilla also provides high levels of antioxidants, which help eliminate free radicals.

1 vanilla bean
½ cup coconut water
½ cup frozen raspberries
½ cup ice
½ cup nonfat Greek yogurt
1 teaspoon lemon juice

Combine all ingredients in a high-power blender or food processor and blend until smooth. Drink immediately.

CALORIES: 120 **FAT:** 0 **CARBS:** 18 **FIBER:** 4 **PROTEIN:** 13

347. VANILLA MELTER

This is a delicious real-vanilla and organic-banana blend that is so good, you may want it every day! One of the reasons I recommend organic produce is because the agricultural chemical residues in non-organic produce act as obesogens by interrupting endocrine functions. Vanillin, an active nutrient in vanilla, helps to release stored body fat.

½ frozen banana
½ cup coconut water
½ cup ice
½ cup nonfat Greek yogurt
1 teaspoon vanilla extract

Combine all ingredients in a high-power blender or food processor and blend until smooth. Drink immediately.

CALORIES: 152 **FAT:** 0 **CARBS:** 24 **FIBER:** 2 **PROTEIN:** 12

348. GOLDEN SPICE

This smoothie is creamy with almond nibbles and layers of spices and flavors. Piperine, the active ingredient in black pepper, boosts turmeric's anti-inflammatory action by up to 2,000 percent by increasing the bioavailability of curcumin.

8 almonds
½ frozen banana
½ cup coconut water
½ cup nonfat Greek yogurt
½ inch fresh turmeric root
1 pinch of ground cardamom
1 pinch of fresh-ground black pepper

Combine all ingredients in a high-power blender or food processor and blend until smooth. Drink immediately.

CALORIES: 180 **FAT:** 7 **CARBS:** 16 **FIBER:** 5 **PROTEIN:** 14

349. DARK CHOCOLATE BANANA

This creamy smoothie has a rich and bitter cocoa flavor. The cocoa contains epicatechin, which helps our bodies burn calories, rather than storing them away as body fat.

1 frozen banana
1 cup plant milk
½ cup nonfat Greek yogurt
2 tablespoons unsweetened cocoa powder

Combine all ingredients in a high-power blender or food processor and blend until smooth. Drink immediately.

CALORIES: 175 **FAT:** 2 **CARBS:** 30 **FIBER:** 4 **PROTEIN:** 12

350. TART CHERRY CREAM

Creamy, pink, and sweet, this is a classic comfort-food smoothie! The cherries used in this recipe contain anthocyanins and proanthocyanidins that help reduce inflammation, thus reducing water weight.

1 cup plant milk
1 cup frozen cherries
½ cup nonfat Greek yogurt
1 teaspoon vanilla extract

Combine all ingredients in a high-power blender or food processor and blend until smooth. Drink immediately.

CALORIES: 170 **FAT:** 3 **CARBS:** 30 **FIBER:** 4 **PROTEIN:** 13

Week 51

Grocery List

- ☐ 4 bananas
- ☐ 1 date
- ☐ ½ cup frozen mango
- ☐ 1½ inches fresh turmeric root
- ☐ ½ cup frozen cherries
- ☐ ½ cup frozen wild blueberries
- ☐ 4½ cups coconut water
- ☐ 3 cups nonfat Greek yogurt
- ☐ 1 teaspoon coconut palm nectar
- ☐ 4 tablespoons unsweetened cocoa powder
- ☐ 3 tablespoons hulled hemp seed
- ☐ 4 almonds
- ☐ 2 tablespoons chia seed
- ☐ 1 tablespoon peanut butter
- ☐ 1 teaspoon instant coffee
- ☐ 1 teaspoon pure vanilla extract
- ☐ 1 pinch of fresh-ground nutmeg
- ☐ 1 pinch of ground cinnamon

351. CREAMY COCONUT

Coconut and banana are a perfect combination in this smoothie, with an edge of chocolate and peanut butter. Cocoa is a rich source of theobromine, which reduces nervous eating and suppresses excessive hunger signals.

1 date
½ frozen banana
½ cup coconut water
½ cup nonfat Greek yogurt
1 tablespoon unsweetened cocoa powder
1 tablespoon peanut butter

Combine all ingredients in a high-power blender or food processor and blend until smooth. Drink immediately.

CALORIES: 210 **FAT:** 8 **CARBS:** 23 **FIBER:** 3 **PROTEIN:** 14

352. COFFEE ALMOND CREAM

This almond cream treat has aromatic layers of coffee and cocoa. The healthful fats from the nuts and yogurt provide energizing amino acids for hours of nutritious fuel.

4 almonds
½ frozen banana
½ cup coconut water
¼ cup nonfat Greek yogurt
1 teaspoon instant coffee
1 tablespoon unsweetened cocoa powder

Combine all ingredients in a high-power blender or food processor and blend until smooth. Drink immediately.

CALORIES: 140 **FAT:** 17 **CARBS:** 20 **FIBER:** 5 **PROTEIN:** 8

353. MEDITERRANEAN MORNING

This smoothie is fresh and aromatic with rich spice flavors. At just 35 on the glycemic scale, coconut palm nectar is a low-glycemic sweetener that minimally affects insulin, the fat storage hormone.

½ frozen banana
½ cup coconut water
½ cup ice
½ cup nonfat Greek yogurt
1 teaspoon coconut palm nectar
1 pinch of ground cinnamon
1 pinch of fresh-ground nutmeg

Combine all ingredients in a high-power blender or food processor and blend until smooth. Drink immediately.

CALORIES: 192 **FAT:** 0 **CARBS:** 30 **FIBER:** 4 **PROTEIN:** 13

354. PURPLE WHIP

This creamy and protein-rich banana blend has blueberries, which provide resveratrol, an anti-inflammatory nutrient that helps with weight maintenance because it keeps fat cells active.

½ frozen banana
½ cup coconut water
½ cup ice
½ cup frozen wild blueberries
½ cup nonfat Greek yogurt
2 tablespoons hulled hemp seed

Combine all ingredients in a high-power blender or food processor and blend until smooth. Drink immediately.

CALORIES: 264 **FAT:** 6 **CARBS:** 30 **FIBER:** 6 **PROTEIN:** 12

355. THE FAT MELTER

The Greek yogurt in this recipe is a protein powerhouse that helps maintain muscle by providing amino acids and probiotics needed to build muscle mass, which helps burn body fat as energy. This protein-packed smoothie can help keep hunger in check for long periods of time.

½ frozen banana

1 cup coconut water

½ cup ice

½ cup nonfat Greek yogurt

2 tablespoons unsweetened cocoa powder

½ inch fresh turmeric root

Combine all ingredients in a high-power blender or food processor and blend until smooth. Drink immediately.

CALORIES: 202 FAT: 2 CARBS: 30 FIBER: 4 PROTEIN: 12

356. SKINNY ELIXIR

Drink up to slim down with this creamy smoothie, designed to melt away water weight. Hemp seed provides omega-3 fatty acids that improve leptin signaling in the brain, which increases fat burning and decreases hunger signals.

1 frozen banana

½ cup coconut water

½ cup nonfat Greek yogurt

1 tablespoon hulled hemp seed

1 teaspoon vanilla extract

½ inch fresh turmeric root

Combine all ingredients in a high-power blender or food processor and blend until smooth. Drink immediately.

CALORIES: 244 FAT: 4 CARBS: 30 FIBER: 4 PROTEIN: 15

357. CHERRY SLUSHY

This cherry-mango smoothie is sweet and cool, with a little turmeric flavor. Melatonin is a hormone found in significant levels in cherries that increases metabolism and improves ability to lose weight by regulating body fat and glucose metabolism.

1 cup coconut water
½ cup frozen cherries
½ cup frozen mango
2 tablespoons chia seed
½ inch fresh turmeric root

Combine all ingredients in a high-power blender or food processor and blend until smooth. Drink immediately.

CALORIES: 230 **FAT:** 7 **CARBS:** 36 **FIBER:** 10 **PROTEIN:** 5

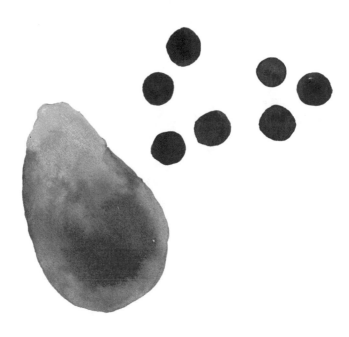

Week 52

Grocery List

- [ ] 3 bananas
- [ ] 2 apples
- [ ] 1 avocado
- [ ] 1 cup watermelon
- [ ] ¼ cup pomegranate arils
- [ ] 2 cups frozen wild blueberries
- [ ] 5 cups frozen mango
- [ ] ¾ cup frozen cherries
- [ ] 1 cup brewed green tea
- [ ] 1 cup coconut water
- [ ] ½ cup nonfat Greek yogurt
- [ ] 4 teaspoons lime juice
- [ ] 10 tablespoons chia seed
- [ ] 2 tablespoons protein powder
- [ ] 1 tablespoon hulled hemp seed
- [ ] 4 teaspoons pure vanilla extract
- [ ] 1 teaspoon coconut extract

358. WATERMELON MANGO

Watermelon juiciness combines beautifully with exotic mango in this vanilla-scented and lightly sweet smoothie. The beta-cryptoxanthin in mango suppresses adipogenesis, which is the creation of body fat cells.

1 cup watermelon
1 cup frozen mango
2 tablespoons chia seed
1 teaspoon vanilla extract

Combine all ingredients in a high-power blender or food processor and blend until smooth. Drink immediately.

CALORIES: 290 **FAT:** 10 **CARBS:** 30 **FIBER:** 16 **PROTEIN:** 6

359. BANANA MANGO DREAM

This perfect, simple blend uses vanilla extract, which has been found to reduce nausea. Vanillic acid in real vanilla extract fights obesity by activating thermogenesis, the heat that releases stored body fat.

½ frozen banana
½ cup frozen mango
½ cup coconut water
½ cup ice
2 tablespoons chia seed
1 teaspoon vanilla extract

Combine all ingredients in a high-power blender or food processor and blend until smooth. Drink immediately.

CALORIES: 274 **FAT:** 10 **CARBS:** 30 **FIBER:** 14 **PROTEIN:** 6

360. APPLE CREAM

This smoothie has a sweet and tropical mango flavor in a creamy base. Apples are a rich source of the natural phytochemical phloridzin, which reduces blood glucose levels and improves lipid metabolism.

½ apple
½ frozen banana
½ cup frozen mango
½ cup nonfat Greek yogurt
¼ cup water
¼ cup frozen cherries

Combine all ingredients in a high-power blender or food processor and blend until smooth. Drink immediately.

CALORIES: 232 FAT: 0 CARBS: 30 FIBER: 9 PROTEIN: 12

361. APPLE ICY

Tart mango with sweet cherries is a perfect flavor combination in this smoothie. Apples provide chlorogenic acid, which induces body fat loss by increasing thermogenesis and lipolysis.

1 apple
½ frozen banana
½ cup frozen mango
½ cup frozen cherries
½ cup ice
1 tablespoon chia seed

Combine all ingredients in a high-power blender or food processor and blend until smooth. Drink immediately.

CALORIES: 302 FAT: 5 CARBS: 25 FIBER: 16 PROTEIN: 3

362. MELLOW MANGO

This light and frosty mango blend is simple and not too sweet. Green tea can be a powerful weight-loss inducer when ingested on a regular basis.

1 cup brewed green tea
1 cup frozen mango
½ cup ice
1 tablespoon hulled hemp seed

Combine all ingredients in a high-power blender or food processor and blend until smooth. Drink immediately.

CALORIES: 148 **FAT:** 4 **CARBS:** 18 **FIBER:** 4 **PROTEIN:** 3

363. COOL TROPICAL BREEZE

This refreshing drink has full-bodied tropical flavors, with tart mango and bright citrus. Mangoes have mangiferin and lactase enzymes, which support digestion.

½ frozen banana
½ cup coconut water
½ cup frozen mango
½ cup ice
2 tablespoons chia seed
3 teaspoons lime juice

Combine all ingredients in a high-power blender or food processor and blend until smooth. Drink immediately.

CALORIES: 262 **FAT:** 10 **CARBS:** 30 **FIBER:** 14 **PROTEIN:** 6

364. MANGO AVOCADO LIME

This recipe is a light and tropical blend. Avocados contain healthful monounsaturated fatty acids, which reduce appetite and help keep blood sugar steady.

½ frozen banana
½ avocado
1 cup frozen mango
1 cup frozen wild blueberries
2 tablespoons chia seed
1 teaspoon lime juice
1 teaspoon coconut extract

Combine all ingredients in a high-power blender or food processor and blend until smooth. Drink immediately.

CALORIES: 330 **FAT:** 14 **CARBS:** 37 **FIBER:** 17 **PROTEIN:** 6

365. SKINNY BERRY POM

This smoothie has weight-loss nutrients galore and is bursting with flavor! Protein makes us feel full and studies have found that protein powder promotes a reduction in adipose tissue (body fat).

1 cup frozen wild blueberries
¼ cup pomegranate arils
½ cup ice
½ cup water
2 tablespoons protein powder
1 tablespoon chia seed
2 teaspoons vanilla extract

Combine all ingredients in a high-power blender or food processor and blend until smooth. Drink immediately.

CALORIES: 240 **FAT:** 6 **CARBS:** 30 **FIBER:** 22 **PROTEIN:** 9

You did it—a year of infusing your body with a daily elixir of nutrients to support weight loss. Congratulations! Pick your favorite recipe and make that your morning drink to help maintain your ideal weight while staying healthy.

SMOOTHIE INGREDIENT REFERENCE LIST

The following ingredient details provide definitions for commonly known ingredients, as well as some of the more unusual items. A few helpful tips for purchasing, preparation, and storage are included here for reference.

AGAVE: Agave nectar is often used as a sweetener. It's similar to honey, high in carbohydrates, and calorie dense. Use sparingly, as it will stimulate insulin, just like table sugar.

ALMONDS: Almonds provide minerals, fiber, B vitamins, phytosterols, and protein. They are a popular nut for making fresh nut milk at home due to their sweet and light flavor.

APPLES: Organic apples are grown without chemicals. Non-organic apples have remained on the Dirty Dozen list of the Environmental Working Group (ewg.org) for many years, because they have a higher pesticide residue than other produce. Remove the core and the stem, leaving the skin intact. Whole fresh apples last for months when stored in a cool dark place. It's best to store them in the garage or refrigerator, as freezing damages the fruit, making it mushy when thawed. Chopped apples can be stored in an airtight glass container for up to a week in the fridge. Reduce browning by tossing with lemon juice before storage. Unsweetened applesauce can be used in smoothies in place of fresh apples.

AVOCADO: Avocados are rich in healthy fats and create a creamy texture in smoothies that helps emulsify the ingredients, so they don't separate in the glass. Use a fresh avocado and look for even green color with no brown spots, as browning indicates the fruit may be overripe. Cut the avocado in half and gently twist it to separate the two halves. Leave the pit in the unused portion. Scoop out the amount of avocado to be used for your smoothie from the other half. Store the unused portion in a wax paper bag in the fridge for up to three days. When ready to use the other half, remove it from the storage bag and remove the pit by sticking it with a knife blade and gently twisting. If the surface of the avocado is discolored or dry, simply cut a thin slice off the top layer to reveal the fresh avocado beneath.

BANANAS: Bananas are the perfect smoothie ingredient, as they blend well and provide a creamy texture, especially when frozen. When shopping for bananas, always buy organic to avoid toxic pesticides, and look for bananas that are yellow, not green, and not overripe or brown. The peel contains weight-loss nutrients, such as melatonin. Add a tablespoon of peel to each smoothie to get these benefits. Keep fresh organic bananas on hand for smoothies. When bananas are green or do not peel easily, they are not ripe yet. Once they have ripened to the stage where they are a uniform yellow color, they can be peeled and then added to a smoothie or placed in a waxed paper bag to be frozen. They will keep for up to three months in the freezer.

BASIL: Fresh basil leaves blend well and give smoothies an herbal scent. Dried basil leaves are available in the bulk section of many grocery stores; they last for months in an airtight glass jar and can be used in smoothies. Fresh basil leaves are preferable, as they are rich in antioxidant oils, they're tender and blend easily, and they add intense flavor and fragrance to smoothies. Whole basil stems can be stored in a glass of fresh water like fresh cut flowers. If you have fresh leaves, they can be wrapped in a damp, clean tea towel to keep them fresh in the crisper drawer for about four days.

BEETS: Cooked beets provide a rich red color, carotenoids, and folate. Beets have a strong flavor that may overpower all other ingredients, so use them sparingly. Washed and peeled raw beets, beet juice, and beet greens can be added to smoothies. All can be stored for up to a week in the refrigerator.

BERRIES: Berries, including blackberries, blueberries, raspberries, and marionberries, can be blended fresh or frozen. Use fresh berries when available, or pick your own and freeze some for later. Frozen berries provide a thick and frosty texture to smoothies.

BLACK PEPPER: Whole peppercorns can be kept in a pepper grinder or pepper mill and freshly ground as needed, which preserves the medicinal properties of their oils. Buy in bulk to be frugal and also because peppercorns are often fresher in bulk due to the fast turnover of bulk products in many co-ops and stores.

BLUEBERRIES: Blueberries are a great way to add flavor, anthocyanin color, 4 grams of fiber, and only 80 calories per cup. As a bonus, laboratory studies have found that common cultivated blueberries reduce the inflammation that promotes insulin resistance, thus providing some protection against metabolic syndrome, type 2 diabetes, and hypoglycemia. Wild blueberries contain an even higher concentration of antioxidants than cultivated blueberries, and they are my favorite smoothie ingredient because they are sweet, rich in flavor, and naturally contain high concentrations of health-promoting phenolic compounds. Cultivated and wild frozen blueberries are available year-round in the freezer section of most co-ops and grocery stores. You can pick your own wild blueberries and use them fresh or freeze them. I keep my freezer stocked with wild blueberries so that I have some on hand for my daily smoothie.

CARDAMOM: Ground cardamom can be purchased in bottles and in the bulk section of your local co-op, but whole cardamom pods are preferable. The oils are protected from oxidation while in their pods, so the seeds stay fresh longer and have a more potent fragrance and flavor.

CARROTS: Cooked carrots blend well and add fiber, carotenoids, and sweet flavor to smoothies. Carrot juice can be made at home with a juicer but should be consumed quickly, as fresh-made carrot juice lasts for just a few days in the refrigerator. Bottled carrot juice is available in most grocery stores; be sure to buy organic and avoid plastic containers, which may contain toxic phthalates.

CASHEWS: The high fat content in cashews makes them ideal for smoothies, as they add a rich and creamy texture as well as healthy oils. They blend well and are a popular nut for making nut milk at home.

CELERY: Celery stalks can be added to smoothies for their B vitamins, electrolytes, and fiber. Use organic celery when possible. To keep celery fresh longer, rinse the stalks, trim the ends, then wrap in a damp, clean tea towel and store in the crisper drawer for up to four days.

CHERRIES: Sweet, tart, dark, and sour cherries all contain anthocyanins and proanthocyanidins that help reduce inflammation and thus reduce water weight. Fresh cherries must be pitted. Frozen packaged cherries are pre-pitted, so you won't have to take the extra step of pitting them as you would with fresh cherries. Cherry juice and black cherry concentrate are available in the juice section of the grocery store. Concentrates are wonderful for smoothies, as they come in small bottles, so there's no need to lug heavy glass bottles of juice, and just a few tablespoons provide loads of flavor, color, and nutrients.

CHIA: Whole chia seeds are tiny, hard seeds that contain soluble fiber, protein, and essential fatty acids. Chia powder blends completely into smoothies. Chia seeds can be pre-ground into powder in a coffee grinder or spice grinder to help them release their fiber more readily in a smoothie, which creates a texture that is similar to pudding. They come in resealable food-storage bags and can be stored in an airtight glass container in a cupboard. If unopened, they can be stored in the refrigerator, but the moisture is damaging to exposed chia, so be sure to store in an airtight container. Seeds generally have a high oil content, so the freezer, which keeps oils safe from light and heat, is the best way to store chia for longer than a month.

CHILE PEPPERS: These hot peppers add zest, depth of flavor, and a little heat on the back of the tongue. Try a small amount the first time you're making a hot pepper smoothie and adjust according to your taste. Remove the stem and the seeds and taste your pepper to make sure it's not too hot before adding it to your smoothie. Fresh hot peppers can be stored for up to a week in the refrigerator.

CILANTRO: Cilantro leaves have a strong distinctive fragrance and flavor, which people seem to either love or hate. Cilantro can always be replaced with parsley in a recipe if you don't love it. Rinse cilantro leaves and chop lightly before blending. If you are using a high-power blender, you can use the cilantro stems as well.

The best way to store cilantro is to rinse it well and, while still wet, wrap it in a clean tea towel and store in the crisper drawer of your refrigerator, where it will stay fresh for up to a week. If your cilantro is starting to look droopy or dried out, simply cut off the bottoms of the stems, rinse with water, and place them in a glass of fresh water, just as you would to bring back a bouquet of wilting flowers. The stalks of cilantro should perk up within a day, at which time the whole bunch can be rinsed in fresh water and stored as above.

CINNAMON: Ground cinnamon powder is the most common form of culinary cinnamon; however, cinnamon sticks are widely available in the bulk section of most grocery stores and can be easily broken into pieces to be added to smoothies for fresh cinnamon flavor and more potent weight loss nutrients. True cinnamon is from the inner bark of the *Cinnamomum verum* tree, but a majority of the cinnamon we buy is actually from the cassia tree. It contains strong oils, so a little goes a long way in terms of flavor.

If your cinnamon powder has been in your cupboard for a while and has lost its flavor, it has also lost its nutritional effectiveness. Just toss it and buy some new ground cinnamon. Purchase from bulk bins when possible to save money and store in your own containers to avoid plastic. Store cinnamon powder in an airtight glass container and out of the light, if possible.

CITRUS: Citrus fruits include oranges, tangerines, limes, lemons, kumquats, blood oranges, mandarin oranges, navel oranges, clementines, and grapefruit. They all provide powerful weight-loss and anti-inflammatory nutrients, which are in the juice, pulp, and, surprisingly, concentrated in the peel. As long as you are using organic produce, you can add a tablespoon of citrus peel to each smoothie. You may want to mince the peel to help it blend. If you have high-power blender like a Vitamix, you can just toss a chunk of peel in and the powerful motor will be able to handle the tough skin. The bioflavonoids are in the pithy white part of the peel, just under the colorful skin. Add as much of this to smoothies as possible, rather than discarding.

Clementines are a variety of the mandarin orange and are a go-to citrus for smoothies because they're easy to peel, seedless, and sweet. Meyer lemons, a cross between an orange and a lemon, smell heavenly, and their juice is a little sweeter and less tart than other lemons. Fresh oranges keep for up to a week in the refrigerator and up to three weeks in the freezer. Once peeled they should be stored in a wax paper bag and can be kept refrigerated, where they will stay fresh for up to four days.

CLOVES: Whole and ground cloves have intense flavor and scent. Just a pinch of clove powder is enough for a whole blender.

COCOA: Unsweetened cocoa powder is a weight-loss superfood due to its polyphenolic compounds. It blends well in smoothies to create healthy alternatives to chocolate milkshakes. It is also available in dark cocoa form, which has a higher level of bioactive nutrients. Look for unsweetened organic cocoa powder. It will last for months in a covered container.

COCONUT: Coconut oils blend easily with other ingredients but, due to their high fat content, should be kept to about a teaspoon per smoothie. Fresh coconut—including the meat, milk, and water—is ideal for smoothie making, but only available in tropical locations. Dried organic coconut flakes and ground macaroon coconut are available from Bob's Red Mill and can be found in most grocery stores. Unsweetened fine macaroon coconut is available in most grocery stores and co-ops and adds a little texture to smoothies, as well as coconut flavor. Ground coconut adds that tropical flavor to smoothies, along with considerable minerals and fiber. Coconut milk adds a richness to smoothies, and cultured coconut milk products provide health-supportive probiotics.

COCONUT PALM NECTAR: When we think of coconut products, we generally think of the coconut's water, milk, or meat, but there's a new coconut product you may be seeing on your co-op shelves: coconut palm nectar. It is made from the sap of coconut palm flower buds. It's specifically used as a sweetener and is showing promise for those looking to balance blood sugar and/or lose weight, as it does not appear to spike blood sugar levels the way most carb-based sweeteners do. It is nutrient dense, high in potassium and magnesium, and low glycemic. It provides a mellow, sweet flavor and dissolves well in smoothies.

Coconut palm nectar is available in a syrup form, which must be refrigerated once opened, and also as dry granules, which should be stored like other granulated sugars, in an air- and moisture-tight container.

COCONUT WATER: Coconut water has a sweet, nutty flavor and provides trace minerals (electrolytes) such as sodium, magnesium, and manganese, as well as concentrated amounts of potassium. It's naturally low in fat, calories, and sugar, so it's an ideal weight-loss smoothie liquid. Look for it in glass bottles rather than plastic bottles. Also, avoid aseptic boxes, which are made with layers of plastic and aluminum that are toxic for our bodies and the environment.

COFFEE: Instant coffee is available in small glass containers; it has a long shelf life and can be stored in the freezer for up to a year. Freeze-dried coffee crystals are ideal, as they are almost as rich in antioxidants as brewed coffee and dissolve easily in liquid. Decaffeinated instant coffee is also available for those who want the coffee flavor without the caffeine. Coffee extracts, such as mannooligosaccharides, are also being studied for their potential as weight-loss nutrients.

Fresh-brewed coffee can be used in place of instant coffee. Use ¼ cup of brewed coffee to replace 1 teaspoon of instant coffee. The beans, whether they're whole or ground, can be stored in the freezer and will stay fresh for months. Brewed coffee can be kept in a glass container in the refrigerator for up to a week.

CRANBERRIES: Cranberries are tart and almost bitter and beg for a little sweetener, which can add calories to a smoothie. Therefore, whole cranberries and cranberry juice should be used sparingly and combined with sweeter fruits to mellow their intensity. Fresh cranberries are only available in the winter and can be stored in an airtight container in the refrigerator for up to two months. However, canned and frozen cranberries are available year-round. Cranberry concentrate and cranberry juice are both widely available.

CUCUMBER: Cucumbers are low in calories. and provide electrolytes, and their flavor blends well with fruits and vegetables, making them an ideal smoothie ingredient. Peel the waxy skin off cucumbers before adding to smoothies. Since cucumbers are highly sprayed with pesticides, buy organic cucumbers, which are grown without chemicals. Choose fresh cucumbers that are firm and without blemishes or soft spots. Store them in the crisper drawer of the refrigerator. Once cut into, cucumbers can be stored in an airtight glass container for about two days.

CULTURED COCONUT MILK: Cultured coconut milk is sold in tubs, just like a yogurt product. The term *cultured* indicates that the product contains healthful probiotics, such as *Lactobacillus acidophilus*.

DATES: Dates are sweet and a great source of fiber, so they can be used as a sweetener that won't spike blood sugar levels, making them a healthy option for those with hypoglycemia or diabetes. Dates also provide minerals, B vitamins, and carotenoids. Medjool dates are widely available and work well in smoothies, as they are soft and blend easily and they provide a mellow, sweet flavor to soften bitter flavors from ingredients like lemons, greens, or pomegranate.

FIBER SUPPLEMENTS: Fiber supplements, such as acacia fiber (gum arabic) and glucomannan (konjac root), help us feel full and reduce our appetite. Blueberry skin powder is not only rich in fiber but also antioxidants. Studies have found that fiber supports weight loss and lowers blood cholesterol. Adding fiber to smoothies is beneficial, as our bodies break down fiber slowly, which lowers the glycemic index of any smoothie it has been added to. For those who have a low-fiber diet, adding a tablespoon of fiber to your daily smoothie can have an almost instant health impact by regulating bowel movements, improving blood sugar, and stabilizing hydration. Be consistent with the amount you use daily so that your body can adjust to your water needs when taking fiber supplements.

Fiber powders are available at food co-ops and supplement stores. They are sold in individual packets and in airtight containers and, when kept dry and cool, will stay fresh for months.

FIGS: Figs act as a sweetener for smoothies and are a great source of fiber, potassium, manganese, and vitamin B_6. Fresh figs can be kept in an airtight container in the refrigerator, but they only last for about two days. They can also be sliced and frozen. Dried figs have a longer shelf life (about one month), especially when refrigerated (several months). Both fresh and dried figs work well in smoothies.

If you're using a high-power blender, dried figs will blend easily. However, some blenders are not able to completely break down dried fruits. If your blender is lower powered, you might opt for fresh figs, which blend much more easily. When using fresh figs, remove the stem and rinse under water, then drop them into smoothies whole.

FIVE-SPICE POWDER: Asian five-spice powder is a blend that typically includes anise, pepper, fennel, cloves, and cinnamon. Each spice is fairly strong on its own and can overpower flavors in a smoothie easily. A pinch of the five-spice blend adds a hint of each pungent flavor, along with small amounts of polyphenol nutrients to boost the overall antioxidant content of a smoothie.

FLAVOR EXTRACTS: Liquid flavor extracts can add a lot of flavor and fragrance to a smoothie, without calories or carbs, with just a few drops. These include pure vanilla, almond, hazelnut, and orange oil extracts. They're available at most grocery stores and have a long shelf life.

FLAXSEED: Flaxseeds are rich in fiber, healthy oils, and protein. Whole seeds are difficult to chew because they're so tiny, therefore ground flaxseed is often preferable. However, its oils are delicate and will oxidize quickly from exposure to heat and oxygen, so freshly grind just the amount you need. Flaxseeds contain essential fatty acids, but note that they also contain phytoestrogens, which can cause a hormonal imbalance for some. (Other essential fatty acid sources that do not affect hormones are avocado, hemp seeds, chia seeds, and borage oil.)

Whole flaxseeds and flaxseed meal are available in most grocery stores. Both whole and ground flaxseeds are available in bags, and whole seeds are available in bulk. Store flaxseed in an airtight container in the freezer, and it will last for months.

GARLIC: Garlic supports the endocrine system and improves thyroid function, thus increasing metabolism. Garlic also contains more than 400 different compounds that kill bacteria, viruses, and fungi. Peel the paper from a clove of garlic and chop it so that a whole clove doesn't get caught under the blender blades. Peeled garlic cloves can be stored in an airtight glass container in the refrigerator for several days.

GINGER: Ginger root is full of flavor, fiber, and active compounds that provide fiber and nutrients that support weight loss. Pickled ginger, powdered dried ginger (available in the spice section of the grocery store), and ginger juice can all be used in place of fresh ginger root.

Fresh ginger root has a strong flavor and a pungent scent. For a subtler ginger accent, try 1 teaspoon of dried powdered ginger.

Fresh ginger root is available in the fresh produce section of most grocery stores. To prepare, use a knife to remove the papery skin and then chop about 1 inch of root, which equals about a tablespoon. Fresh ginger root can also be chopped and then pressed through a garlic press to extract its flavorful juice. If you have a high-power blender, you may be able to use the ginger without peeling. Unpeeled fresh ginger root lasts for about a week in a cool dry place, such as the crisper drawer of your refrigerator. To keep ginger fresh longer, store the unpeeled root in a wax paper bag in the freezer, where it will stay fresh for months. When you need fresh ginger, you can pull it out of the freezer, grate some into your recipe, and then return the root to the freezer. The peel will grate easily when frozen.

GRAPES: Grapes are very sweet, so a small amount adds a lot of flavor. They also add powerful anti-inflammatory nutrients, such as anthocyanins and resveratrol, to smoothies. Freeze whole seedless grapes so you'll have some of these delicious little flavor packs on hand when you need to sweeten up a smoothie. Of course, seedless grapes make for a smoother, and generally preferable, smoothie texture. It is also possible to use grapes that have seeds, which are packed with antimicrobial oils that kill fungus and bacteria. Their seeds blend easily with a high-power blender.

GREEK YOGURT: Greek yogurt has a creamy texture, and is high in protein. Many are low in sugar and contain no chemicals. For centuries, the Greeks have strained their yogurt to remove extra liquid, which increases the amount of protein by weight. Greek yogurt has roughly twice as much protein as ordinary yogurt, and it's delicious! Read yogurt labels and look for organic products with no added sugar or food coloring. Use nonfat yogurt to replicate the recipes in this book. Look for glass containers and taste-test yogurts until you find the brand you like best. Yogurt can be kept in the fridge for about five days once it's been opened.

GREEN TEA: Brew green tea for no longer than two minutes, as this allows for the maximum nutrient infusion into the tea water without the bitter elements.

GREENS: Greens are the leaves of plants, including turnips, kale, and beets. Fresh young garden greens, such as kale and spinach, add delicate flavor to a smoothie. These leaves provide minerals and chlorophyll, which support weight loss. Buy organic greens when possible. Rinse and wrap them in a damp, clean tea towel and store in the crisper drawer of your refrigerator for up to three days.

HAZELNUTS: Hazelnuts, which are also known as filberts, are flavorful and sweet. Whole nuts can be added to smoothies made in high-power blenders, or hazelnut milk can be used in smoothies to add flavor and nutrients. You can use store-bought hazelnut milk or make your own. Freshly made hazelnut milk is incredibly delicious, and it's easy to make.

HEMP: Hemp seeds (aka hulled hemp seeds) have a mild, nut-like flavor and a creamy texture when blended in smoothies. Hemp seeds are rich in protein and essential fatty acids. They are sold as ground protein powder; however, hulled hemp seed is ideal for smoothies because of its milder flavor and creamy texture when blended. Both hulled hemp seed hearts and hemp protein powder are available from the Bob's Red Mill line of products in most grocery stores, as well as online. These products are ready to eat right out of the package. No prep necessary. Just pour them into your smoothie. They can be stored in the freezer for up to a year.

Milk made from hemp seeds is creamier and richer than most nut milks due to the seeds' essential fatty acid content. Hemp milk comes in an aseptic package that has a long shelf life until opened.

HOLY BASIL: Tulsi, or holy basil, is a type of basil that contains more ursolic acid, which has been shown to increase muscle and reduce body fat, than common basil. It also contains rosmarinic acid, a natural phenolic that supports metabolism and reduces inflammation. Holy basil plants can be grown in your garden or in pots on a porch. Fresh holy basil is available in some grocery stores in the produce section, and dried holy basil is available in the bulk section of many grocery stores. If your local market does not yet carry dried holy basil, you may want to request it, as it is available through bulk suppliers, such as Frontier Co-op (frontiercoop.com). To keep basil stalks fresh, trim the stems, place them in a glass of fresh water, and keep them out on the counter, just as you would fresh flowers.

HORSERADISH: Fresh or grated bottled horseradish products can be used in smoothies. This root of the cabbage family is spicy and heats up the digestive tract, improving digestion. Fermented horseradish provides probiotics, and the flavor works well in vegetable-based smoothies.

ICE: Adding ice to smoothies gives them a frosty texture and more water for hydration, but it also dilutes the flavors a bit and is not necessary. Smoothie enthusiasts seem to either love or hate the addition of ice. You decide. Store-bought ice is usually not made from filtered water and not intended for consumption, just for coolers. Use filtered tap water for making ice cubes or hook up a filtration system to your automatic ice maker. Filtering tap water with a solid carbon filter improves the flavor of the water, and it will also remove heavy metals and other chemicals, including chlorine.

JUICE: Liquid extractions, such as juices, nectars, and juice concentrates, can be found in shelf-stable glass bottles and in the freezer section, and often, fresh-squeezed juices are found in the produce section of the grocery store. They add a lot of flavor, color, and nutrients to smoothies. The alternative is using whole fresh produce, rather than packaged products. Fresh produce is more nutritious and means less packaging. And with whole foods, it's possible to buy from the produce section, pick fresh produce from your own garden, or purchase at a farmers' market, which means no added ingredients, just wholesome produce.

Concentrates are basically juices with much of the water removed, so you can buy a small bottle and add just a tablespoon or two to a smoothie to get the same flavor you would from a cup of juice. Nectars are also more concentrated than juices and often have fruit pulp, so they have a thicker texture. Think unfiltered, fresh-squeezed orange juice versus reconstituted orange juice from the freezer. However, these concentrates and nectars are sometimes higher in sugar than juice, so be sure to read labels. Only get those in glass bottles to avoid plastic, as these liquids are acidic and leach phthalates.

KIWI: Kiwifruit provides vitamin C and a tart flavor but is often sour unless you are able to get it locally and ripe off the vine. Balance the sour flavor with sweet fruit, such as berries. Fresh, ripe kiwi can be used with skin intact in high-power blenders. However, some blenders have a hard time with kiwi skin, in which case the skin can be removed by cutting a kiwi in half and using a spoon to scoop out the green flesh. Store unused kiwi in an airtight container in the refrigerator for up to a week.

MANGO: Fresh or frozen mango can be added to smoothies and contains high levels of weight-loss carotenoid nutrients. The skin is a medicinal powerhouse, providing even higher levels of antioxidant nutrients than the fruit, so add a tablespoon of the skin to each mango smoothie. Be sure to buy organic to avoid toxic agricultural chemicals. The skin and pit must be removed from fresh mangoes before adding to the blender. Frozen mango is ideal, as it has been pre-chopped, and the pit and skin have been removed. Unripe mangoes can be kept at room temperature for up to a week as they ripen. Once ripe, they can be stored in the refrigerator for up to a week. When they've reached their peak ripeness, remove the skin and the pit and chop the sweet yellow fruit, which can then be stored in a wax paper bag and frozen for months.

MELONS: Honeydew, cantaloupe, watermelon, Crenshaw, and other melons are all sweet additions to smoothies. They provide electrolytes, antioxidants, and provitamin A substances to smoothies, with a lot of sweet flavor. Remove the rind and seeds and use fresh, or chop and freeze for later use.

MILK: Animal milks, such as cow and goat milk, are less nutritious than plant milks, as they contain saturated fats and byproducts from farming practices, such as bovine growth hormone, stress hormones like cortisol, and antibiotic residue. They also contain lactose, which is milk sugar that is hard for most adults to digest. In fact, adult humans are not meant to consume animal milks, which are of course produced by mother animals for their infants. Our bodies need the nutrients in plants, so plant-based milks are more nutritious for us, and also happen to be better for the environment.

MINT: There are many types of mint, each with its own particular flavor. Taste your mint before adding it to your smoothie to make sure you like the flavor, and so you can adjust the amount depending on its level of intensity. Fresh mint leaves contain oils that are often very pungent. Use sparingly, as they dramatically change the flavor of smoothies. Fresh mint leaves are sold in the produce department of most grocery stores. Rinse and add directly to smoothies.

Keep mint stalks fresh by cutting off the bottom inch of the stems, which allows them to take up fresh water. Then place them in a glass of fresh water, just as you would with cut flowers, where they will stay fresh at room temperature for up to a week. Be sure to keep the water fresh by changing it daily. If you've already removed the leaves from the stalks, the leaves can be rinsed and wrapped in a damp, clean tea towel and stored in the crisper drawer of the refrigerator for about a week.

NUTMEG: Nutmeg's complex flavors come from its oils. Some varieties contain more than fifty different compounds. Whole nutmeg is the most potent and preferable form, as it can be grated as needed, which preserves the oils. Ground nutmeg is available in the spice section of the grocery store and in bulk. Ground nutmeg is rich in oils that oxidize from light, air, and heat, so keep it in an airtight container and in a cool, dark place. Ground nutmeg will retain its flavor and fragrance for up to a year when stored properly.

NUTS: Nuts have a high oil content, which means they can oxidize (become rancid) from heat and air exposure. Store them in airtight containers and they will stay fresh for weeks. They will also stay fresh for months when stored in airtight glass jars in the freezer. Just a tablespoon of nut butter per smoothie adds richness, protein, healthy plant oils, and minerals. Whole nuts will grind well in high-power blenders. Fresh-ground nut butters can be purchased at many co-ops and whole-food stores. If you are buying premade nut butter, look for products made with only nuts—no sugar, no hydrogenated oils, and no preservatives.

OATS: Rolled oats are pre-steamed and soften easily when combined with liquids, so they blend well. Steel cut and other raw, uncooked forms of oats, such as oat berries, have tough fiber that won't blend easily. Those who are following a gluten-free diet may be interested to know that there are gluten-free rolled oats available in the Bob's Red Mill line of products, in packages and in bulk.

PAPAYA: There are two types of papaya, the red-fleshed, which is rich in lycopene, and the yellow-fleshed, which is rich in beta-carotene. These carotenoids support endocrine function and weight loss. The easiest way to prepare a ripe papaya for smoothies is to cut it in half lengthwise and scoop out the seeds. Then use a large spoon to scoop out the flesh for your smoothie and toss the skin.

PEANUTS: The flavor of peanut butter is a comfort to many of us who grew up eating peanut butter sandwiches. Healthy fats in peanuts give them their wonderful creamy texture when ground into peanut butter. Whole peanuts blend into a creamy paste in high-powder blenders. Just a tablespoon or two per smoothie serving will add flavor and a little protein. Peanuts can be stored in an airtight container in the freezer for months. Be on the lookout for peanut butter varieties labeled aflatoxin-free, as they have been tested for the highly allergenic aflatoxin mold and are the least allergenic. Peanut butter can be stored for about a month at room temperature but should be kept in a cool, dark place, such as a pantry or cupboard. Peanut butter will stay fresh for months in the refrigerator.

PEAR: Most pears taste great in smoothies. Asian pears are especially sweet and juicy and provide ample fiber. Pears are rich in fiber and antioxidant polyphenolic compounds. Due to their mild flavor, they work equally well in vegetable or fruit smoothies. Remove the stem and core before blending, unless you have high-power blender, in which case your blender can easily blend the whole pear. Pears ripen quickly and only last for a few days once they're cut into. Store cut pears in airtight containers in the refrigerator for up to three days.

PEPPERS: Colorful fresh hot peppers are nutritious, and the hotter they are, the more weight-loss action their nutrients provide. Mild peppers, such as bell peppers, provide antioxidants, such as vitamin C and carotenoids, but the hot peppers have been well studied for their ability to control insulin and treat obesity. Cayenne pepper (fresh, powder, or flakes) is a powerful weight-loss spice, and just a pinch will do. Hot sauces that contain hot peppers also impart their natural weight-loss benefits, even in small doses.

PINEAPPLE: Fresh pineapple is intensely sweet when ripe and adds a heady, tropical aroma to smoothies. Remove the skin and core of fresh pineapple or use canned pineapple or pineapple juice. Store pineapple in a glass container with a lid for up to three days in the refrigerator. I use frozen pineapple, which is sold in the freezer section of most grocery stores, specifically for smoothies. It's sweet and ripe and flash-frozen, so the individual pieces pour out easily into the blender, rather than being frozen together.

PLANT MILKS: Milks made from rice, soy, hemp, flaxseed, and the like are collectively referred to as plant milk in this book. Use your favorite milk in any recipe that calls for plant milk. Plant milks are often made from nuts due to their rich oil content, which gives the milk a creamy texture. Nut milks are healthy beverages made from ground nuts, such as almonds, cashews, and hazelnuts, as well as seeds like hemp, flax, and chia. Plant milks are available in various flavors and fat levels, including plain, vanilla, low-fat, and full-fat versions.

POMEGRANATE: Pomegranate arils (seeds) are jewel-like in appearance and juicy. Whole arils can be purchased in the freezer section of most grocery stores and are much easier to use than a whole pomegranate, which you'll need to mine for its seeds. Pomegranate juice and pomegranate concentrate are also available in the juice section of the grocery store. If you opt for using a fresh whole pomegranate, the uncut fruit will last for a few weeks at room temperature and longer in the refrigerator.

To remove the edible portion of the pomegranate, the arils, you'll need to cut the fruit into quarters and carefully pull the arils out of the white material. Collect the arils in a bowl, and when you have about a quarter cup, pour them into your smoothie.

PROBIOTIC POWDER: Probiotics are live bacteria supplements that adhere to the lining of our digestive tracts and support digestion and healthy weight, among many other benefits. Probiotic powders are much more affordable when purchased in bulk, and the strains that are sold in bulk happen to be the most effective weight-loss-supporting strains.

PROTEIN POWDERS: Pea, rice, soy, hemp, pumpkin seed, and chia protein powders add concentrated protein to smoothies. Protein powders can be stored at room temperature for several weeks, but they stay fresh for months when stored in the freezer. They can be stored in their original container, as long as it has an airtight lid. Look for organic and low-sugar products.

PRUNES: Prunes are dried plums. They can be used to sweeten a smoothie without added refined sugar and provide the bioactive compound ursolic acid, which improves muscle mass and weight loss. Prunes are also famous for their ability to regulate bowel movements. Just add one to your daily smoothie to get these life-changing benefits.

PUMPKIN: Freshly cooked pumpkin adds cancer-fighting mixed carotenoids and fiber to smoothies. If you happen to have freshly cooked pumpkin on hand, certainly try it in a smoothie; otherwise, just buy canned pumpkin, which is already cooked and ready to use. Cooked pumpkin or leftover canned pumpkin can be stored in an airtight glass container in the refrigerator for up to a week, and in the freezer for months.

Pumpkin seeds are highly nutritious and one of our richest vegan sources of zinc, which supports metabolism and muscle development.

SPARKLING WATER: Carbonated water made with CO_2, such as San Pellegrino or that made using home carbonation machines, can be added to smoothies to give them a fizzy effect. Adding the sparkling water after blending will preserve the bubbles and keep your drink from going flat when blended.

SQUASH: All cooked squash contains fiber and carotenoids and blends well in smoothies, adding flavor, nutrients, and texture. There are many varieties, such as acorn, delicata, and butternut. To prepare squash for smoothies, rinse it, cut off the tough skin, then chop and steam the flesh until tender. The seeds are often discarded, but squash seeds are actually very nutritious. They're a rare source of the mineral zinc, which supports weight loss.

STAR ANISE: The pods of star anise are perfect star-shaped husks that contains shiny spice seeds with a licorice flavor. The seeds can be added to smoothies, as can star anise powder.

STAR FRUIT: Star fruit, which is also known as carambola, has a sweet but acidic flavor that gives smoothies an exotic flair. Yellow and waxy, carambola is a juicy and tannic fruit that is an excellent smoothie ingredient. Carambola provides antioxidants, potassium, vitamin C, and polyphenolic compounds. It is available at specialty markets and occasionally in the produce section of grocery stores.

Carambola is a tropical fruit that should be used fresh, not frozen, and can be added directly to smoothies. No preparation is necessary, as the seeds are small and the skin is soft enough to blend easily, so there is no need to peel first. Look for yellow star fruit (not green), which are at the peak of ripeness, but avoid those with brown spots, which indicate they may be too ripe. Starfruit can be stored in an airtight container in the refrigerator for up to a week.

STONE FRUIT: Fresh whole stone fruit, like cherries, nectarines, black velvet apricots, plums, and peaches, adds silky texture, loads of carotenoid nutrients, and fiber to smoothies. Stone-fruit nectars add a lot of pulp and luscious flavor and texture to smoothies. Always buy organic stone fruit, as it is typically highly sprayed with chemical pesticides. The skin can be left on when adding to smoothies, but the pits must be removed from stone fruits. You can pit and freeze them, or you can buy pre-pitted frozen fruit, which is available in most grocery stores now. Once the pit is removed, these fruits can be stored in a covered glass container for several days in the refrigerator. To store longer than a few days, pit and freeze them in a wax paper bag.

STRAWBERRIES: Strawberries with a deep red coloring are riper and sweeter and contain more nutrients than less ripe berries with lighter coloring. Strawberries that are not organic are most certainly sprayed with toxic pesticides throughout their life cycle. Buy organic strawberries for better flavor, increased nutrient levels, and to avoid agricultural chemical residue. Wild strawberries are much sweeter than cultivated berries.

Remove the green tops from strawberries, rinse, and add to smoothies, or store them in wax paper and a zip-top bag to freeze them for future use. Frozen strawberries provide a frosty texture to smoothies, and they're easy to keep on hand, as they last for about a year in the freezer.

SWEETENERS: Sweeteners are rarely needed in smoothies and some can add calories, so it's a good idea to keep them to a minimum. Whole fruits and dried fruits, like dates, can be used to add sweetness instead—they naturally contain fiber, which gives them a lower glycemic load. The addition of carbohydrate-based sweeteners, like honey, agave, beet sugar, and cane sugar, should be minimized, because they increase fat storage. In a particularly bitter recipe, such as one with grapefruit juice or pomegranate arils, add sweet fruit to balance the flavors, rather than actual sweeteners.

Avoid synthetic chemical sweeteners, such as Equal (aspartame), Sweet'N Low (saccharin), Splenda (sucralose), and NutraSweet (aspartame), as studies have proven that they increase weight gain, cause headaches, and contribute to joint pain, and many of them increase the risk for cancer. Alcohol sugars, such as xylitol, erythritol, and maltitol, are very sweet and nontoxic and are not easily absorbed into the bloodstream, so they don't stimulate insulin production. Just a teaspoon of xylitol will take the edge off a blender full of bitter or sour produce. Alcohol sweeteners also provide some health benefits, such as reducing dental cavities and feeding flora in the digestive system.

Liquid sweeteners can be stored in the cupboard for months, and refrigeration extends their shelf life even further. Coconut palm nectar is sold as granulated sugar and as a syrup. Xylitol and erythritol are sold as granules, and maltitol is available as a powder or syrup. Most sweeteners can be stored in a cool, dry place for many months, even after they've been opened.

TEA: Black tea, green tea, chai tea, and herbal teas, such as chamomile and peppermint, taste great, contain no calories, and provide powerful nutrients that support weight loss and health. Loose-leaf tea or tea bags can be used to brew tea for smoothies.

The trick with caffeinated tea, such as green or black tea, is steeping it lightly, which will infuse your water with all the polyphenol nutrients before the bitter substances and caffeine have a chance to be extracted from the leaves. To do this, simply steep tea leaves—about 1 tablespoon of loose leaf in a tea ball or two tea bags—in water that is slightly cooler than boiling temperature. Steep in a large glass pitcher with as much water as you like. Remove tea leaves after two minutes, and then chill the tea in the refrigerator for up to five days to use in smoothies. Freeze some of your brew in ice cube trays so you'll have access to green tea, even when you're too busy to brew a pot.

TOMATILLOS: Tomatillos provide a high level of carotenoids because they are not overly hybridized. In 2017, scientists reported on their discovery and analysis of a fossil tomatillo found in the Patagonia region of Argentina, dated to 52 million years ago. This ancient food can be grown in your yard or purchased in most grocery stores. To prepare them for a smoothie, just remove the papery husk and rinse.

TOMATOES: Tomatoes contain all four major carotenoids: alpha- and beta-carotene, lutein, and lycopene. These essential nutrients are found in concentration in eye tissue, brain tissue, and body fat, where they are needed for optimal vision, cognitive function, and fat metabolism, respectively. To prepare tomatoes, simply remove the stem and leaves, if any, and rinse.

TURMERIC: Turmeric is a root grown in South Asia that is ground and used extensively as a culinary and medicinal spice. It has a mild, bitter flavor and is an ideal addition to all weight-loss smoothies, as it helps reduce water weight. Turmeric contains an active compound called *curcumin*, a powerful anti-inflammatory agent. Turmeric is used in India as part of the daily diet, to prevent edema and inflammation.

Fresh turmeric root is available in the produce department of most grocery stores. The flavor of the fresh root works well with most smoothies. The bioactive nutrients are more powerful in the fresh root than in dried powder. However, ground turmeric powder is still very powerful as an antioxidant and anti-inflammatory. Dried turmeric is available in the bulk section of most co-ops and can be stored in an airtight container for months. Be careful when handling turmeric powder, as the yellow color stains cloth and some countertop materials.

VANILLA: Vanilla beans are the seed pods of the vanilla orchid. Real vanilla extract is generally made from tropical vanilla beans native to Mexico, Central America, and the Caribbean. Whole beans can be added to smoothies when using a high-power blender. However, if your blender has a hard time with tough fibers, use real vanilla extract or prep beans by cutting them open and scraping out the seeds from inside, and then discard the husk. Use this fragrant "vanilla goo" in your smoothie. There is nothing else like it on the planet.

Vanilla beans sold in packaging like bags or bottles can be expensive, but when purchased from bulk bins, they're surprisingly affordable, because they don't weigh much. Whole vanilla beans can be purchased from most co-ops in their bulk sections.

WATER: Purifying water with a solid carbon filter at the tap removes toxins, such as heavy metals, as well as chlorine. Filtering water also improves its flavor and smell. Use filtered water to make ice cubes, as well.

WATERMELON: Fresh and frozen watermelon can be used in smoothies. Frozen watermelon gives smoothies a frosty texture. When fresh watermelon is available, prep it for freezing so you'll have some on hand for months. Simply remove the rind, cut into chunks, and freeze in a wax paper food-storage bag or sealed glass container.

YOGURT: Avoid yogurts that contain lots of sugar and food coloring. Look for yogurt with less than 10 grams of sugar per serving. Greek yogurt generally has a higher protein level and is available in a non-fat form.

XYLITOL: Xylitol is a low-calorie alcohol sweetener that is a low-glycemic sweetener option for those with blood sugar concerns. It has a cool flavor and dissolves well. Xylitol granules can be stored in a cupboard for about a year.

GLOSSARY OF TERMS

AFLATOXIN: Common toxins produced by fungi that grow on peanuts. Aflatxoins are a trigger of peanut allergies.

AMINO ACIDS: Amino acids, often referred to as the building blocks of proteins, are precursors for other molecules in the body.

ANTHOCYANINS: Colorful flavonoid nutrients that have potential health effects against aging, inflammation, metabolic disorders, and bacterial infections.

ANTIOXIDANT: A molecule that inhibits the oxidation of other molecules, which may provide protection against dementia, diabetes, rheumatoid arthritis, and heart disease.

ASEPTIC PACKAGING: This is a manufacturing process in which both a food product, such as milk, and its packaging are sterilized separately and then combined and sealed in a sterilized atmosphere. Products in aseptic packaging do not need to be refrigerated until the package is opened, which gives them a long shelf life.

BETA-CAROTENE: A reddish-orange pigment that is a type of carotene found chiefly in orange, dark green, yellow vegetables and fruits such as carrots, sweet potatoes, and spinach. Beta-carotene is converted to vitamin A in the body.

BIOACTIVE/BIOACTIVITY: A bioactive substance is one that has a biological effect.

BIOAVAILABILITY: The portion of a substance, such as a vitamin, mineral, or photochemical, which enters the blood circulation when it is introduced into the body where it is able to have an active effect.

BIOFLAVONOIDS: *see* flavonoids

BLOOD SUGAR: The level of sugar in the bloodstream, which indicates how effectively our bodies are using sugar from the food we eat to create energy. Blood sugar testing is a common and simple test that those with diabetes use to determine whether they need to eat food or take insulin.

CAROTENOIDS: Carotenoids are plant pigments responsible for bright red, yellow, and orange hues in many fruits and vegetables.

CARVACROL: A phenol found in essential oils of various mints such as thyme and oregano.

CULTIVATED: Refers to foods that are agriculturally grown for consumption. For example, most blueberries are cultivated and grown on farms, whereas wild blueberries are collected from bushes growing in their natural environment.

DIABETES MELLITUS (DIABETES): A disorder of the metabolism in which the pancreas isn't making enough insulin or the cells don't respond to the insulin that is produced, resulting in high blood sugar levels (hyperglycemia).

ELECTROLYTES: Minerals, such as sodium, potassium, calcium, magnesium, chloride, and phosphate, which control electrical conduction and hydration in our bodies. Fruits, fruit juices, and coconut water are excellent natural sources of these minerals.

ELLAGIC ACID: A natural antioxidant found in many fruits and vegetables, such as blackberries, cranberries, pomegranate, raspberries, strawberries, grapes, and peaches.

ELLAGITANNINS: Natural antioxidants that provide vitamin C, vitamin K, and free radical–scavenging polyphenols.

FLAVONOIDS: Plant pigments, such as quercetin, which occur naturally in onions and citrus fruit. They strengthen skin and blood vessels, thus reducing risk for aneurisms, bruising, and varicose veins. Also known as bioflavonoids.

FLAVONOLS: A class of flavonoids found in many fruits and vegetables. They include quercetin and kaempferol, which play an important role in our liver function and in the detoxification of environmental toxins and medications.

FOLATE: A B vitamin (aka B_9) that plays a primary role in cell division and is naturally occurring in foods such as leafy greens, sunflower seeds, orange juice, pineapple juice, cantaloupe, honeydew melon, grapefruit juice, bananas, raspberries, strawberries, and tomato juice.

FREE RADICAL: An atom, molecule, or ion that is highly reactive, meaning it can cause damaging reactions to occur in the body. Antioxidants are the nutrients that bond to them, rendering them inactive and harmless.

GENETICALLY MODIFIED ORGANISMS (GMOS): Fruits, vegetables, dairy, and now even meats that have been manipulated by chemical corporations in a process called *genetic modification*. The actual genetic material of these foods has been altered. They should be avoided when possible, as they carry health risks, such as higher chemical residue and food reactions (allergies). Foods that are labeled organic are a healthier choice, as they are non-GMO.

GLYCEMIC: Glycemic literally means "causing glucose (sugar) in the blood." Blood glucose levels are affected by the amount and type of carbohydrates consumed. Glycemia is the related noun meaning glucose or sugar in the blood.

GLYCEMIC INDEX: The Glycemic Index (GI) is a relative ranking of carbohydrate in foods according to how they affect blood glucose levels. Carbohydrates with a low GI value (55 or less) are more slowly digested, absorbed and metabolized and cause a lower and slower rise in blood glucose and, therefore usually, insulin levels.

GLYCEMIC LOAD: A number that estimates how much a given food will raise a person's blood sugar after eating or drinking it. The glycemic load is determined based on the food's glycemic index minus its fiber load.

GLYCOGEN: The storage of sugar as bundles of glucose in muscle and the liver, where our bodies access it when needed, such as when we strenuously exercise or in times of starvation.

GLYCOLIPIDS: Glycolipids are lipids with a carbohydrate attached. Their supports cell membranes and facilitate cellular recognition, which is crucial to the immune response.

HORMONES: The chemical messengers that regulate our endocrine systems.

HYDRATION: Hydration levels indicate how much water is in our bodies and how well we are able to absorb water and maintain water levels. When we are low in water, we can become dehydrated, which can cause physical symptoms, such as headaches, false-hunger signals, joint pain, and backaches.

HYPOGLYCEMIA: An imbalance in blood sugar that can cause symptoms such as weakness, fatigue, and brain fog. When we have low (*hypo*) blood sugar (*glycemia*), we need to eat or drink carbohydrates to raise our blood sugar to a healthy level.

INFLAMMATION: A condition that can cause swelling, edema, redness, and heat in body tissues. It can also cause puffiness, distended stomach, and puckering in the thighs, which we often think of as cellulite.

INSULIN: The hormone made by the pancreas that pulls sugar from the bloodstream into cells to be used as energy. Those who are insulin-dependent take insulin injections to manage their blood sugar levels.

LINALOOL: Linalool is a naturally occurring terpene found in many flowers and spice plants. It has been studied for its health benefits as an anti-inflammatory, pain reducer, antibacterial agent, and anti-epileptic.

LIPOLYSIS: The breakdown of lipids (fat) for the body to use as energy.

LYCOPENE: Lycopene is a carotenoid—a natural pigment that gives some vegetables and fruits their red color. It is an antioxidant, which means it is a substance that protects against cell damage.

MELATONIN: The hormone that regulates sleep (circadian rhythms). It is also an antioxidant that protects our cells from genetic damage.

METABOLIC SYNDROME: A group of disorders, such as obesity and insulin resistance, that increase the risk for heart disease and diabetes.

METABOLISM: Generally refers to the digestion of foods and their transport throughout the body.

NECTAR: Fruit nectars, such as mango, papaya, and blueberry, are richer, sweeter and thicker than most fruit juices. They are unstrained and contain more pulp.

NEUROTRANSMITTER: A chemical substance that is released at the end of a nerve fiber by the arrival of a nerve impulse which communicates with other cells.

NORADRENALINE: A hormone and a neurotransmitter that controls many biological functions, including our focus, fight-or-flight response, and heart rate.

OLEANOLIC ACID: A naturally occurring triterpenoid found in plants such as garlic and basil, which provides protection of the liver and improves diet-induced obesity by modulating fat metabolism.

OXIDATION/OXIDATIVE STRESS: Oxidative stress is an imbalance between free radicals and antioxidants in your body. Free radicals are oxygen-containing molecules with an uneven number of electrons that can affect cells in unhealthy ways.

PANCREATIC BETA CELLS: The cells of the pancreas that produce the hormone insulin. Insulin grabs up sugar in the bloodstream and carries it into the cells, where it can be used as energy or stored as body fat.

PHYTONUTRIENTS: These are natural chemicals that are found in plants.

PHYTOSTEROLS: Naturally occurring cholesterol-lowering plant compounds found in nuts, vegetables, fruits, and berries.

POLYPHENOLS: Naturally occurring substances found in grape and berry skins, grape seeds, cinnamon bark, pomegranate arils, cloves, tea leaves, red wine, coffee, and chocolate. When these nutrients are modified by intestinal microflora, they provide benefits such as reducing inflammation and improving metabolism.

PROANTHROCYADINS: Proanthocyanidins are natural compounds, in a group of compounds called polyphenols, that give many fruits and flowers their red, blue, or purple colors.

PROBIOTICS: Live, health-promoting bacteria taken as supplements or in fermented food products, such as yogurt and kefir. These bacteria are necessary for proper digestion and help us to balance our hormones and absorb nutrients. They also protect us from unhealthy bacteria, viruses, and fungi.

RECEPTORS: A specialized cell or group of nerve endings that responds to sensory stimuli and can bind with substances such as hormones, antigens, drugs, neurotransmitters, nutrients, phytochemicals, and toxins.

ROSMARINIC ACID: Rosmarinic acid is a naturally occurring phenol antioxidant found in herbs such as rosemary, oregano, sage, thyme, and peppermint. It has antiviral, antibacterial, anti-inflammatory, and anti-oxidant properties.

TANNIC: An astringent or slightly bitter flavor often associated with tannins.

TANNINS: Tannin is a naturally occurring polyphenol found in plants, seeds, bark, wood, leaves, and fruit skins. Tannins have been reported to help hypertension, high cholesterol levels, and immune function.

TERPENE: Terpenes are a large and diverse class of organic compounds, produced by a variety of plants, that produce aroma and flavor.

THERMOGENESIS: Thermogenesis is the process of heat production in organisms.

THIAMINE: Also known as vitamin B_1, thiamine is needed for eyesight, building neurotransmitters, and proper functioning of our cardiovascular system. If we become deficient in this nutrient, we may experience symptoms such as malaise, irritability, and confusion.

TOXIN: A poisonous substance that is usually very unstable and notably toxic when introduced into the tissues, and typically capable of inducing antibody formation.

TRYPTOPHAN: An essential amino acid necessary for the production of serotonin, melatonin, and niacin.

URSOLIC ACID: Found naturally in apples and apple peel, basil, bilberries, cranberries, peppermint, rosemary, oregano, thyme, and prunes. Ursolic acid increases muscle mass gain and induces fat burning.

REFERENCES

Acheson, KJ, Blondel-Lubrano A, Oguey-Araymon S, Beaumont M, Emady-Azar S, Ammon-Zufferey C, Monnard I, Pinaud S, Nielsen-Moennoz C, Bovetto L. (2011) Protein choices targeting thermogenesis and metabolism. *American Journal of Clinical Nutrition.*

Alam MA, Kauter K, Brown L. (2013) Naringin improves diet-induced cardiovascular dysfunction and obesity in high carbohydrate, high fat diet-fed rats. *Nutrients.*

Alghasham AA. (2013) Cucurbitacins—a promising target for cancer therapy. *International Journal of Health Science (Qassim).*

Allen RW, Schwartzman E, Baker WL, Coleman CI, Phung OJ. (2013) Cinnamon use in type 2 diabetes: an updated systematic review and meta-analysis. *Annals of Family Medicine.*

Asgary S, Rastqar A, Keshvari M. (2018) Weight Loss Associated with Consumption of Apples: A Review. *J Am Coll Nutr.*

Aviram M, Rosenblat M. (2013) Pomegranate for your cardiovascular health. *Rambam Maimonides Medical Journal.*

Azarpazhooh A, Lawrence HP, Shah PS. (2011) Xylitol for preventing acute otitis media in children up to 12 years of age. *Cochrane Database Systematic Review.*

Azevedo MI, Pereira AF, Nogueira RB, Rolim FE, Brito GA, Wong DV, Lima-Júnior RC, de Albuquerque Ribeiro R, Vale ML. (2013) The antioxidant effects of the flavonoids rutin and quercetin inhibit oxaliplatin-induced chronic painful peripheral neuropathy. *Mol Pain.*

Babu PV, Liu D, Gilbert ER. (2013) Recent advances in understanding the anti-diabetic actions of dietary flavonoids. *Journal of Nutritional Biochemistry.*

Bártíková H, Skálová L, Dršata J, Boušová I. (2013) Interaction of Anthocyanins with Drug-metabolizing and Antioxidant Enzymes. *Current Medicine Chemistry.*

Bendtsen LQ, Lorenzen JK, Bendsen NT, Rasmussen C, Astrup A. (2013) Effect of dairy proteins on appetite, energy expenditure, body weight, and composition: a review of the evidence from controlled clinical trials. Advances in Nutrition: *An International Review Journal.*

Bertoia M, Rimm E, Mukamal K, Hu F, Willet W, Cassidy A. (2016) Dietary Flavonoid Intake and Weight Maintenance: Three Prospective Cohorts of 124,086 US Men and Women Followed for Up to 24 Years. *BMJ.*

Breslavsky A, Frand J, Matas Z, Boaz M, Barnea Z, Shargorodsky M. (2013) Effect of high doses of vitamin D on arterial properties, adiponectin, leptin and glucose homeostasis in type 2 diabetic patients. *Clinical Nutrition.*

Cao GY, Yang XW, Xu W, Li F. (2013) New inhibitors of nitric oxide production from the seeds of Myristica fragrans. *Food and Chemical Toxicology.*

Cao ZY, Ma YN, Sun LH, Mou RZ, Zhu ZW, Chen MX. (2017) Direct Determination of Six Cytokinin Nucleotide Monophosphates in Coconut Flesh by Reversed-Phase Liquid Chromatography-Tandem Mass Spectrometry. *J Agric Food Chem.*

Chaiittianan R, Sutthanut K, Rattanathongkom A. (2017) Purple Corn Silk: A Potential Anti-Obesity Agent With Inhibition on Adipogenesis and Induction on Lipolysis and Apoptosis in Adipocytes. *Journal of Ethnopharmacology.*

Cherniack EP. (2011) Polyphenols: planting the seeds of treatment for the metabolic syndrome." *Nutrition Journal.*

Chirumbolo S. (2013) Dietary Assumption Of Plant Polyphenols and Prevention Of Allergy. *Curr Pharm Des.*

Chowdhury KP. (2020) Health Benefits of Green Tea and Herbal Teas: A Comparative Review. *Our Heritage Journal Academic Press.*

Da Silva ST, Dos Santos CA, Bressan J. (2013) Intestinal microbiota; relevance to obesity and modulation by prebiotics and probiotics. *Nutrición Hospitalaria.*

Danhauer JL, Johnson CE, Corbin NE, Bruccheri KG. (2010) Xylitol as a prophylaxis for acute otitis media: systematic review. *International Journal of Audiology.*

Delzenne NM, Neyrinck AM, Cani PD. (2011) Modulation of the gut microbiota by nutrients with prebiotic properties: consequences for host health in the context of obesity and metabolic syndrome. *Microbiology Cell Factories.*

Denis MC, Furtos A, Dudonné S, Montoudis A, Garofalo C, Desjardins Y, Delvin E, Levy E. (2013) Apple peel polyphenols and their beneficial actions on oxidative stress and inflammation. *PLoS One.*

Devkota S, Layman DK. (2010) Protein metabolic roles in treatment of obesity. *Current Opinion in Clinical Nutrition & Metabolic Care.*

Dinstel RR, Cascio J, Koukel S. (2013) The antioxidant level of Alaska's wild berries: high, higher and highest. *Int J Circumpolar Health.*

Di Perro F, Bressan A, Ranaldi D, Rapacioli G, Giacomelli L, Bertuccioli A. (2015) Potential Role of Bioavailable Curcumin in Weight Loss and Omental Adipose Tissue Decrease: Preliminary Data of a Randomized, Controlled Trial in Overweight People With Metabolic Syndrome. *Eur Rev Med Pharmacy Sci.*

Duan L, Tao HW, Hao XJ, Gu QQ, Zhu WM. (2009) Cytotoxic and antioxidative phenolic compounds from the traditional Chinese medicinal plant, Myristica fragrans. *Planta Medicine.*

Espín JC, Larrosa M, García-Conesa MT, Tomás-Barberán F. (2013) Biological significance of urolithins, the gut microbial ellagic Acid-derived metabolites: the evidence so far. *Evidence Based Complementary and Alternative Medicine.*

Evans JA, Johnson EJ. (2010) The Role of Phytonutrients in Skin Health. *Nutrients.*

Ferrarse R, Ceresola ER, Preti A, Canducci F. (2018) Probiotics, Prebiotics and Synbiotics for Weight Loss and Metabolic Syndrome in the Microbiome Era. *Eur Rev Med Pharmacol Sci.*

Fiamoncini J, Turner N, Hirabara SM, Salgado TM, Marçal AC, Leslie S, da Silva SM, Deschamps FC, Luz J, Cooney GJ, Curi R. (2013) Enhanced peroxisomal ß-oxidation is associated with prevention of obesity and glucose intolerance by fish oil-enriched diets. *Obesity Journal.*

Flamini R, Mattivi F, De Rosso M, Arapitsas P, Bavaresco L. (2013) Advanced knowledge of three important classes of grape phenolics: anthocyanins, stilbenes and flavonols. *International Journal of Molecular Science.*

Fujii M, Nakashima H, Tomozawa J, Shimazaki Y, Ohyanagi C, Kawaguchi N, Ohya S, Kohno S, Nabe T. (2013) Deficiency of n-6 polyunsaturated fatty acids is mainly responsible for atopic dermatitis-like pruritic skin inflammation in special diet-fed hairless mice. *Experimental Dermatology.*

Gray B, Steyn F, Davies PS, Vitetta L. (2013) Omega-3 fatty acids: a review of the effects on adiponectin and leptin and potential implications for obesity management. *European Journal of Clinical Nutrition.*

Haddad JJ, Ghadieh RM, Hasan HA, Nakhal YK, Hanbali LB. (2013) Measurement of Antioxidant Activity and Antioxidant Compounds under Versatile Extraction Conditions: II. The Immuno-Biochemical Antioxidant Properties of Black Sour Cherry (Prunus cerasus) Extracts. *Anti-Inflammatory & Anti-Allergy Agents in Medicinal Chemistry.*

Halim EM, Mukhopadhyay AK. (2006) Effect of Ocimum sanctum (Tulsi) and vitamin E on biochemical parameters and retinopathy in streptozotocin induced diabetic rats. *Indian Journal of Clinical Biochemistry.*

Hotta M, Nakata R, Katsukawa M, Hori K, Takahashi S, Inoue H. (2010) Carvacrol, a Component of Thyme Oil, Activates PPAR and Suppresses COX-2 Expression. *Journal of Lipid Research.*

Hou J, Zheng D, Fan K, Yu B, Xiao W, Ma J, Jin W, Tan Y, Wu J. (2012) Combination of mangiferin and dipeptidyl peptidase-4 inhibitor sitagliptin improves impaired glucose tolerance in streptozotocin-diabetic rats. *Pharmacology.*

Howatson G, Bell PG, Tallent J, Middleton B, McHugh MP, Ellis J. (2012) Effect of tart cherry juice (Prunus cerasus) on melatonin levels and enhanced sleep quality. *European Journal of Nutrition.*

Hulsken S, Martin A, Mohajeri MH, Homberg JR. (2013) Food-derived serotonergic modulators: effects on mood and cognition. *Nutrition Research Review.*

Hurley CF, Hatfield DL, Riebe DA. (2013) The effect of caffeine ingestion on delayed onset muscle soreness. *Journal of Strength Conditioning Research.*

Hursel R, Westerterp-Plantenga MS. (2013) Catechin- and caffeine-rich teas for control of body weight in humans. *American Journal of Clinical Nutrition.*

Islam MS, Indrajit M. (2012) Effects of xylitol on blood glucose, glucose tolerance, serum insulin and lipid profile in a type 2 diabetes model of rats. *Annals of Nutrition and Metabolism*.

Jeena K, Liju VB, Kuttan R. (2013) Antioxidant, anti-inflammatory and antinociceptive activities of essential oil from ginger. *Indian Journal of Physiology and Pharmacology*.

Junco JJ, Mancha A, Malik G, Wei SJ, Kim DJ, Liang H, Slaga TJ. (2013) Resveratrol and P-glycoprotein Inhibitors Enhance the Anti-skin Cancer Effects of Ursolic Acid. Molecular Cancer Research.

Kelley DS, Adkins Y, Reddy A, Woodhouse LR, Mackey BE, Erickson KL. (2013) Sweet bing cherries lower circulating concentrations of markers for chronic inflammatory diseases in healthy humans. *Journal of Nutrition*.

Khan V, Najmi AK, Akhtar M, Aqil M, Mujeeb M, Pillai KK. (2012) A pharmacological appraisal of medicinal plants with antidiabetic potential. *Journal of Pharmacology and Bioallied Science*.

Krishnaswamy K. (2008) Traditional Indian spices and their health significance. Asia Pacific *Journal of Clinical Nutrition*.

Kujawska M, Ignatowicz E, Ewertowska M, Markowski J, Jodynis-Liebert J. (2011) Cloudy apple juice protects against chemical-induced oxidative stress in rats. *European Journal of Nutrition*.

Kunkel SD, Elmore CJ, Bongers KS, Ebert SM, Fox DK, Dyle MC, Bullard SA, Adams CM. (2012) Ursolic acid increases skeletal muscle and brown fat and decreases diet-induced obesity, glucose intolerance and fatty liver disease. *PLoS One*.

Kunnumakkara AB, Bordoloi D, Padmavathi G, Monisha J, Roy NK, Prasad S, Aggarwal BB. (2017) Curcumin, the Golden Nutraceutical: Multitargeting for Multiple Chronic Diseases. *Br J Pharmacol*.

Kurola P, Tapiainen T, Sevander J, Kaijalainen T, Leinonen M, Uhari M, Saukkoriipi A. (2011) Effect of xylitol and other carbon sources on Streptococcus pneumoniae biofilm formation and gene expression in vitro. *APMIS*, formerly *Acta Pathologica, Microbiologica et Immunologica Scandinavica*.

Landberg R, Sun Q, Rimm EB, Cassidy A, Scalbert A, Mantzoros CS, Hu FB, van Dam RM. (2011) Selected dietary flavonoids are associated with markers of inflammation and endothelial dysfunction in U.S. women. *Journal of Nutrition*.

Latif R. (2013) Health benefits of cocoa. *Current Opinion of Clinical Nutrition and Metabolism Care*.

Lee CM, Su YH, Huynh TT, Lee WH, Chiou JF, Lin YK, Hsiao M, Wu CH, Lin YF, Wu AT, Yeh CT. (2013) Blueberry Isolate, Pterostilbene, Functions as a Potential Anticancer Stem Cell Agent in Suppressing Irradiation-Mediated Enrichment of Hepatoma Stem Cells. *Evidence Based Complementary and Alternative Medicine*.

Leidy HJ, Ortinau LC, Douglas SM, Hoertel HA. (2013) Beneficial effects of a higher-protein breakfast on the appetitive, hormonal, and neural signals controlling energy intake regulation in overweight/obese, breakfast-skipping, late-adolescent girls. *American Journal Clinical Nutrition.*

Levi JR, Brody RM, McKee-Cole K, Pribitkin E, O'Reilly R. (2013) Complementary and alternative medicine for pediatric otitis media. *International Journal of Pediatric Otorhinolaryngology.*

Li R, Liang T, Xu L, Li Y, Zhang S, Duan X. (2013) Protective effect of cinnamon polyphenols against STZ-diabetic mice fed high-sugar, high-fat diet and its underlying mechanism. *Food and Chemical Toxicology.*

Lucarini R, Bernardes WA, Ferreira DS, Tozatti MG, Furtado R, Bastos JK, Pauletti PM, Januário AH, Silva ML, Cunha WR. (2013) In vivo analgesic and anti-inflammatory activities of Rosmarinus officinalis aqueous extracts, rosmarinic acid and its acetyl ester derivative. *Pharmaceutical Biology.*

Majdalawieh AF, Carr RI. (2010) In vitro investigation of the potential immunomodulatory and anti-cancer activities of black pepper (Piper nigrum) and cardamom (Elettaria cardamomum). *Journal of Medicinal Food.*

Manganaris GA, Goulas V, Vicente AR, Terry LA. (2013) Berry antioxidants: small fruits. providing large benefits. *Journal of Science, Food and Agriculture.*

Martín MA, Fernández-Millán E, Ramos S, Bravo L, Goya L. (2013) Cocoa flavonoid epicatechin protects pancreatic beta cell viability and function against oxidative stress. *Molecular Nutrition and Food Research.*

Martín MA, Ramos S, Cordero-Herrero I, Bravo L, Goya L. (2013) Cocoa phenolic extract protects pancreatic beta cells against oxidative stress. *Nutrients.*

McCormack D, McFadden D. (2013) A review of pterostilbene antioxidant activity and disease modification. *Oxidation Medicine and Cellular Longevity.*

Meinke MC, Friedrich A, Tscherch K, Haag SF, Darvin ME, Vollert H, Groth N, Lademann J, Rohn S. (2013) Influence of dietary carotenoids on radical scavenging capacity of the skin and skin lipids. *European Journal of Pharmacology and Biopharmacology.*

Mohamad NE, Yeap SK, Abu N, Lim KL, Zamberi NR, Nordin N, Sharifuddin SA, Long K, Alitheen NB. (2019) In vitro and in vivo antitumour effects of coconut water vinegar on 4T1 breast cancer cells. *Food Nutr Res.*

Mulabagal V, Lang GA, DeWitt DL, Dalavoy SS, Nair MG. (2009) Anthocyanin content, lipid peroxidation and cyclooxygenase enzyme inhibitory activities of sweet and sour cherries. *Journal of Agriculture and Food Chemistry.*

Nakamura A, Fujiwara S, Matsumoto I, Abe K. (2009) Stress repression in restrained rats by (R)-(-)-linalool inhalation and gene expression profiling of their whole blood cells. *Journal of Agriculture and Food Chemistry.*

Nissen L, Emanueledi C, Gianotti A. (2020) Prebiotic potential of hemp blended drinks fermented by probiotics. *Food Research International.*

O'Neill Rothenberg D, Zhou C, Zhang L. (2018) A Review on the Weight Loss Effects of Oxidized Tea Polyphenols. *Molecules.*

Panchal SK, Ward L, Brown L. (2013) Ellagic acid attenuates high-carbohydrate, high-fat diet-induced metabolic syndrome in rats. *European Journal of Nutrition.*

Parim B, Harishankar N, Balaji M, Pothanaa S, Sajjalaguddam R. (2015) Effects of Piper Nigrum Extracts: Restorative Perspectives of High-Fat Diet-Induced Changes on Lipid Profile, Body Composition, and Hormones in Sprague-Dawley Rats. *Pharm Diol.*

Pérez-Jiménez J, Neveu V, Vos F, Scalbert A. (2010) Identification of the 100 richest dietary sources of polyphenols: an application of the Phenol-Explorer database. *European Journal of Clinical Nutrition.*

Pimentel GD, Micheletti TO, Fernandes RC, Nehlig A. (2019) Coffee intake and obesity. *Treatment of Abdominal Obesity (Second Edition).*

Ping H, Zhang G, Ren G. (2010) Antidiabetic effects of cinnamon oil in diabetic KK-Ay mice. *Food and Chemical Toxicology.*

Pongcharoen S, Warnnissorn P, Leṛtkajornsin O, Limpeanchob N, Sutheerawattananonda M. (2013) Protective effect of silk lutein on ultraviolet B-irradiated human keratinocytes. *Biology Research.*

Račková L, Cupáková M, Tažký A, Mičová J, Kolek E, Košt'álová D. (2013) Redox properties of ginger extracts: Perspectives of use of Zingiber officinale Rosc. as antidiabetic agent. *Interdisciplinary Toxicology.*

Ranasinghe P, Pigera S, Premakumara GS, Galappaththy P, Constantine GR, Katulanda P. (2013) Medicinal properties of 'true' cinnamon (Cinnamomum zeylanicum): a systematic review. *BMC Complementary and Alternative Medicine.*

Rao VS, de Melo CL, Queiroz MG, Lemos TL, Menezes DB, Melo TS, Santos FA. (2011) Ursolic acid, a pentacyclic triterpene from Sambucus australis, prevents abdominal adiposity in mice fed a high-fat diet. *Journal of Medicinal Food.*

Rastmanesh R. (2011) High polyphenol, low probiotic diet for weight loss because of intestinal microbiota interaction. *Chemical Biology Interaction.*

Rendeiro C, Vauzour D, Rattray M, Waffo-Téguo P, Mérillon JM, Butler LT, Williams CM, Spencer JP. (2013) Dietary levels of pure flavonoids improve spatial memory performance and increase hippocampal brain-derived neurotrophic factor. *PLoS One.*

Ritter AV, Bader JD, Leo MC, Preisser JS, Shugars DA, Vollmer WM, Amaechi BT, Holland JC. (2013) Tooth-surface-specific effects of xylitol: randomized trial results. *Journal of Dental Research.*

Ruchkina IN, Fadeeva NA, Parfenov AI, Shcherbakov PL, Gubina AV, Poleva NI, Khomeriki SG, Chikunova BZ. (2013) The role of small bowel microflora in the development of secondary lactase deficiency and the possibilities of its treatment with probiotics. *Terapevticheskiĭ arkhiv.*

Sangai NP, Verma RJ, Trivedi MH. (2012). Testing the efficacy of quercetin in mitigating bisphenol A toxicity in liver and kidney of mice. *Toxicology and Industrial Health.*

Sartang MM, Bellissimo N, Totosy de Zepetnek JO, Brett NR, Mazloomi SM, Fararouie M, Bedeltavana A, Famouri M, Mazloom Z. (2018) The Effect of Daily Fortified Yogurt Consumption on Weight Loss in Adults With Metabolic Syndrome: A 10-Week Randomized Controlled Trial. *Nutr Metab Cardiovasc Dis.*

Savignac HM, Corona G, Mills H, Chen L, Spencer JP, Tzortzis G, Burnet PW. (2013) Prebiotic feeding elevates central brain derived neurotrophic factor, N- methyl-d-aspartate receptor subunits and d-serine. *Neurochemistry International.*

Sesso HD, Wang L, Ridker PM, Buring JE. (2012) Tomato-based food products are related to clinically modest improvements in selected coronary biomarkers in women. *Journal of Nutrition.*

Shimizu T, Torres MP, Chakraborty S, Souchek JJ, Rachagani S, Kaur S, Macha M, Ganti AK, Hauke RJ, Batra SK. (2013) Holy Basil leaf extract decreases tumorigenicity and metastasis of aggressive human pancreatic cancer cells in vitro and in vivo: potential role in therapy. *Cancer Letters.*

Shoba G, Joy D, Joseph T, Majeed M, Rajendran R, Srinivas PS. (1998) Influence of Piperine on the Pharmacokinetics of Curcumin in Animals and Human Volunteers. *Planta Med.*

Shui G, Leong LP. (2004) Analysis of polyphenolic antioxidants in star fruit using liquid chromatography and mass spectrometry. *Journal of Chromatography A.*

Siddiqui S, Kamal A, Khan F, Jamali KS, Saify ZS. (2019) Gallic and vanillic acid suppress inflammation and promote myelination in an in vitro mouse model of neurodegeneration. *Mol Biol Rep.*

Siddiqui WA, Shahzad M, Shabbir A, Ahmad A. (2018) Evaluation of Anti-Urolithiatic and Diuretic Activities of Watermelon (Citrullus Lanatus) Using in Vivo and in Vitro Experiments. *Biomed Pharmacother.*

Sowjanya K, Manjula R, Ratna, Vaishnavi V, Sai B. Keerthi, Divya K. (2019) In-Vivo Antioxidant Activity of Hibiscus plantifolius Stems. *Research Journal of Pharmacy and Technology.*

Srinivasan K. (2014) Antioxidant potential of spices and their active constituents. *Critical Review Food Science Nutrition.*

Stohs SJ. (2017) Safety, Efficacy, and Mechanistic Studies Regarding Citrus Aurantium (Bitter Orange) Extract and p-Synephrine. *Phytother Res.*

Stull AJ, Cash KC, Johnson WD, Champagne CM, Cefalu WT. (2010) Bioactives in blueberries improve insulin sensitivity in obese, insulin-resistant men and women. *Journal of Nutrition.*

Taghizadeh M, Farzin N, Taheri S, Mahlouji M, Akbari H, Karamali F, Asemi Z. (2017) The Effect of Dietary Supplements Containing Green Tea, Capsaicin and Ginger Extracts on Weight Loss and Metabolic Profiles in Overweight Women: A Randomized Double-Blind Placebo-Controlled Clinical Trial. *Ann Nutr Metab.*

Tang M, Armstrong CL, Leidy HJ, Campbell WW. (2013) Normal vs. high-protein weight loss diets in men: effects on body composition and indices of metabolic syndrome. *Journal of Obesity.*

Tavares L, Figueira I, McDougall GJ, Vieira HL, Stewart D, Alves PM, Ferreira RB, Santos CN. (2013) Neuroprotective effects of digested polyphenols from wild blackberry species. *European Journal of Nutrition.*

Tchantchou F, Graves M, Ortiz D, Rogers E, Shea TB. (2004) Dietary supplementation with apple juice concentrate alleviates the compensatory increase in glutathione synthase transcription and activity that accompanies dietary- and genetically-induced oxidative stress. *Journal of Nutrition Health and Aging.*

Valussi M. (2012) Functional foods with digestion-enhancing properties. *International Journal of Food Science and Nutrition.*

Viladomiu M, Hontecillas R, Lu P, Bassaganya-Riera J. (2013) Preventive and prophylactic mechanisms of action of pomegranate bioactive constituents. *Evidence Based Complementary and Alternative Medicine.*

Walker AW, Lawley TD. (2013) Therapeutic modulation of intestinal dysbiosis. *Pharmacology Research.*

Wang X, Zhang F, Yang L, Mei Y, Long H, Zhang X, Zhang J, Qimuge-Suyila, Su X. (2011) Ursolic acid inhibits proliferation and induces apoptosis of cancer cells in vitro and in vivo. *Journal Biomedical Biotechnology.*

Wedick NM, Pan A, Cassidy A, Rimm EB, Sampson L, Rosner B, Willett W, Hu FB, Sun Q, van Dam RM. (2012) Dietary flavonoid intakes and risk of type 2 diabetes in US men and women. *American Journal of Clinical Nutrition.*

Willoughby D, Hewlings S, Kalman D. (2018) Body Composition Changes in Weight Loss: Strategies and Supplementation for Maintaining Lean Body Mass, a Brief Review. *Nutrients.*

Woo HD, Kim J. (2013) Dietary flavonoid intake and smoking-related cancer risk: a meta- analysis. *PLoS One.*

Yang X, Yang S, Guo Y, Jiao Y, Zhao Y. (2013) Compositional characterization of soluble apple polysaccharides, and their antioxidant and hepatoprotective effects on acute CCl4-caused liver damage in mice. *Food Chemistry Journal Elsevier.*

Ying X, Chen X, Cheng S, Shen Y, Peng L, Xu HZ. (2013) Piperine inhibits IL-ß induced expression of inflammatory mediators in human osteoarthritis chondrocyte. *International Immunopharmacology.*

Yishai Levy, Baruch Narotzki, Abraham Z Reznick. (2017) Green Tea, Weight Loss and Physical Activity. *Clin Nutr.*

Zanuto R, Siqueira-Filho MA, Caperuto LC, Bacurau RF, Hirata E, Peliciari-Garcia RA, do Amaral FG, Marçal AC, Ribeiro LM, Camporez JP, Carpinelli AR, Bordin S, Cipolla-Neto J, Carvalho CR. (2013) Melatonin improves insulin sensitivity independently of weight loss in old obese rats. *Journal of Pineal Research.*

INDEX

ABOUT THE AUTHOR

Daniella Chace, MSc, CN, is a clinical nutritionist, radio show host, and eco-lifestyle educator. She specializes in personalized medical nutrition therapy, with an emphasis in toxicology and whole food nutrition for disease management.

She is the author of more than twenty nutrition books, including *What to Eat if You Have Cancer* (McGraw-Hill, 2006), *More Smoothies for Life* (Clarkson Potter, 2007), *Healing Smoothies* (Skyhorse, 2015), *Breast Cancer Smoothies* (HCI, 2016*), Superfood Smoothie Bowls* (Running Press, 2017), and *Beat Breast Cancer* (Skyhorse, 2020).

She is the creator of NADb, a medical nutrition research database, and the iPhone application iEat for Life: Breast Cancer. She is the host of the podcast *Nutrition Matters*, available on NPR and iTunes. She lives in Port Townsend, Washington, where she sees clients in her private practice. She is currently writing a book about toxins found in the home and creating her first children's book, which is about plastic in the ocean.

Follow Daniella on Instagram @daniellachace and on Facebook via Daniella Chace. Sign up for her newsletter to get tips and recipes for staying healthy and feeling great!